TALES
FROM
THE
SKIPPER

TALES FROM

EDITED BY H. K. RIGG

BARRE PUBLISHERS, BARRE, MASSACHUSETTS

Library of Congress Catalog Card No. 68-17072
Copyright © 1968 The Skipper Publishing Co., Inc.
Composed and printed in the United States of America

ACKNOWLEDGEMENTS

The following is a list of credits for those articles which appeared in one form or another in various publications. The titles have been changed in some instances but the content remains basically the same as the original.

The Sea and the Wind That Blows — E. B. White
This essay, which was first published in "The Ford Times," was reprinted in "The Skipper" in December 1963, and in this book, with permission of the author and of Harper & Row, who published it in *An E. B. White Reader,* edited by William W. Watt and Robert W. Bradford, in 1966.

The Ledge — Lawrence S. Hall
Reprinted by permission of Lawrence Sargent Hall. First published in "The Hudson Review," Volume XI, No. 4, winter 1958-59.

On the Knees of the Gods — Joseph Conrad
This article first appeared as Chapter VII and VIII of *Mirror of the Sea* published by J. M. Dent & Sons, Ltd. of London. It is reprinted here with the permission of the publishers and the trustees of the Joseph Conrad Estate.

Home to the Meadow — Farley Mowat
From *The Dog Who Wouldn't Be* by Farley Mowat © 1957. Reprinted with permission of Atlantic-Little Brown and Company.

The Bottoms-up Riddle — Frank Barcus
Reprinted from *Fresh Water Fury* by Frank Barcus copyright © Wayne State University Press, 1960. Published here by permission of the Wayne State University.

v

CONTENTS

PREFACE

One of the attendant rewards of producing a monthly publication is getting the readers' response to the selection of editorial content. If you get none — not even unfavorable comments — you are in trouble. Fortunately, THE SKIPPER, since its inception in 1947, has been blessed with a plethora of letters, mostly complimentary, on our choice of material.

When the decision was made to bring out an anthology of the best yarns and articles that we have published, the selection was most difficult to make. Actually we were in the fortunate position of having an excess of good material which, to meet the exigencies of book publishing, had to be boiled down from several hundred potential candidates to a mere thirty-two. As a consequence of this attrition, many of our finest contributions had to be eliminated for one reason or another.

From the outset, THE SKIPPER's editorial policy has been to serve up a varied literary fare, or balanced diet of *belles-lettres* — humor, fiction, semi-technical pieces, historical presentations, photo-essays, and re-prints and pre-prints of classics. These are what we have decided should be part of the yachting literary scene. We have also from time to time gone into the graphic arts rather extensively. Many stories and articles that leaned heavily on illustrations, photographs or cartoons had to be eliminated for economic reasons in this book.

Full marks and chief credit for what literary success THE SKIPPER has achieved should be given to Victor Jorgenseon, our Managing Editor. Vic has always worn the dual hat of Chief of the Copy Desk and is solely responsible for all of the fine cutting, editing, and re-arranging that is so vital in the eventual success of any piece of writing. And incidentally, some of the best literary gems that have appeared in THE SKIPPER are those that have appeared in "Flotsam and Jetsam" from Vic's agile pen. Unfortunately, most of them are too brief and topical to stand alone in this volume.

We are grateful to the various publishers, and holders of copyrights, who have allowed us to again use some of the immortal works from the past. Our feeling is that these pieces deserve constant exposure, particularly for the edification of the younger generation.

Finally, credit is also due the many contributors, authors, and artists who have given their talents to THE SKIPPER for a mere pittance, allowing us to make this contribution to American yachting annals.

H. K. RIGG
Editor

CHAPTER I

The Sea and The Wind That Blows*

E. B. WHITE

WAKING or sleeping, I dream of boats — usually of rather small boats under a slight press of sail. When I think how great a part of my life has been spent dreaming the hours away and how much of this total dream life has concerned small craft, I wonder about the state of my health, for I am told that it is not a good sign to be always voyaging into unreality, driven by imaginary breezes.

I have noticed that most men, when they enter a barber shop and must wait their turn, drop into a chair and pick up a magazine. I simply sit down and pick up the thread of my sea wandering, which began more than fifty years ago and is not quite ended. There is hardly a waiting room in the east that has not served as my cockpit, whether I was waiting to board a train or to see a dentist. And I am usually still trimming sheets when the train starts or the drill begins to whine.

If a man must be obsessed by something, I suppose a boat is as good as anything, perhaps a bit better than most. A small sailing craft is not only beautiful, it is seductive and full of strange promise and the hint of trouble. If it happens to be an auxiliary cruising boat, it is without question the most compact and ingenious arrangement for living ever devised by the restless mind of man — a home that is stable without being stationary, shaped less like a box than like a fish or a bird or a girl, and in which the homeowner can remove his daily affairs from shore as far as he has the nerve to take them, close-hauled or running free — parlor, bedroom, and bath, suspended and alive.

Men who ache all over for tidiness and compactness in their lives often find relief for their pain in the cabin of a thirty-foot sailboat at anchor in a sheltered cove. Here the sprawling panoply of The Home is compressed in orderly miniature and liquid delirium,

*©The Ford Times, 1963

suspended between the bottom of the sea and the top of the sky, ready to move on in the morning by the miracle of canvas and the witchcraft of rope. It is small wonder that men hold boats in the secret place of their mind, almost from the cradle to the grave.

Along with my dream of boats has gone the ownership of boats, a long succession of them upon the surface of the sea, many of them makeshift and crank. Since childhood I have managed to have some sort of sailing craft and to raise a sail in fear. Now, in my sixties, I still own a boat, still raise my sail in fear in answer to the summons of the unforgiving sea. Why does the sea attract me in the way it does? Whence comes this compulsion to hoist a sail, actually or in dream? My first encounter with the sea was a case of hate at first sight. I was taken, at the age of four, to a bathing beach in New Rochelle. Everything about the experience frightened and repelled me: the taste of salt in my mouth, the foul chill of the wooden bathhouse, the littered sand, the stench of the tide flats. I came away hating and fearing the sea. Later, I found that what I had feared and hated, I now feared and loved.

I returned to the sea of necessity, because it would support a boat; and although I knew little of boats, I could not get them out of my thoughts. I became a pelagic boy. The sea became my unspoken challenge: the wind, the tide, the fog, the ledge, the bell, the gull that cried help, the never-ending threat and bluff of weather. Once having permitted the wind to enter the belly of my sail, I was not able to quit the helm; it was as though I had seized hold of a high-tension wire and could not let go.

I liked to sail alone. The sea was the same as a girl to me — I did not want anyone else along. Lacking instruction, I invented ways of getting things done, and usually ended by doing them in a rather queer fashion, and so did not learn to sail properly, and still cannot sail well, although I have been at it all my life. I was twenty before I discovered that charts existed; all my navigating up to that time was done with the wariness and the ignorance of the early explorers. I was thirty before I learned to hang a coiled halyard on its cleat as it should be done. Until then I simply coiled it down on deck and dumped the coil. I was always in trouble and always returned, seeking more trouble. Sailing became a compulsion: there lay the boat, swinging to her mooring, there blew the wind; I had no choice but to go. My earliest boats were so small that when the wind failed, or when I failed, I could switch to manual control — I could paddle or row home. But then I graduated to boats that only the wind was strong enough to move. When I first dropped off my mooring in such a boat, I was an hour getting up the nerve to cast off the pennant. Even now, with a thousand little voyages notched in my belt, I still feel a memorial chill on casting off, as the gulls jeer and the empty mainsail claps.

Of late years, I have noticed that my sailing has increasingly become a compulsive activity rather than a source of pleasure. There lies the boat, there blows the morning breeze — it is a point of honor, now, to go. I am like an alcoholic who cannot put his bottle out of his life. With me, I cannot not sail. Yet I know well enough that I have lost touch with the wind and, in fact, do not like the wind any more. It jiggles me up, the wind does, and what I really love are windless days, when all is peace. There is a great question in my mind whether a man who is against wind should longer try to sail a boat. But this is an intellectual response — the old yearning is still in me, belonging to the past, to youth, and so I am torn between past and present, a common disease of later life.

When does a man quit the sea? How dizzy, how bumbling must he be? Does he quit while he's ahead, or wait till he makes some major mistake, like falling overboard or being flattened by an accidental gybe? This past winter I spent hours arguing the question with myself. Finally, deciding that I had come to the end of the road, I wrote a note to the boatyard, putting my boat up for sale. I said I was "coming off the water." But as I typed the sentence, I doubted that I meant a word of it.

If no buyers turns up, I know what will happen: I will instruct the yard to put her in again — "just, till somebody comes along." And then there will be the old uneasiness, the old uncertainty, as the mild southeast breeze ruffles the cove, a gentle, steady, morning breeze bringing the taint of the distant wet world, the smell that takes a man back to the very beginning of time, linking him to all that has gone before. There will lie the sloop, there will blow the wind, once more I will get under way. And as I reach across to the black can off the point, dodging the trap buoys and toggles, the shags gathered on the ledge will note my passage. "There goes the

[3]

old boy again," they will say. "One more rounding of his little Horn, one more conquest of his Roaring Forties." And with the tiller in my hand, I'll feel again the wind imparting life to a boat, will smell again the old menace, the one that imparts life to me: the cruel beauty of the salt world, the barnacle's tiny knives, the sharp spine of the urchin, the stinger of the sun jelly, the claw of the crab.

CHAPTER II

The Ultimate Wave

FRANK ROBB

THERE are other names for it — the "occasional freak sea," the "abnormal wave," the "catastrophic sea." Even the staid Admiralty Pilot books refer gloomily to the existence of "giant seas" — although they steadfastly refuse to give any estimates of height, nor any counsel on what action should be taken on meeting the monster.

What we are to understand by this is a wave that differs from a normal wave in size and/or form in such a manner as to make it particularly dangerous to ships of all sizes. There can be no doubt that such waves do occur, although with any luck a man might spend a lifetime at sea without running into one.

Their normal breeding place is the high latitudes and the tropical hurricane zones, and the blame for many a "lost without trace" tragedy can be laid on them.

Once only have I seen such a wave, and then I was — fortunately — not at sea, but standing on a rock on the beach at Cape Hangklip in South Africa. There was a full gale blowing, and it had kicked up a tremendous sea which I was watching with some professional curiosity and wondering how a small boat would have fared in such weather. No skipper would have been carrying sail in such wind, of course, and any boat large or small would have been uncomfortable; but I judged that a good small boat properly handled would have ridden it out either running with warps trailing, lying beam-on (hulling), or riding to a sea-anchor.

I was feeling comfortable about this — and then I saw the Ultimate Wave, and have never since been casual when aboard a small boat in a big sea.

It rose far out, perceptibly higher than the surrounding seas, but what caught the eye was not so much the height but the shape, for the forward face of the wave appeared to be a vertical wall of water, and its general appearance was entirely at variance with ordinary gale seas.

Most people have seen how a big sea steepens on meeting shallow water, and how eventually (if the sea is big enough) the whole crest curls over and falls headlong down into the trough with a thunderous roar. Well, this sea looked like that, but with the horrid difference that it was falling continuously, so that it seemed like some white waterfall sweeping across the ocean at, perhaps, thirty knots or more.

The speculation is inevitable — what happens to a small boat lying relatively stationary when it meets a vertical wall of water moving at thirty knots?

It is this subject I want to discuss, and we have to aid us the evidence of a number of people who claim that they know what happens from bitter experience — having learned the hard way.

Among these are the crews of such yachts as *Typhoon, Sandefjord, Les Quatre Vents* and *Coimbra,* all of whom believe they encountered such a sea with results varying from the exciting to the disastrous.

The latest of these is Miles Smeeton, who tells of two such occurrences in his book "Once Is Enough." This is a book in grand contrast to many other yachting stories written by lubbers who put to sea in cranky, parish-rigged abortions and get deservedly clobbered in weather that a competent boat and master would take in their stride.

Briefly, the *Tzu Hang* was a good little boat, 42-feet over-all, not particularly fast, but with sea-kindly lines. Her crew were Smeeton, his wife, and young John Guzzwell. The yacht was well found, sound, well equipped, well handled by experienced seamen.

She had safely ridden out many savage gales, and although at this time they were bound east around the notorious Cape Horn they were reasonably confident of their own ability and of the qualities of their craft. Even when, nearing the Horn, they were caught in very heavy weather and forced to run under bare poles and towing warps, they were happy enough in the knowledge that their boat had carried them safely through weather as bad or worse.

And then, without warning, a great sea took the *Tzu Hang* and

[6]

pitchpoled her stern-over-stem in a brutal somersault that left her a dismasted, waterlogged wreck with her decks swept clear, doghouse gone, and indescribable chaos below. How they crept into a Chilean port under jury rig and remasted and refitted their boat makes a brave and fascinating story.

But it does not end there. Once more they set course for the Horn — without John, who could no longer spare the time.

Once again they hit the inevitable big depression. On this occasion they were understandably a little chary about running before it, warps or no warps, and preferred to lie beam-on, without any sail set — which is generally taken to be a perfectly seamanlike habit.

And once more the Big Sea got them — this time rolling the boat contemptuously over like a barrel, and again leaving her a barely floating derelict. How they made port again unaided finishes a remarkable story.

From this and from other accounts we can form a fairly clear picture of what happened in each case — and in every case the picture is similar. The moving wall of water rushes on the boat. Even before it reaches her, it picks up warps (if they are being towed) and carries them forward in loose bights to lessen or perhaps completely nullify their drag.

If she is riding stern-to she is swiftly brought into a stern-up, bows-down position. The bow digs in and, partly by the momentum of her heavy keel and partly by the onward rush of the sea itself, she is thrown over to crash either on her deck or, perhaps, on her beam ends should the heavy keel above take charge and wrench her over.

Bow-on, the same thing must happen; and if lying beam-on, the boat is simply rolled over with the wave passing over it.

It would appear from accounts that if one has to make a choice in the matter it is preferable to be rolled rather than pitchpoled, but in either event you will be lucky to escape at all, and almost sure to suffer dismasting and fairly severe damage.

It is an upsetting thought in every way. It goes against the grain to believe that a condition can exist in which no amount of skill courage, vigilance, or equipment can save a small vessel from catastrophe. The majority of cruising men tend to avoid this conclusion, I think. They will affirm that the boat in question was running too fast, that she was pooped, or maybe broached broadside-to

[7]

and was rolled by the following sea when off balance — but few seem prepared to admit that a boat can actually be somersaulted.

But in Smeeton's book there is a photograph of a sea taken from a battleship hove-to in Denmark Strait, and I defy any deep-sea man to look at it without feeling a chilly grue run down his spine, and without admitting that, if such waves occur, anything at all can happen to a small boat unlucky enough to be in their path, including pitchpoling. I have discussed this business recently with a number of men with long experience in off soundings cruising. All of them to whom I showed that photograph regarded it with horrified awe, and thereafter tended to regard it sidewise — and briefly. I have found general agreement that no ship on the Seven Seas could encounter a wave of that height and *shape* without *at least* being swept from stem to stern and suffering more or less severe damage.

As far as small boats are concerned, all felt that it was unlikely or downright impossible for any boat under one hundred feet to rise to it and breast it. Most felt — as I do — that waves traveling at speed and with a forward slope in excess of forty-five degrees are simply not surmountable by any boat at all — and that includes the *Queens*. The boat would rise to it as far as possible, but within seconds would either go through it or be smashed down — depending on size.

Faced with the problem of a wave that cannot be surmounted, one casts about for some method of getting through it with the least possible damage. It seems that running with warps or hulling are not good ideas at all. What to do? How about oil? Supposing that oil would have much effect on waves of this shape — which seems doubtful — it would surely require a devil of a lot of oil. And the snag is that because freak seas give no warning of their approach, you would have to spread large quantities of oil all the time on the off-chance that you will meet one. I suppose an oil tanker could afford that. A cruising yacht would never have that much oil available — although Smeeton suggests rather hesitantly that large built-in storm-oil tanks *might* help. Nobody knows, and on the whole it does not seem to be a practicable solution.

The one device we have not yet dealt with is a sea-anchor. After considerable argument, sometimes heated, most of the deep-sea chaps seemed to feel that, although a sea-anchor was not the solution, the use of one might be described as making the best of a bad job. Even here there are nasty snags. In the first place, let no-one suppose that a sea-anchor helps a boat to *rise* to a sea. On the contrary, depending from which end it it streamed, it does exactly the opposite, keeping the boat stem- or stern-heavy. But it would at least tend to pull the boat *through* the wave stem or stern first, which should end in less damage than somersaulting or rolling over — although one finds it difficult to believe you would have any masts left after the performance. Anyway, you would probably stay right-side up. But — and a big but — what size sea-anchor is required to hold a small boat not only head (or stern) to sea, but also to counteract her buoyancy *and* the dynamic force of a great wave traveling at speed, so as to *pull* the boat right through the wave and out on the other side?

And — when you have worked that one out — what are you going to make it of? Where are you going to stow it? What are you going to use as an anchor cable? And — and this is a good one — to what part of the boat do you propose to belay this cable? I have had some experience with sea- anchors, and I suggest that you make the cable fast to some part of the boat that you can spare.

That is as far as the discussion has got to date. Only two people have offered really intelligent solutions. One suggested sticking to inland dinghy sailing, while the other — after a nervous glance at that photograph — felt that peanut farming in Kenya offered a way out. After another quick look he added "in one of the *higher* parts of Kenya."

The problem is academic as far as most of us are concerned, but for some it may not remain so — because there are plenty of people (including myself) who propose to indulge in at least one more deep-sea, long reaching cruise before we swallow the anchor. It would be nice to think that some time in the future the master of some little boat battling a heavy gale could regard the approach of the Ultimate Wave not helplessly, but with some degree of confidence.

CHAPTER III

The Paid Hand Racket

EV MORRIS

THIS piece is not calculated to make the author popular in too many forecastles, or among the larcenous marine establishments that deal in pocket picking by the kick-back method, but it has needed writing for some time. The boss himself suggested the title and that should give you some idea how *he* feels on the subject of today's professional yacht hands. It might also tip you off that kid gloves will be conspicuously absent in the treatment of this unpleasant topic.

Neither author nor editor expects to effect, or even to touch off any reform, but it is just barely possible that the bright light of publicity will direct yachtsmen's attention to a situation in which they have quite a stake, and one which is getting no better rapidly.

It could be, too, that after reading this, some of the waterfront bums masquerading as yacht captains will, until the novelty wears off, give their owners something more for their money than a reluctant smile, a lot of malarkey about how overworked they are and a good gypping on boat yard and ship chandlers' bills. Experience, however, warns against such optimism.

This is not to suggest, mind you, that all paid hands are good-for-nothings who privately refer to their employers as suckers and treat them accordingly. There are still a few good ones of the old school left, and some of the new, postwar crop who have integrity, pride in their jobs, respect for the man who pays them and are thoroughly competent boatmen and seamen as well.

Unfortunately, they seem to be a small minority, and a dwindling one at that. The reasons for this are too complex to be studied at length in this article. They would make a splendid basis for a master's or PhD thesis in sociology, or economics, or, as the skipper of THE SKIPPER might contend, criminology.

[10]

THE PAID HAND RACKET

Your agent has discussed the matter with a number of yachtsmen whose careers extend from the period when there were precious few sailing or power yachts of any size which did not have a paid complement forward until the present, when there are precious few which have any professionals at all.

He has likewise seen for himself the differences which time has wrought in the crewing of yachts, for he has been shipmates with many professionals, both of the old company and the modern.

What follows then will be the first hand observations bolstered with the impressions of others in a position to know. There will be an attempt, of course, to explore the whys and wherefores of the problem, but none to offer a solution. That involves too many intangibles, not the least of which are the vagaries of human nature, for we are dealing with human beings here and many of their weaknesses.

If I seem to be unimpressed with a good portion of the present crop of yacht professionals, it is because I have been spoiled. I have had the good fortune to be shipmates with many more really good ones than those who are mediocre or just plumb no good. Perhaps unjustly, I judge them all by Vernon, with whom I was lucky enough to be shipmates in the early thirties.

Vernon was a Deer Islander, a wiry, agile little State of Maine man who ran a 65-foot staysail schooner for a fine, distinguished and thoughtful New York sailing enthusiast who was a thorough-going gentleman of the old school. The owner was a kind, understanding person who appreciated quality and was willing to pay for it.

Vernon lived forward with Benny, a large strong young fellow who did the heavy work, and Clarence, a Newfoundlander who was a wizard in the galley and an enthusiastic volunteer on deck.

Vernon and his employer were friends, good friends who enjoyed mutual respect, loyalty and esteem. Neither presumed on this friendship, which lasted until the owner's death. Vernon never tried to insinuate himself into things that went on aft, and I never recall hearing the boss try to tell Vernon how to do his job. The result was an extremely happy ship, a beautifully kept one which never experienced a gear failure growing out of neglect or carelessness. In the days when schooners were commonplace rather than unusual in racing fleets, this one used to win more than her share of prizes.

[11]

Vernon was well paid for those times. He drew full salary from fitting out time in the spring until de-commissioning in the fall and received a retainer during the winter he spent on Deer Isle in the little house built out of his savings. He earned his pay for he was as prideful as he was competent and he protected his owner in every possible way.

Vernon supervised the laying up of the boat and its preparation for launching in the spring. He did as much work himself as he could get the shipyard to let him do and he oversaw the rest of it with a sharp eye and sharper tongue. He made it a point to see that his owner got full value in every item on the bill. Vernon and Clarence did the marketing for the ship and never bought twice from anyone who offered a kick-back. "I figure that a fellow who does that is a crook." Vernon used to say. "He's got to make that percentage up somewhere so its tacked onto the owner's bill. I don't deal with crooks. If you do, you get to be one yourself."

Vernon was a simple, straightforward, proud little man of impeccable integrity. He had a more modest explanation, though, for his attitude toward his job and employer. One night when we were standing an anchor watch together, he told me: "Mr. A—— is the finest man anyone could work for. All the years I've worked for him he's always treated me well and fairly. A fellow can't ask more. Everything I have in this world I owe to him and this job. Least a fellow can do is to play square with a gentleman like him.

"Even if I didn't feel this way, wouldn't I be a fool to cheat him and risk losing this job? It's a small thing, mebbe, but we eat the same food forward as you do aft. Mr. A—— insists on it. Says there ain't no reason why we should eat different. They ain't all like Mr. A——, though. You know Mr. G——, the tightwad that owns—— (Vernon named a slightly larger schooner that we made a habit of beating without the help of our time allowance). Well, I was up to the market this evening when he came in, bought a mess of steaks for his afterguard and then told the butcher he wanted some stew beef for his crew.

"Well, sir, mebbe I shouldn't a done it, but I sidles up to him and I sez: 'Mr. G——, now I know what's the matter with your boat. If you fed your crew the way Mr. A—— feeds us you might win more races.' I left him chewing that one over. Didn't seem to like it none, he didn't."

Perhaps there's a moral here somewhere, or at least a tip on how to handle hired hands. The late Henry B. Nevins, who most certainly was in a position to know both sides of the situation, used to say: "It takes a certain amount of money for a man to live properly and support a family decently. Hence a man who is hiring a yacht captain or hand should pay him enough so as not to invite trouble."

What he was implying, of course, was that the properly paid professional would not have to augment his income by grafting on yard, market, uniform and laundry bills. Of course, there are those, no matter how well paid, who consider bites into the hands that feed them as "legitimate" graft.

Maybe there aren't enough Mr. A——s left in yachting. There certainly aren't enough Vernons. What few of them still exist largely prefer sailing jobs to motorboating even though they are more work. That's because your genuine sailing hand, for all of his grumbling, is not happy unless he is with sailing vessels and sailing people.

A chap who is about as close to the professional sailor situation as anyone the writer knows – he hires, fires and administers them for yacht owners who have neither the time nor inclination to attend to such details themselves – recalls that not so many years ago half the boats in any yachting haven of importance had professionals aboard. Today, he points out somewhat sadly, you would be lucky to find half a dozen paid hands in the whole fleet in any such harbor.

The reasons for the change appear to be three: (1) economic, (2) social, (3) technical. The first, perhaps, is the most important because its impact was felt first and led more or less naturally to the others. At least that is the way it looks to this observer of the yachting scene. Scholars preparing theses for doctorates in seafaring social studies may argue otherwise ... and be right.

Before the grim depression of the early Thirties; the newer and higher taxes; the union-inspired restrictive legislation which made it virtually impossible for Americans to own and operate large steam, diesel and sailing yachts – there was a grand fleet of such vessels under the American flag.

Their usefulness, their contributions to the prosperity of the

[13]

marine industry and shoreside communities do not concern us here. That is another study in itself. But what we are interested in is the fact that each of these splendid ships had an appropriate complement of professionals on deck, in the black gang and the steward's department. Almost invariably their captains and chief engineers, and frequently mates and assistants, were licensed as such.

It was in these large sailing and power vessels — the *Migrants*, *Vemas*, *Atlantics*, *Alohas*, *Corsairs*, *Nourmahals*, *Vikings* and *Orions* — and their more numerous, somewhat smaller sisters that the Scandinavian immigrants, Down East fishermen and the smattering of Nova Scotians and Newfies who manned them got their schooling as yacht sailors.

The depression, with its accompanying trend toward small yachts, if any at all, dried up this source of professional yachting talent at the same time that it did away with the necessity for any great quantity thereof.

Even before the demise of the big yachts, the coasting trade in sail had become all but extinct and canvas as a means of propulsion had virtually disappeared from the fishing fleet. These changes meant that scarcely anyone was being brought up to make his living hauling on sheets and halyards, wielding a marlinspike, using a fid, or palm and needle; another source of good materials had succumbed to mechanical progress.

Came the war and booming business in its wake and the better, handier boatmen found out that they could make a lot more money fishing and lobstering, too, and not so many young Scandinavian immigrants were interested in taking up yachting as a career.

Consequently, when yachting in both power and sail won more and more converts in the post-war years and some of the old timers who had been beached temporarily got back into the sport with new boats, there was a shortage of reliable, competent, experienced hands available for hire.

The few really good top hands and qualified captains who were still willing to go to sea, particularly in sailing yachts, were snapped up quickly at salaries which they had only dreamed about in the pre-war era. Many owners, hopefully, or desperately, signed on one chronic drunk or mediocre cast-off after another. Most of these unfortunates (the owners, that is) gave it up as a bad job after a while and swapped their boats for something small enough to run without a paid hand, or quit the sport.

Back in the Twenties and Thirties, wages were nothing to cause people to turn to the sea for a livelihood, but the pay was in keeping with the times and sailors got their food, uniforms and laundry to boot. Licensed personnel was remunerated on a higher scale, of course.

Captains of the capital ships in our yachting fleet, many of them master mariners with unlimited tickets, were paid something like $500 a month and found to supervise the operation, maintenance and business of vessels carrying close to forty men.

Today it is all you can do to get a "captain" — the quotes are intentional — for a 45 or 50-foot power cruiser for that money. Most of them will hold out for $600. And what do they do for this kind of gelt? Engine repairs? Routine hull maintenance? Keep the ship's gear in order? Are you kidding?

If the engines need a going over, the chances are ten-to-one that Dandy Andy, the "captain," will have a repairman come aboard. If the bright work needs rubbing down and a touch of varnish, the shipyard gets the job. Do the topsides need a dab of paint here and there? Another job for the shipyard. And, if the boat happens to be berthed at one of the more high faluting, accent-on-service marinas, Dandy Andy doesn't even wash down, swab and chamois his charge. Tch, tch. That's for menials, not for "captains." So a shoreside crew takes care of it — for a fee, of course.

Then what, you ask, does this bird do to earn his keep? Well, when the owner goes out for a little spin or a short fishing trip, Dandy Andy will turn on the gas, start the engines and steer the boat. Actually, he's nothing much more than a water-borne chauffeur and he has the same attitude toward his owner's yacht as the paid driver has toward the boss' car. It is a means of making an easy living plus all that the traffic will bear on the side in the way of nips from the owner's bottles, cigars from his humidor and "gifts" from the shipyards, laundries, food merchants and gasoline stations whom he has favored with the ship's business.

Your reporter knows one old-time yachtman who does considerable cruising on the East Coast — New England in the summer, Florida and such in the winter. This chap having had paid hands of

[15]

his own and swapped information with others who have kept a man or two aboard their vessels, gets somewhat choleric when he discusses the present-day professional — professional merely because he gets paid, you understand.

"I figure that it costs you $1200 a year for a man before you pay him a nickel of his salary," says he. "You have his uniforms to buy, his laundry to provide and his food to pay for. I doubt that even the best paid hand today saves his owner half his salary in shipyard bills by doing jobs that he could do himself, or should do."

This same yachtsman also has a very low opinion of the ability of the current crop of power cruiser professionals. He is convinced, from long and close-up observation of the species, that too many of them are not seamen by any stretch of imagination and that only a few of them know the piloting rules and the fundamentals of safety at sea.

"These fakers have foisted themselves on innocent new cruiser owners as experienced, competent mariners. They couldn't fool a real yachtsman for five minutes, but they sure do fool the poor souls who go for these three decks, no bottom, motorized showcases. By the time these chaps find out what a wretched excuse for a captain their employee is, their bankroll, and sometimes their boat, has taken a dreadful beating.

"But I've got a cure for this situation," he went on. "I think that it has considerable merit. Let the Coast Guard examine applicants and issue licenses to yacht captains just the same as it examines applicants and issues tickets to merchant marine deck officers and engineers. You can not take a merchant ship out unless you've got a ticket, so why should you be allowed to run a yacht for hire unless you have satisfied the Coast Guard that you know your job?"

When our noble law-givers start thinking about making a few more political jobs and squeezing more money out of taxpayers by requiring state or federal licenses for pleasure boat operators, they might give the suggestion in the preceding paragraph priority. Why not start with the group that is paid to do a job?

With the changing times, the paid hands themselves have changed. Twenty years and more ago, a hand on a yacht did a lot of things besides looking after the physical welfare of the boat and its equipment. Like as not, he washed dishes, did a bit of plain cooking and made up the bunks. In many respects, he was more of a servant than sailor.

There was a sharply drawn line between the forecastle and the owner's country and the professionals never went aft except on business. When the owner was aboard, they worked, lived and took their leisure forward. There was nothing in common between cabin and forecastle.

Now, because the social structure of American life has changed, the line of distinction between employer and employee is badly blurred if not obliterated. The present-day paid hand might be a college lad working to get money to help him through school. Servility is no part of his make-up and the chances are that he is at least as much a gentleman as his boss. Or the professional might be a New England Yankee, an independent sort of cuss who knows his job thoroughly, takes his responsibilities seriously, has pride in his work and kow-tows to no one.

He's worth his weight in gold to any owner, but he needs tactful handling. He won't work for anyone he doesn't respect — not for long, anyway — and he won't stand being patronized.

The chap I mentioned some paragraphs back — the one who sometimes acts as ship's agent for owners who have other things on their minds — was commenting on the situation over a spot of sherry a while back.

"To go to sea in comfort — that means a good-sized yacht — today takes money, big money," he said. "A lot of people with that kind of money don't want paid hands around; not paid hands as you and I knew them. They'd rather have a college kid or two on board to do the rough work and, instead of treating him like a hired hand, they'd probably make him part of the family temporarily. The old caste system afloat has broken down completely.

"Then, quite often, owners don't want any strangers on board. They want privacy and the whole ship to themselves. And there are those who just don't want to accept the responsibility involved in carrying a hand or two, particularly these modern jokers who want health insurance, hospitalization, overtime and what not along with everything else."

He went further into the reasons why there are not so many professionals afloat as there used to be. "More people know more

[17]

about boats than they did fifteen, thirty years ago," he declared. "They know more about taking care of them too, and don't consider it below their social status to do a little work on board.

"In the old days, there were plenty of yachts that could not have left their moorings if they hadn't had paid crews. The owners simply didn't know how to handle the vessels and most certainly would not have lifted a finger to help in the operation. We have a few like that nowadays, but not so many. They're mostly new money people who go in for fancy power boats because they want to impress someone or make a big splash socially. These are usually the people who get taken for the works by some smart operator of a captain, who puts up with a lot of pushing around for the sake of what he can milk out of a good thing.

"You know, this business is not all one-sided. Sure there are a lot of minor racketeers in the yacht manning business, but there are a lot of owners who have only themselves to blame. I used to run a big yawl for a millionaire who, when he called up and said he wanted the boat at a certain place at a certain time with cocktails, canapes and a six course dinner for four or eight, got what he wanted. He spent money like water on himself and on entertainment, but he had no consideration for those who worked for him.

"One night, the boat was to meet him at Larchmont at six with just such a spread as I have described. The yacht was there, looking like a dream. The steward had everything ready below, everything from cocktails and hors d'oeuvres to savory and liqueurs. Well, the owner sent word out at seven that he'd be delayed. Later on he sent out a launchman with the word that he'd be out presently. Finally at eleven o'clock, stone-drunk in the club, he sent out word that he had changed his mind and wasn't coming. So most of that dinner — and it must have cost a mint — had to be thrown away. And that same owner only a week before had refused to allow the captain to raise a deckhand's wages five dollars a month. You can imagine the morale of that crew.

"Sailors get this sort of thing in moderation of course, on some of the modern fancy power boats. That's why what few old-timers there are still around, prefer sailing jobs. They believe that a sailing yacht owner is likely to be more understanding of a man's problems and more considerate of his crew. I suppose that this grows out of the feeling that most sailing folks have for others of the fraternity. The fact that a fellow does it for a living doesn't make him any less eligible if he's a decent chap and a real sailorman.

"The younger professionals want no part of sailboats — the exceptions being mostly kids who have been brought up in junior yacht clubs and are trying to earn a little college money. The others don't want to stop, mend, dry and stow sails; splice halyards and sheets — even if they knew how — and do all the little jobs that a sailing yacht captain does to keep a boat ready for racing or cruising.

"They want to do things the easy way and after they're on board for a while the owner is very likely to get the impression that his boat is being run for the convenience of the paid hand, rather than for him. The next thing you know, after a few experiences of this kind and the usual sideline gypping, the owner gets discouraged and moves ashore.

"This kind of a captain literally drives men out of yachting. He simply kills the goose that laid his golden eggs. I don't know how much longer this sort of thing can go on." he concluded sadly.

Neither do we, but probably until yacht owners smarten up, demand competence and integrity on the part of their professionals, and run the Dandy Andys off the plank.

CHAPTER IV

My Friend Wilbur

KATHERINE MCINNIS

SUMMER came to Crab Creek as swiftly as the geese fly north, and with just as little warning. Right away business began to hum at the boatyard and everybody wanted to get ahead of everybody else. All I heard from morning to night was: "Hank, how soon can you haul my boat? . . . Hank, there seems to be a leak in my shaft log. . . . Mr. Robbins, will you order me a new carburetor? . . . Hank, my generator isn't charging like it should."

Oh, it was Hank this, and Hank that, until I felt like a duck trying to walk across the creek on ice. For every step forward I skidded backwards and sat on my tail feathers.

Well, a man can't satisfy everybody, especially if he's running a boatyard shorthanded. Of course, I did have Hobby. Hobby is my engine man and a right good mechanic he is, too. Why, he talks to those motors just like they were human. Loves 'em like children, he does. But I needed another pair of hands to help with the hauling and painting. Good help is always scarce, and sometimes even poor help. Finally someone told me about a kid named Wilbur who did odd jobs and painting in Summerville, so I drove over there and located this Wilbur up on a ladder painting his old man's house.

He was quite a small, skinny youngster, maybe eighteen or twenty, but the minute I saw him I thought — there's my forepeak man — he'll just fit up under those deck beams. He can easy coil himself down in the rope locker, or under the sink, or behind the w.c., or any place aboard where there's hardly enough room to work. I had heard of midgets being hired to work inside airplanes where no full-sized man could squeeze himself, and although Wilbur was no midget, his lean body looked as though it could wiggle into narrow spaces.

Wilbur had so much paint on his overalls and his cap that I

[20]

wondered what he had been putting on the house, or if there was any paint left in the bucket. He didn't bother to get down off the ladder, but just hooked his arm over a rung and leaned there solemnly looking down at me with his big round, China-blue eyes. He hadn't ever worked in a boatyard, he said, and he wasn't too sure he wanted to, but I told him that painting boats wasn't any different from painting houses except you had to be kind of an acrobat to reach all the out-of-the-way places.

"Crab Creek is too far away," he objected.

"What's fifteen miles?" I asked him. "You've got a jalopy, haven't you?"

Then I told him that we had the best boatyard on the Eastern Shore, which was kind of laying it on thick, even though to me it was the best boatyard in Maryland. After awhile I got him to promise that he would come over next week and help me.

The day Wilbur arrived at Crab Creek, he just took one look around and said disappointedly, "Why, it ain't nawthin here. What have you got except a few docks and a litty-bitty old boat shop?"

Well that kind of gave me a slow burn.

"Look, Wilbur, we got everything here. The boatyard is kind of a social center in these parts. Sure, it's small, but we're busy all the time. And it ain't just with fishing boats either. We got some nice yachts, too. Then there's the county dock right next to us where the trucks come every day from Philadelphia to buy all the crabs and oysters our watermen can catch. And there's The Beeches, which is always crammed chock-a-block with summer folks. But the main thing is, Wilbur, we got people, and where you've got people, you've got the whole world in a nutshell. I guarantee you, there's more excitement goes on here than in Summerville. It's a friendly place where everybody knows everybody else."

"Yeah, and everybody knows everybody else's business, I bet," said Wilbur, looking as if he had just bit into a sour pickle.

For a young man, Wilbur is right sarcasket.

"You take a tip from me, Wilbur, and just keep your eyes and ears open. There's no better place to start living than right here. You don't want to be dead before they buy your coffin do you?"

After me lecturing at him every day, sure enough he began to take a kind of grudging interest in the place, only he wouldn't admit it. One morning we were slapping copper paint on the bottom of a deadrise fishing boat, enjoying the smell of the paint, and talking while we worked. Wilbur kept one eye on the row of chairs on the bank under the locust trees where the summer folks came and went, and I watched the docks so as not to miss anything. Pretty soon I noticed a tall, spare figure that looked familiar yet somehow different.

"Why, Cap'n Tilgh, I didn't recognize you in that new outfit."

"Say, what d'you know, he's got a haircut at last," kidded Wilbur. "Bet you had to pay double to get all that hair chopped off."

Cap'n Tilgh ran a gnarled hand over his closely cropped head. "Yes-sir, I went to the barber and asked for a estimate." He expanded his chest like a man who had just closed a million-dollar deal. "Figured he could do the work all right so I give him the job."

"But what's the big idea of getting dressed up like a dude?" Cap'n Tilgh usually wore a blue shirt and dungarees like the rest of us Crab Creekers, and to see him in a shiny new pair of khaki trousers and a neat khaki shirt, not to mention the loud necktie, was a sure sign that something was in the wind.

"What are you fixing to do, Cap'n Tilgh? If I didn't know you, I'd say you was courting." I winked at Wilbur.

But instead of laughing, Cap'n Tilgh scowled and muttered something about, "Ain't going to let that old fool get ahead of *me.*" I had expected him to laugh, and that kind of left me with my mouth hanging open, but he just clammed up, and directly he turned on his heel and stalked off.

Just then Hobby came into the shop with a monkey wrench in his hand. "What the hell is eating him?" he asked, waving the wrench towards Cap'n Tilgh.

"Hanged if I know, but we'll probably find out soon as we see Uncle Ed. He can't keep anything to himself. . . . You see what I mean, Wilbur? A man can get a good education by paying attention to other folks' problems. He can learn psychology."

"Sounds just plain nosey to me," Wilbur grunted.

What could you do with a boy like that? We went back to our painting and didn't say anything to each other for a while. Our brushes kept time together, *slup-slup, slup-slup.* I was thinking and

[22]

MY FRIEND WILBUR

I could see Wilbur putting two and two together. Pretty soon it came out.

"You reckon he meant Uncle Ed when he said 'old fool'?"

"Yeah I guess so. Them two old men been calling each other 'fool' and worse for years."

"Well, do you know of any old dames on the loose around here?"

"Can't say as I do at the minute, Wilb, but it looks like there must be one somewhere close by. I can't think of any other reason in the world why Cap'n Tilgh would get dressed up."

My mind just sort of drifted along as I worked and I began to think about Uncle Ed. He had been a sort of a handy-man around the neighborhood and made his living by carpentering and a little fishing. He had outlived two wives, and a couple of years ago at the ripe old age of eighty, he had decided to build himself a pleasure boat — a sailboat, of all things. Said he was figuring on going to Florida for the winter. As a ship's carpenter, he was a butcher, and the boat turned out to be sort of a cross between a skipjack, a house-boat, and a barge. Nobody thought he'd ever get it finished, but by gum, he did. It even floated. We celebrated by throwing a humding-er of a launching party. You'd a thought the boat was a real fancy yacht if you'd been at that party. As Cap'n Tilgh said later at a meet-ing of the Crab Creek Pilots Association, the beer cans and the bour-bon bottles were getting so thick on the bottom of the creek that it took knowledge to navigate these parts.

Uncle Ed named his boat the *Tomfoolery*, and that's exactly what all the Crab Creekers thought it was. One day he arrived carrying all his belongings in two bulging suitcases and a burlap bag and moved aboard the boat for good. Said he couldn't stand rattling around in a big old empty house any longer. Of course, Cap'n Tilgh was specially scornful of the *Tomfoolery* because he was an old-time waterman and knew a good boat when he saw one. He had worked all up and down the Bay on oyster dredges, buy-boats, and the old Bay freighters. He had a little money saved up, so he didn't have to go crabbing and oystering any more except when he felt like it. He owned one of the local type of long, lean deadrise boats with saucy flaring bows, but he kept her so purty she looked like a pleasure boat. 'Course, in a way she was, because Cap'n Tilgh sure got a lot of pleasure out of her.

[23]

It wasn't more than half an hour later when I heard the sound of an old one-lunger engine, "chigga-chugga-wuffoo-CHUH, chigga-chugga-wuffoo-CHUH." I didn't even need to see who it was because I knew it was Uncle Ed in his fishing boat, the *Mabel Grace*. Wilbur couldn't understand how I could tell who was coming just by the sound of their engines.

"Them motors all sound alike to me," he said. "They all sound like they had a set of broken dishes inside."

"Trouble is you don't have a refined ear like me," I told him. "Motors all sing a different tune. It's the sweetest music in the world to me. Now you take Cap'n Tilgh's boat. He's got a good motor, but it's timed different. It percolates real slow and quiet when he's got it throttled down, and it just whispers, 'chiffoo-WEFFoo, chiffoo-WEFFoo-chiffoo-WEFFoo.'" Wilbur looked at me like he thought I was going plumb crazy. Seemed to me like that boy just didn't have any imagination.

The *Mabel Grace* was Uncle Ed's work boat. She was an old log canoe which had been stripped of her rigging and had been left abandoned and half-awash up in the rushes at the head of the creek. Uncle Ed had salvaged her tired hull and converted her to power — if you could call that hunk of rusty iron sitting on the engine bed "power." It was an ancient single-cylinder Unreliable which he had scrounged out of another wrecked boat. He had worked over it and patched it up with baling wire, bits of wood and friction tape until it finally ran, although the Lord knew why, but only Uncle Ed knew her combination.

The *Mabel Grace* bumped gently alongside the gas dock and Uncle Ed made fast her lines. He was a short man with a long goose-neck and a little head which worked on a swivel. His eyes were bright as a chipmunk's, and when he laughed — which was often — he gurgled and gasped like a strangling fish. I always expected to see his tonsils come up with the next breath.

"What's he wearing rubber boots for?" demanded Wilbur.

"He *always* wears rubber boots, that's why." I sauntered down on the dock to crank out a few gallons of gas for him. "Where you off to this time of day, Uncle Ed? How come you aren't crabbing?"

"Have to go to town. Do an errand."

"Sounds mighty urgent to me," I hinted, hoping he would tell

[24]

me what he was going to do, but he never let out a word. Uncle Ed is one of the talkingest men in Crab Creek, and when he don't talk, something is the reason why.

He leaned over and spun the heavy flywheel with a knowing hand. The engine only coughed. I settled down comfortably on a piling to watch the operation. He spun the fly-wheel several times with no result. He cussed. Then he kicked the carburetor with his foot and spun the wheel again. Old Unreliable just coughed and sputtered. He cussed some more.

"Maybe she's out of time," I suggested.

"Naw, she ain't getting gas. I been having trouble with dirt in my gas line."

"No wonder, Uncle Ed. That tank of yours was twenty years old when you snitched it out of a car at the junk yard ten years ago. It's probably plugged full of rust. You better clean out your filter."

"Don't have no filter." He shoved his greasy cap back on his head and jerked his neck nervously. Reaching a long arm down under the seat, he pulled out a pint of bourbon and set it down on top of the engine box.

"Goddarn it! Guess I'll have to."

Hobby strolled along the dock just then with a carburetor in his hand. "Whatsa matter, Uncle Ed, won't she run on gasoline anymore?" he chuckled.

Uncle Ed skooched down and rummaged in his tool box for a wrench and commenced to disconnect his gasoline feed line. Quickly, so as not to spill any more gas than necessary, he put the end of the tubing in his mouth and blew, puffing his cheeks out with the effort. Burbling noises sounded in the tank. Finally he stopped blowing and sucked. Making an awful face, he hurriedly spat out a mouthful of gasoline and frantically grabbed the bottle of bourbon and downed a good slug. My guts turned over in sympathy. Keeping his thumb over the end of the line as long as he could, he joined the two pieces of tubing together and swiftly tightened the sleeve with the wrench. I threw a couple buckets of water into the bilge to wash down whatever gasoline had spilled, and Uncle Ed silently pumped it overboard. After a safe interval he gave the fly-wheel another spin. The motor sputtered encouragingly.

[25]

"Well, I guess it's time," observed Uncle Ed, his voice sounding as mournful as a whistling buoy.

"Time for what?" I asked.

"When I'm madder'n the devil and ready to give up trying, if I make like I'm going to get out of the boat, she'll always start." He put one foot on the gunwale and leaned his weight on it, and then turned quickly and grabbed the fly-wheel like a crazy man, and I'll be dod-gasted if that ornery engine didn't start. I like to fell in the creek I laughed so hard. Uncle Ed threw off the lines, shoved the stick forward, and chugged off down the creek. He had the combination all right.

I went back to my painting. As I said, we were awfully busy at the boatyard. Along about ten-thirty, the men began to come back to the county dock with their morning's catch of crabs. There was a good deal more laughter than usual and I kept hearing Uncle Ed's name so I hustled down on the dock to find out what the joke was.

"What's Uncle Ed done now?" I asked Ben as he hoisted up a bushel basket full of the biggest jimmy crabs you ever see.

"Well sir," said Ben, "as I was coming in the creek I see Uncle Ed going out. The cruiser *Juanita* was coming in, and Uncle Ed he heads right for her and I see there was a woman in the cockpit waving at him. Well Uncle Ed, he takes off his cap real polite and waves and hollers. He's so busy waving that he don't look where he's going and he runs hard aground on the sandbar right by the flasher. Oh man he was really aground! I went to help him, but when I told him he ought to leave the women alone at his age, danged if he didn't get real mad and wouldn't let me pull him off. Fur as I know, he's still there. I can't figure what's got into him."

"Well, I can. Him and Cap'n Tilgh have got their eyes on this woman and those two Romeos are trying to do each other out."

"Well-I'll-be-a-dirty-name!" said Ben, flabbergasted.

Someone poked me in the ribs and there was Wilbur looking like he had important news. "Take a look at who's setting up on the bank."

I did, and there sat Cap'n Tilgh with a right smart-looking lady, not too young and not too old — well preserved, I guess you'd say. They were sitting in the lounge chairs as friendly as you please,

[26]

and even from here I could see she was impressed at what he was telling her.

"He's telling her stories about how he went around Cape Horn."

That I'd like to hear. Cap'n Tilgh ain't never been outside the Bay. *Say, how do you know what he's telling her?"*

"Oh, I just kind of moseyed by and listened."

You know, I began to think maybe there was hope for that boy.

Hobby came by laughing to himself. "Looks like Cap'n Tilgh has netted a fish while Uncle Ed is setting on the sand bar."

The weeks flew by as they do in the summer when a man is working hard every day. Wilbur turned out to be a pretty good news scout and found out a number of things which saved me a lot of time. The lady's name was Perkins, "Miss Dor'thy" they called her. She was a widow from Baltimore, a real citified lady. Cap'n Tilgh brought her into the shop one afternoon. I noticed that he was carrying a folded canvas deck chair in one hand and a picnic basket in the other.

"Miz Perkins, meet Mr. Robbins." I dusted off my hand on the seat of my pants and held it out to her.

"Oh, Mr. Robbins," she cooed, "I have always loved the smell of fresh new wood. It reminds me of the late Mr. Perkins. He used to like to whittle."

I was working on a new row-boat that day and the cedar sure did smell good.

"And I do think shipbuilding is the most romantic occupation in the world. Is that a sailing boat you are building?"

I didn't see much of anything romantic about my work — me sweating away in my ramshackle shop. Naturally I liked it — I wouldn't do anything else, but I was no shipbuilder and anybody could see that a plain old ordinary rowboat was not a sailboat.

"Well, no, ma'am, this here is just a little flat-bottomed skiff.'"

Cap'n Tilgh was swaggering around like a young buck. "If Uncle Ed inquires, tell him we'll be over at Heron Island." He winked wickedly at me, and raised both eyebrows, wrinkling his forehead so that his cap rode up and down on his head.

"Just think, Mr. Robbins, in all my life I have never been picnicking on an island, and it was one of my dearest dreams as a child. After all these years, Captain Tilghman is the gentleman who is going to gratify that wish." She smiled sweetly at Cap'n Tilgh. "Well, goodbye, Mr. Robbins, so nice to have met you. We'll be off now in the *Blue Teal* — such a romantic name."

Wilbur and I watched them go down the dock. "She's got him right under her thumb. That's the trouble with women. They make a man look like a fool," said Wilbur, and he banged his hammer down on a nail extra hard. "I think it's silly, specially at their age — them two old love coots. People can't fall in love when they get that old, can they?"

I looked at Wilbur, amazed at his ignorance. "Why, of course they can. Especially when time is running short. Particularly men. There ain't a man alive who isn't interested in love right up to his dying day, Wilbur. You wait and see."

"Well, anyways," said Wilbur, "it sure looks like Cap'n Tilgh was way ahead and Uncle Ed didn't have a chance."

"You can say that again." A mournful voice from the back of the shop startled us out of a year's growth. There was Uncle Ed looking like he had gone hunting and left his shells at home. He watched glumly until the *Blue Teal* disappeared around the point down the creek. Funny thing, here was Uncle Ed as mum as an oyster, and Cap'n Tilgh, who was ordinarily not much of a talker, was talking up a storm under the widow's spell.

Hobby came staggering into the shop carrying a battery. "Whatsa matter, Uncle Ed, won't she go out on a picnic with you?"

"Durn right she won't. She won't step her foot in the *Mabel Grace*. She says its too dirty. Besides, I don't have any yacht chairs in my boat."

"Now let's not get bitter. You ain't exactly dumb. Why don't you put your brains to work and think up some way to get ahead of Cap'n Tilgh?"

Uncle Ed snorted and jerked his neck nervously.

"Why don't you fix up the *Tomfoolery* and ask Miz Perkins to go to the regatta with you?" suggested Wilbur unexpectedly.

"That's only two weeks away."

"Yeah," I added, "but you can do a lot in two weeks, if you want to."

[28]

Uncle Ed looked thoughtful. "Mebbe you're right, boys. I'd orter try, anyhow." And off he clumped in his rubber boots.

During the next fortnight, Wilbur began to spend a good deal of his spare time with Uncle Ed on the *Tomfoolery*. But no matter how many times I tried to find out, they wouldn't either one of them tell me whether Miz Perkins had actually been invited to go to the regatta yet. I couldn't help having the feeling that those two were up to something, though.

Regatta day dawned clear and bright. There was a brisk northwesterly wind blowing and the sky was full of little white puffy clouds. Even way up here at the head of the creek the branches of the pine trees were waving, which meant there was right much wind out in the river. Everybody clears out of Crab Creek at regatta time and this year was no exception.

The first person I saw that morning was Uncle Ed. He had brought the *Tomfoolery* alongside the main dock just astern of the *Blue Teal,* and he and Wilbur were busy making her as ship-shape as they knew how. They even had the sails bent on — just for looks. As a sailboat, the *Tomfoolery* hadn't been much of a success.

Most of the racing boats, including the log canoe, *Emma H.,* had been towed down to the yacht club the night before so as to be all ready for the starting gun at ten o'clock. Ben was skippering the *Emma* and his crew consisted of Hobby and some young folks from The Beeches — just green hands, though. That was why the *Emma* never won any races.

By now people were milling around on the dock. Several cruisers were getting ready to leave. People were shouting back and forth not to forget this, or be sure to bring that. Mothers were looking for their children and the children were looking for other children, and fathers were saying for Pete's sake to hurry up or they'd all be late, and don't forget the beer and fried chicken.

The minute I saw Cap'n Tilgh appear in spandy-clean white ducks looking like a regular yachtsman, I was sure the widow must be going with him. It looked like Uncle Ed had lost out again, but if that was the case, I couldn't figure out why he and Wilbur looked so happy.

"You going with me, Hank?" called Cap'n Tilgh.

"Sure thing, if you have plenty of room."

[29]

"The more the merrier, my dear Mr. Robbins," chirped Miz Perkins, who arrived at that moment with two friends. We all settled ourselves on board the *Blue Teal* and looked expectantly at Cap'n Tilgh, waiting for him to start the motor. He pushed the starter button with a flourish and beamed at Miss Dor'thy. Nothing happened. He pushed it again. Still nothing happened. Cap'n Tilgh looked puzzled as well as mad. "Had her going yesterday," he muttered, "I can't understand it." He took the cover off the engine and gave it a quick once-over. We could see that he didn't relish the idea of tinkering with the motor on account of his elegant white clothes. He pushed the starter button once more, but no luck. By this time he was purple in the face trying to hold back in the presence of ladies.

Uncle Ed called over in a gentle, innocent voice, "Something wrong, Tilgh? Need any help?"

"You mind your own business and take care of that floating hotel of yours!"

I took out my watch and saw that it was nine o'clock. "Holy smoke, Cap'n Tilgh, we'd better transfer to another boat if we're going to make the regatta. You haven't time to overhaul this engine."

"Well, why don't we go with Uncle Edward?" suggested Miz Perkins. "How fortunate that he's right here and *his* motor is already going."

Cap'n Tilgh's temper exploded like a cork popping out of a bottle. He said he wasn't going to the regatta if he had to go in that blankety-blank scow, and if that blankety-blank son-of-a-bilge-crawler thought he was seaman enough to carry passengers, he'd snag his anchor, *etc., etc.*

"Captain Tilghman! I am surprised at you. Yes, and disappointed, too. The late Mr. Perkins never used strong language. I do not approve of it. And if you do not wish to come with us, I am sure that Uncle Edward will excuse you."

Well, the upshot of it was, we all piled into the *Tomfoolery* — including Cap'n Tilgh, who was scared to death he was going to be left behind — and started on our way out the creek and up the river. Cap'n Tilgh sat on the deckhouse and sulked while Miz Perkins was so sweet to Uncle Ed that I was afraid he would run us aground any minute. He was right back to being his most talkingest self.

[30]

Wilbur lounged about the deck not saying much of anything. Every now and then I would catch his eye and he would look up the mast or out over the water and just whistle softly.

Anyhow, we made it to the regatta in the nick of time. With a northwesterly astern, even the *Tomfoolery*, tub that she was, made good time. We anchored off the entrance to Long Creek opposite the yacht club where we could see everything. I guarantee you, there were some lively races that day.

On the *Tomfoolery* we all had enjoyed ourselves, in spite of Cap'n Tilgh being a litle stand-offish. By four o'clock things were mostly over, and we had finished our beer and most of our fried chicken, so it was time to head back home. Fortunately the wind had moderated a bit, but even so, we had to slog into head seas and I kept my fingers crossed that the motor on *Tomfoolery* would keep perking. Uncle Ed was so busy talking to Miz Perkins as we neared the dock in Crab Creek that he didn't slow down quite as soon as he should have. When he did put the engine in neutral, the boat was carrying too much way. The situation finally dawned on him and he grabbed the lever and threw her in reverse. But when the lever came right off in his hands, he just stood there frozen with horror, his mouth open, and his Adam's apple working up and down. The *Tomfoolery* slid along, headed straight for a $20,000 power cruiser.

I forgot to mention that on the end of our dock is a little shanty which used to be a "Chic Sale" before the health department got so fussy about pollution and things. Ever since then we've used it as a storage shed for oil, alcohol, and other marine gear.

"Put her in reverse, you damn fool!" bellowed Cap'n Tilgh, who was in the bow making ready with the lines.

" I can't! I can't!" yelled Uncle Ed, hopping up and down in the cockpit. "My reverse gear's broke."

"Hard a-port! Hard a-port!" I shouted, and although Uncle Ed shoved the tiller over with all his strength, it was too late.

There was a terrible crash and a slow, rending sound. Then it was so quiet you could have heard a minnow flip. When I dared to open my eyes, I saw that the *Tomfoolery* had missed the power cruiser by inches, but her bowsprit had stove in the back of the little shed and gone right through and come out the door on the other side. The bowsprit, being high, and the shed not fastened down very securely, it lifted the shed right off the dock, and there was the *Tomfoolery* with the old privy hanging down from her bowsprit. Cans of oil were rolling off the dock and splashing down into the water.

As soon as we found out that there was not much damage except to the privy and Uncle Ed's pride, we all began to laugh — even Uncle Ed. We all laughed so long and so hard that I don't know who was in worse shape, those aboard the *Tomfoolery,* or the audience on the dock. Tears were running down Ben's face as he leaned against the gas pump. Hobby was doubled up over a piling and was gasping for breath. Cap'n Tilgh was in such a weakened condition that he had to be helped ashore.

Next morning when all the excitement had died down, first thing Wilbur says to me is, "Look at what's going on out there," and he pointed to the *Tomfoolery,* where Cap'n Tilgh was helping Uncle Ed chop the remains of the privy off the bowsprit.

"Well, I'll be a son-of-a-gun! Looks like they're friends again."

"Don't you know what happened last night?"

I shook my head. "Well," said Wilbur, plainly enjoying himself, "Cap'n Tilgh and Uncle Ed were setting on the porch keeping company with Miz Perkins, when this Cadillac drives up and a man gets out — big, gray-haired man smoking a cigar. He gets out of his car, yanks open the screen door, and just walks right in. He acts like he don't even notice Cap'n Tilgh and Uncle Ed.

"'Dossie,' he says — that's what he called her, Dossie — 'I'm tired of all this foolishness, and I won't put up with it any longer. For the last time I'm asking you, are you coming back to Baltimore and marry me, or aren't you?'

"She just says, 'Yes, Harold,' meek as a lamb. The minute she says that, Cap'n Tilgh and Uncle Ed fell all over theirselves trying to get out the screen door at the same time. And after they'd gone it was awful quiet on the porch."

For a minute I was struck dumb. "What I can't understand is how you know all this stuff, Wilbur."

"Well, uh — er — uh, I just happened to be standing behind the crepe myrtle bush."

I couldn't help chuckling. "You see what I mean now, don't

[32]

you, Wilbur? About people and things?" He just stood there grinning.

Suddenly a thought occurred to me. *"By the way, just what did you and Uncle Ed do to Cap'n Tilgh's engine?"* Wilbur jumped and looked guilty. Then he began to laugh. "Oh, we just stuck a couple of pins in the ignition wires and shorted them out."

How that boy had changed!

CHAPTER V

A Nervious Breakdown

THURLOW MCLAUGHLIN

This un-edited piece of Americana was faithfully recorded by Captain Thurlow McLaughlin, a true Down-East seaman, who submitted this story with the following apologies: "I spent most of my time as a sailor, not as a writer. I have plenty of stories, but they are hard for me to put them down on paper as they should be."

The editors feel that to have blue-pencilled Captain McLaughlin would have destroyed much of the flavor of this episode.

THe *Abbie Bowker*, was a small three masted schooner, built for the southern trade, to carry lumber from the southern states to New York, and other northern ports. As she did not pay expenses in the southern trade, the owners started her carrying lime from Rockland Maine to Boston and New York. Then she made her home port in Rockland, Maine. That was the center of the lime trade at that time.

The *Abbie Bowker* did not do much better in the lime trade from Rockland. So the owners started her the second time carrying lumber and coal, or any other cargo, that they could get to carry from any port in Maine. She was turned into a down east lumber schooner. The trip that I was on her, we took a load of lumber from Calais Maine to a port called Warren in the state of Rohd Island.

I had the idea that the ship was all right, when I went aboard of her the first time. For she had an engine on her forward deck, to hoist the sails and to pump all of the bilges. That was a big help on a schooner. We would not have to pull all the sails up by hand, or we would not have to pump the ship out by hand.

The third day after the *Abbie Bowker* arived into Calais, they were loaded, I had shiped aboard of her and we were towed down river to what is called Devels Head. That is where the St. Croix river starts to widen out. When the schooner was abreast of Red Beach, we had all the sails set. We also had a fair wind all of the way down the river to Eastport. On ariving at Eastport, our fair wind had changed into a head wind, and head tide.

So the Captain anchored there for the night to wait for a fair wind. The Captain did not want to take a chance of trying to get through the Lubec Narrows in a head wind and tide. Neather did he want to get out into the Bay Of Fundy in the night time. The Bay Of Fundy is a tricky place in the best of times.

The next morning early we heaved up the anchor and set the sails. We started out around East Quady Head, instead of trying to get through the Lubec Narrows. East Quady Head is on the northern end of Campbellow Island. We had a head tide that was too strong to start through the Lubec Narrows. After sailing out side into the Bay Of Fundy, the wind was dead ahead again, so we had to tack back and forward all day long. I have seen the wind change there three times in one hour. By four in the afternoon we had sailed only as far as West Quady Head. Which is only a few miles from the Lubec Narrows. The captain went in under the lee of West Quady head to anchor for the night.

The next morning we had an eastrly wind, which is a fair wind for us. So we set sail again that morning at daybreak. By early afternoon we were off Bar Harbor. We had made good time. The captain could see where there was a big storm coming up from the north east. The captain would not take any chances with an north easter on that part of the coast. Going in behind some islands we anchored to get out of the storm the best we could. The captain put both port and starboard anchors out.

The storm lasted for three days before it died down. It was a good one. Being in behind some islands did not do much good, for we were tossed around quite a lot. When the storm did die out we set sail to go around Cape Cod. The captain would not go through the Cape Cod canal, as he did not want to pay for the toll. He wanted to make the trip as cheep as he posably could. He was trying to make the schooner pay more than expenses for the trip.

We sailed around the cape all right without any trouble. Sailing down past Vinard Haven and heading into Long Island Sound

[35]

for New Port Rohd Island, we had a fair wind. The fair wind lasted us into the port where we were going to unload the lumber.

While we were off New Port, some men came aboard of us, off a motor launch, to talk to the captain. They wanted to charter the schooner to take some pictures of her. For they were going to make some moving pictures of a sea story. And they had to have a schooner in the picture. The captain would not listen to them, as he had to get permission from the owners. Which would take too long to get. The schooner would look fine in a moving picture. For she was built on good lines. She looked more like a yacht, than she did a down east lumber schooner.

After docking in Warren Rohd Island, it took us three days to unload the lumber off her. We had to unload the lumber by hand, as there were no dericks on the dock. Also it was tide work. After the cargo was discharged the captain made aragements, to take a load of coal from Perth Amboy New Jersey, to Friendship Maine. Just as soon as we had the lumber unloaded, we sailed out of Warren Rohd Island and headed down Long Island Sound for Perth Amboy, where we were to load the coal.

We did not have much of a crew on the *Abbie Bowker*. I was the only man befor the mast. On a three masted schooner there should be at least three men befor the mast. The captain took his son along with him to be the mate of the schooner. He was only nineteen years of age. We had the cook help us with the sails when ever we were getting under way. As the sails were light, and we had an engine to heave them up, we did not have too much trouble when ever we set the sails. Besides the captain, that is all the crew that we had. It being in the summer, the captain took his wife and daughter along with him to give them a vacation.

After loading the coal at Perth Amboy for Friendship Maine, we had a tug tow us up through Hell Gate to the open waters of Long Island Sound. It is a nice sail through the sound in the summer time, when all of the yachts are sailing around there. It is a pretty sight especially when the yachts are racing.

The wind was very light going up the sound, so it took us two days to get to Block Island. The wind changed at Block Island from the west to the east north east. We had a head wind. I knew then that we were in for a spell of fog. It will always get foggy there in a

[36]

easterly wind. But the fog did not set in until some time during the first part of the night. It was befor twelve oclock, for I was off watch form eaight oclock until twelve oclock midnight. It did not get foggy up till the time that I went off watch at eaight in the evening.

I never did know exactly what time the fog realy did set in. I slept all through my watch below forward in the forecastle. I slept there all by myself. For the mate and the cook slept in the cabin aft. The mate had just started forward to call me to go on watch when it happened. The captain had been stearing for Vinard Haven to anchor out of the fog. We were going to stay there untill the fog cleared up, so that we could go around Cape Cod. The steamer *Bunker Hill* was sailing past Vinard Haven at the same time. But the captain or the mate did not see the *Bunker Hill* or its lights in the fog. They said that they did not even hear the *Bunker Hill* blow its whistle.

Befor the mate could get forward to call me, the *Bunker Hill* smashed into our bow. It cut the figure head, the cutwater, and bowsprit off us as clean as if they had been sawed off us. The *Bunker Hill* had hit us about ten feet from where I was sleeping at the time. The *Bunker Hill* stoped to see what damage that they had done to us, gave us their name and then they went on to New York.

It was on a Fourth Of July night. Beleave me I seen fire works for that Fourth Of July. I could see fire works all around me for a minuet. The mate did not have to call me, for I was wide awake when the *Bunker Hill* ramed into us. The shock of the bump, threw me out of my bunk. What a good thing that I had all my clothes on. It is a habbit with the sailors on a schooner to sleep with all of their clothes on. For they do not know what time that they will have to get out in a hurry. Any emengerency can happen on a schooner at any time.

When I went out on the deck, the captain told me to get aft as soon as I posable could and help launch the yawl boat. I ran aft to where the mate and the cook was getting the yawl boat ready to put into the water. The cook helped the captains wife and daughter into the boat befor we started to lower it into the water. Then after we had seen that the two women was all right, we lowered the yawl boat into the water. I slid down the falls into the forward end of the boat to take the foward falls off. The cook jumped into the after end of the Yawl to ship the tiller and to take the after fall off the boat.

The captain was still on the deck, looking every thing all over. He told us not to leave the side of the schooner untill he had tried the pumps, to see how bad she was leaking. The schooner did not seem to be setteling any into the water. The captain had the idea that we were not leaking any. The captain was gone five or ten minuets when he came back to where we were. He said to us, "The schooner is not leaking any. I can not get one drop of water out of the bilges. You might just as well come aboard for we are not sinking." The schooner did not have any holes below the water line we had found out later.

The mate, the cook, and myself climbed back aboard the schooner. Then we hellped the captains wife and daughter aboard. We made the yawl boat fast to the after rail of the schooner so that it would be handy if we needed it again in a hurry. The cook went forward to see what damage was done to his gally, and to make coffee for all hands. We all needed coffee by this time for every one of us was about to have a nervious breakdown.

The captain anchored the schooner right where we were laying. For we could not go any father with the foward end of the schooner off, and the bowsprit draging in the water. The masts were all loose and swaying around. Also the fog was so thick that we could not see where we were going. Every one was expecting another ship to come along at any time and sink us. We were anchored in the middle of the chanel of Vinard Sound.

I was talking to the cook while he was making the coffee. He told me that when he was helping the captains daughter, into the yawl boat, that all the clothes that she had on was her fathers fur coat. She had been sleeping in her bunk when the acadent happned and that she had not had any clothes on when she fell asleep. She did not have time to put her clothes on after the *Bunker Hill* had hit the schooner. It was a good thing for her, that we did not have to leave the schooner and go ashore, for she would not have any clothes to wear if we did.

When daylight came we started to clear away the wrekage. And tie up the sails. It took us the biggest part of the day to do that. We spent the rest of the day, putting a sail around the bow to keep the water out all that we could. As we were to be towed to Friendship Maine, where we were bound for. We did not want any water to get into the hold if we could help it. It took us till long after dark to finish the job.

Then there was the masts to reset and tighten them up so that they would not sway around too much. We did not start that job till the next day. All of the stays had to be tightened. The formast had to have different stays on her, for all the jib stays were gone with the bowsprit.

We had to waite for three days befor a tug came to tow us to Friendship. When the job was just finished of getting the schooner ready, the tug showed up. Towing was the hardest part of the trip. The water was going into the holds faster than we could pump it out with the engine. The hand pumps had to be used also to keep the water down in the holds and to keep the schooner from sinking. The tug towed us to Friendship in two days. Which was good time for a dead tow. The captain could not help the tug with any of the sails. He was afraid that the sails would take the masts out of the schooner.

I payed off the *Abbie Bowker* in Friendship. A bad trip was over with and I was glad to get off that schooner. It was almost the last down east schooner that I had ever sailed on. Two months on that schooner, was too much for me.

CHAPTER VI

The Last Blackbirder

JOSEPH GORDON

AMONG the unusual tales of the sea is the little known story of the *Wanderer,* last of the American slave ships, and one of the few to start life as a trim schooner yacht. Her history ran the gamut from pleasure craft to slaver, to U.S. Navy cruiser, to hospital ship and finally to coaster.

If ships were endowed with a living spirit, and sometimes it ssems they are, it might be said that she was touched with sin, she did penance for the evil that had taken place on her decks, and after a period of righteous living, went the way of all ships. Now her story.

Launched on June 19, 1857, just a little over a hundred years ago, at Setauket, Long Island, the *Wanderer* was built by W. J. Rowland for Colonel John D. Johnson, wealthy citizen of Louisiana and a summer resident at Islip, Long Island. At the time Johnson was a member of the New York Yacht Club, which was then only some thirteen years old.

Wanderer's measurements will give you some idea of the stage upon which were played the unusual scenes soon to follow. The schooner yacht was a 246-ton craft, one of the largest pleasure boats of her time. She was 98 feet on the waterline, 114 feet overall; 26 feet 6 inches beam, 10 feet 6 inches draft. Her foremast was 83 feet high and her main 84 feet, her fore topmast 34 feet and main topmast 35 feet, her bowsprit extended 17 feet outboard, with jib-boom, 36 feet.

Captain Thomas B. Hawkins, her first sailing master, superintended her construction, and one can guess that he lavished much affection on this new nautical creation that was taking shape on the blocks. In due course of time she was held one of the fastest sailing yachts afloat. Her speed and maneuverability were later to help her outstrip and evade the naval slave patrols as she sped her cargo of miserable humans across the South Atlantic.

In April of 1858, two months short of a year after she was launched as a pleasure craft, the *Wanderer* was purchased by Captain William C. Corrie, newly elected member of the New York Yacht Club. Captain Corrie, it was later revealed, was only a part owner. Others joining in the venture were Charles A. L. Lamar of Savannah; N. C. Trowbridge of New Orleans; Captain A. C. McGhee of Columbus, Georgia; Richard Dickerson of Richmond, Virginia, and Benjamin Davis of Charleston, South Carolina.

As soon as the exchange had been effected, Captain Corrie made sail for Charleston. On board were Captain Egbert Farnham as supercargo, and Captain Semmes, brother of Captain Rafael Semmes of the Confederate Navy, as sailing master. In Charleston *Wanderer* was secretly converted for slaving; tanks holding twelve thousand gallons of water were installed and the hold was modified to carry some eight hundred slaves.

With the burgee of the New York Yacht Club still flying, Corrie headed south for the Island of St. Helena and Africa. Ostensibly *Wanderer* was on a pleasure cruise. The graceful little vessel skimmed the waters of the ocean like a giant albatross, and all were charmed with the ease of her handling.

Departing St. Helena, the *Wanderer* made for a rendezvous with a slave trader on the Congo River. Passage was quickly made but just off the mouth of the Congo *Wanderer* fell in with the British warship *Medusa* on the search for slavers along the African coast. Captain Corrie ran alongside. With the club burgee at the fore and the American flag at the main Captain Corrie was going to play the part of a pleasure yachtsman to the hilt. And Corrie and his crew played their parts well.

A newspaper account of the meeting told how the ships accompanied each other for several days with officers reciprocating visits to each other. Places ashore were visited together and even a race between the two ships was held in which the *Wanderer* won handily. Corrie must have been a superb actor, for one story told how the British were invited below to see if the schooner were not, indeed, a slaver and this suggestion was met with uproarious laughter. What a joke to suspect this elegant vessel for a slaver! Finally the ships parted ways and *Wanderer* continued up river to the barracoons, the wretched slave corrals where the imprisoned natives were held shackled until the smugglers arrived.

Corrie arranged to take on board some seven hundred and fifty negroes, mostly youngsters from thirteen to eighteen years of age. Experience had shown that the younger ones were better able to stand the rigors of the dreadful voyage jammed in the 'tween decks.

Many have had the experience of being crammed into the holds of transports and liberty ships during World War II when every inch of space had to be utilized, but no humans, before or since the slave trade, were packed like so many matchsticks for so long a voyage. Between refuse and sickness and the dead and the dying no wonder the slaveships took on the indescribable odors that could not be scrubbed away, and which, it has been said, were often detected by the nostrils even before the ships were sighted.

With her cargo of "black ivory" aboard, the *Wanderer* cleared for Savannah, Georgia, and Lamar's plantations. She made a swift voyage, eluding both British and U.S. patrol vessels. Now the problem was to smuggle the slaves ashore.

Under cover of darkness Captain Semmes navigated the Ogeechee to a big swamp. There he anchored and communicated with Lamar in Savannah. Lamar, according to plan, arranged a grand ball for the military forces at the fort, and again under cover of darkness the *Wanderer* crept along the watercourse into the Savannah River and upstream to Lamar's plantations, where the prisoners were put ashore and placed in charge of older negro slaves for dispersion about the countryside.

But all did not go smoothly. Word of the smuggling venture soon spread and the slaver and her crew were apprehended. A court case followed, but, as was usual in the slave cases of the times, the owners escaped punishment. The *Wanderer,* strange to relate, was sold at auction at one-fourth her original value as a merchant schooner — her buyer, her former owners. As for the slaves who had been bought for cheap trade goods — beads and bandanna handkerchiefs — they were eventually sold for about $600 to $700 apiece. *Wanderer's* first voyage showed a handsome profit.

It wasn't long, however, before the nefarious dealings of Corrie came to the attention of the members of the New York Yacht Club. On February 3, 1859, Corrie was expelled from the organization and the *Wanderer's* name effaced from the club's squadron list.

The *Wanderer* is believed to have made three trips in all for slaves. On the homeward run of her second voyage she was run aground between Jekyll and Cumberland Islands in Georgia but sustained little damage. A number of slaves were drowned trying to escape but eventually a large number of the survivors were sold at auction in New Orleans.

On her final slave voyage under a Captain D. S. Martin in October, 1859, the *Wanderer* put to sea hurriedly without sufficient provisions or equipment. She made a fast run across the Atlantic to the Azores. Here she sighted government patrol vessels and changed course for Funchal in the Madeiras. Provisions were now beginning to run low so Martin spoke a French barque and went on board to arrange to buy the needed supplies. This was just the opportunity the mate had been waiting for. All through the crossing he had been subjected to the captain's abuse, made even more oppressive by the captain's abundant use of alcohol. Now he would be rid of the captain and end a voyage for which he had little heart. Taking over command, the mate gave orders to make sail for the States. The *Wanderer* was delivered to the U.S. marshal in Boston.

Again the *Wanderer* was subject to litigation. Lamar claimed that Martin had stolen the vessel. Again the vessel was put up for auction, and again Lamar was able to purchase *Wanderer* for a fraction of her original cost. Lamar took the *Wanderer* south to be repaired; later she was to be sent to Havana and sold. But then came the Civil War. Lamar, a patriotic southerner, bent his efforts toward raising a southern regiment. He died in the cause of slavery in battle.

To finish out her story: *Wanderer* was captured by Federal forces at Key West in May, 1861, and converted to a Union patrol vessel. After several patrols in the Gulf of Mexico, orders came to utilize her as a hospital ship. Now *Wanderer* cared for the sick and wounded — a sharp contrast to the days when the reek of sickness and death and hopeless misery were in the air about her. Now she was atoning for her sins by offering life and hope to suffering mankind. Finally, with the war at end and slavery abolished forever from the United States, *Wanderer* was declared unseaworthy and listed to be sold once more.

In due course of time *Wanderer* found herself in the coconut trade sailing between the islands off the coast of Honduras and the United States. In December of 1868 while beating up the coast in a heavy gale, *Wanderer* was driven ashore at Cape Henry, Virginia, off the mouth of the Chesapeake. But the *Wanderer* died hard. Her wounds were patched and on January 31, 1869, she was issued a new register out of Philadelphia in the name of *S. S. Scattergood* of that city. For two years she sailed the waters of the blue Caribbean in the West Indian fruit trade. Her end came on January 21, 1871, when she went ashore at Cape Maisi on the east end of Cuba. She was thirteen years, seven months and two days old.

CHAPTER VII

Ten Dollars and Found

MARC T. GREENE

IN the days immediately before the first World War, when two and three-masted coasting schooners were as familiar to every New England port as clippers in San Francisco Bay in the eighteen fifties, four lay close together beside wharves piled high with lumber at Machias, a far Down East village almost within sight of the Bay of Fundy.

Machias is on the river of the same name, a dozen miles from the sea. A diminutive tug brought the laden craft down to Machias-port where they awaited a favorable "slarnt" of wind. Lumber and laths were piled high on their decks until only a yard of freeboard remained. The lowers had to be reefed so the booms might clear the deck-load.

This was the condition on the three-master *Flora Condon* when I, hitch-hiking through Maine, sought a temporary job on her that would get me back to Rhode Island. Her age was as uncertain as that of a dowager duchess. She was of an era even then on its way out. Each winter the ruthless western ocean took heavy toll of her kind. Freight rates went ever lower and, to eke out a livelihood from this hard and dangerous calling, the schooner owners, often the skippers themselves, risked more and more — overloading, undermanning and underfeeding, jockeying recklessly with the sea, chancing "one more trip" in uncertain autumn weather.

The *Flora Condon's* skipper was a stoutish fellow of middle years. His little goatee seemed to bristle as he noted me standing on on the wharf.

"Wouldn't want to ship, I s'pose? Need another hand. Ain't got but three so far. One's the cook. Ever be'n to sea? Know the compass?"

I started to box it.

"All right. Steer, can ye? Wa'l, give ye ten dollars an' found for the trip. Goin' to Bristol, Rhode Island. Ever be'n there?"
I said I had.
"All right. Shuck yer co't n' weskit, and git to work."

By the time we were at sea a few days later, my unaccustomed hands were blistered and my back ached. The *Flora Condon,* like the others of her venerability, leaked. It required almost constant attention at the pumps to keep her afloat. These were hand-operated by long iron levers, which by back-breaking labor were worked up and down until the pumps sucked, indicating that the water in the bilges was below the danger level — for the time being.

It was mid-September. The "Line Storm" was due and the aspect of the western sky as we cleared Machias Bay gave reason to fear that it was at hand.

It was! How the five of us — the cook, a Nova Scotian, was the best all-round man — kept the ancient *Flora Condon* from turning over, I can in nowise record. Being full of lumber, she could not, of course, sink. But she could capsize, as not infrequently happened to the lumber-coasters. So far as we were concerned that would have been just as bad.

But the coasters were built as solidly as a British East Indiaman and even in advanced age, say upwards of two-score years, their endurance was amazing. The *Flora Condon's* had outlasted mine by considerable, before, after a toilsome and several times uncertain fortnight, we entered Narragansett Bay. Once, off the dangerous Peaked Hill Bars on Cape Cod, we had been compelled to throw overboard half the deck-cargo to keep afloat. This was no uncommon thing. It was said in those days that no dweller along the back side of Cape Cod ever had to buy any lumber. All he needed, the tide brought to him.

Lumber was the principal cargo and about the safest, all things considered. The worst and most dangerous was paving-stone. So dangerous that only the most reckless skippers in the most unseaworthy schooners — generally small two-masters — would have anything to do with it. Caught, say, in an easterly off Cape Cod, the stone-laden coaster stood little chance. The records show that one of them was lost for every other disaster from all causes.

But the little schooner *Polly* survived them all. You can see her disintegrating remains today when the tide is low in the mud of a Down East port. Her age, admittedly great, was a matter of difference of opinion. There were those who insisted she had been a privateer in the War of 1812. In any case, her oaken ribs were hard as iron and even more durable. Her planking was two-and-a-half-inch seasoned white pine. She was said to have been on and off every reef along the Maine Coast, but the only evidence of it were such dents and gashes as you might find in a much-used washtub.

For the foregoing and others reasons, the *Polly* used to be known up and down the coast as the "Ark". One of the other reasons was the character of her crew. In her last years these included four old men. Each was full-bearded and patriarchal. Humorists of the Maine coast referred to the skipper as Noah, and to his three assistants as Shadrach, Meshach and Abednego. But the ancient craft, blunt-nosed and time-scarred, wallowed and lurched her way up and down the coast for many a year, April to snow-fly. The long experience of her antique crew seemed to balance their waning strength.

But more curious craft even than the old *Polly* took the water for the first time on the Maine coast, birth-place of the American wooden ship. From a considerable familiarity with the records, I should say the strangest of all was the flat-bottomed centerboard schooner *Enigma* which cleared the Kennebec for the first time in October, 1865.

Now anybody will agree that *Enigma* was a queer, possibly an ominous, name for a ship. It was chosen by the man who built and sailed her, the redoubtable Captain James T. Morse of Bath, for whom there was later called a very popular side-wheel steamer that used to connect with the Boston-Maine steamers at Rockland for Bar Harbor.

Captain Morse "calculated" to carry general cargoes from New England down to the Gulf and to bring them into shallow-water harbors along the coast between Pensacola and the mouth of the Mississippi.

Everybody around Bath shook his head dubiously when the *Enigma* sailed, deep laden with a cargo of Aroostook potatoes and a deckload of lumber. "You take that kind of a b'ot an' that kind of a name, an' anything can happen," was the general opinion.

Anything did happen! The *Enigma*, with her crew of five,

[47]

put in at Charleston, South Carolina, after eleven days during which old Father Neptune appeared tolerant of this affront to his grim power. Here much of the potato cargo was unloaded, leaving an empty space in the hold which, strangely enough, was to decide the fate of the five-man crew.

For before the ship had reached the Florida littoral, Captain Morse had found it necessary to reef-down and try to ride out a gale. Now the schooner's behavior became decidedly enigmatic. She fought it out for awhile, and then a terrific sea came along. Passing, left the *Enigma* bottom-side up.

Now follows an adventure almost, if not entirely, unparalleled in the annals of the sea. The five men were below at the time of the upset and they found themselves locked in a small space, in total darkness, with seawater creeping slowly in upon them. The overhead of the little cabin was now the deck. The men were entrapped. Few would have held out, but the Yankee sailor of those days wasn't easily vanquished.

To shorten the story, Captain Morse feeling about in the darkness, came upon an old hatchet.

"Up to that moment," he said later, "I hadn't figured there was a chance for us. But now an idea came to me. If we could cut through the bulkhead that separated the cabin from the after-hold we should be in a space three feet higher than our present trap."

The bulkhead, luckily, was soft pine, and vigorous work by desperate men at last made a hole big enough to crawl through. They had, of course, to work entirely by feeling and once, thrown off his balance by a heavy lurch of the upside-down craft, Captain Morse cut a deep gash in the hand of one of his men.

Hopes of survival were still dim, but the imprisoned men fought on. Bye and bye, there came a terrific crash. Masts, deckload and galley had separated from the hull at the same time. Captain Morse and his men, who could do nothing now, waited in fear and exhaustion.

But the weather outside calmed and when daylight came they found the disappearance of the galley had left a hole in the hatch beneath it. Through this hole a little light filtered though it was under water.

"Then I got the idea," said Captain Morse, "of cutting through

[48]

the inside skin of the schooner, as we had cut through the bulkhead."

Using the dulling hatchet by turns, they at last succeeded in making a hole about two feet by one. They now had to be sure that the air which had thus far sustained them did not escape, in which case the craft would have sunk at once.

With some of their clothing they plugged the place where the hatchet had pierced the outer planking. Then they cut around the hole until the wood was almost transparent. The remainder of that night, their third in black captivity, they rested. Next morning, with a large scantling found in the hold, they knocked out the cut planking and climbed through the hole onto the outside of the hull.

But even now their sufferings were not over. Incredible as it seems — yet it is all on the record in Bath — they spent three more days clinging to the hull before being sighted and taken off by the English brig *Peerless,* enroute from Philadelphia to Cuba. The men recovered, and Captain Morse returned to the sea for twenty years, not without many more stirring adventures.

That is the kind of men who manned New England sailing craft in the old days. They never thought of giving up while there was a breath of life or a glimmer of hope left. It was the breed that made Yankee clippers like the *Flying Cloud* and the *Lightning* undisputed mistresses of the seas.

Nothing daunted those New England men of the wooden ships. They were as tough as the oak ribs of their craft. Their competence as sailors was on a par with that of the carpenters and fitters who put their ships together, and nothing in history ever has, or ever will, surpass either in their respective callings. Their era is one of the glories of America.

But the record is darkened by tragedies and mysteries. Both tragic and mysterious was the affair of the Bath-built five-master *Carrol A. Deering,* found by the Coast Guard aground on the Outer Hatteras Shoal, in January, 1921.

The *Deering* was one of a famous fleet, built at Bath and other places along the Maine coast. She was bound north with lumber from southern ports. Off Hatteras there had been several days of impenetrable fog. When at last it lifted, there stood the big schooner, all sails set, looming up in the murk like another Flying Dutchman.

The seas were heavy and the Coast Guard boat could not approach for several more days. When the men did board her they found a set-up much like that of the so-called "mystery" of the *Marie Celeste* which, in the opinion of many sea-farers, was boarded by Barbery pirates and her company carried away into captivity.

Anyway, what had become of the Bath schooner's crew? On the galley table was an unfinished meal, no sign of life except a couple of half-starved cats. But the wheel rudder-housing and all navigational gear had been smashed. The ship's papers, the chronometer, some of the stores, and the clothes of the officers were gone.

In some ways here was a mystery without precedent. Other than the foregoing there was no signs of violence, but two of the small boats were gone, their falls hanging loose. Curiously, all lights, both side and running, were burning. The ship was so hard on the shoal that efforts to get her off were hopeless. She gradually broke up and following a heavy February gale, she disappeared.

But the element of mystery was deepened when, a few weeks later a bottle came ashore near Bunton, North Carolina. In it was a note, "*Deering* captured by boat. Taking off everything. Crew hiding but no chance to escape." There was no signature, simply *Deering*. What did this mean, if indeed it was genuine? No one has ever known, and more speculations have been made than about the fate of the aforesaid *Marie Celeste*. Of Captain Wormsley, a Portland, Maine, man, and his crew of eleven, nothing was ever heard.

The *Deering* was, by maritime standards, almost a new ship, built in the war period, a money-maker during her short life, until in the middle Twenties, the bottom dropped out of the sail-carrying trade and left many a good vessel, still young, to disintegrate on the mudflats. You see them all along the Maine coast, and two at Wiscasset, one of Maine's loveliest villages, are a familiar sight to summer tourists driving along U. S. Route 1. Fine four-masters they were, the *Hesper* and the *Luther Little*, built by the federal government during the first World War. The government sold them to a man named Winter of Auburn, Maine, owner of the little two-foot-gauge railroad that operated between Wiscasset and the interior. The scheme was to bring lumber down on the railroad and load it

[50]

on the schooners. But this fell through and neither of them ever left Wiscasset.

The big Maine-built five-master *Cora F. Cressey* made several coastwise voyages and then came to an ignominious end — first as a showboat in Boston Harbor and then as a lobster-pound near the little village of Breman on the Medomak River in Maine, where she is today. To those who have known and loved the splendid things of sail, she is a pathetic spectacle; to the summer tourist, merely quaint.

On the New England coast three towns were renowned throughout the world and their names were familiar in all the ports thereof — Bath, Searsport and Thomaston. Bath's fame, however, rested mainly on the great Sewall steel ships like the *Arthur Sewall* (disappeared in 1902 somewhere off the Horn), the *Edward Sewall*, the *Dirigo* (in which Jack London made his round-the-Horn voyage described in "The Mutiny of the *Elsinore*"), the *Kenilworth* and the *Erskine M. Phelps*. The era of these ended at the turn of the century, and then commenced what was widely hailed as a renaissance of sail.

More than two-score three-, four-, and five-masters resulted from this. They took the water at Yarmouth, from the famous yards of Giles Loring and others, and from there eastward at a dozen places — Wiscasset, Boothbay Harbor, Damariscotta, Thomaston, Rockland, Searsport, Harrington, Millbridge, Calais and Waldoboro (the far-famed Winslow fleet and some of the Palmer, hailed from there, including the big *Davis Palmer*, lost on The Graves at the mouth of Boston Harbor on Christmas night, 1909, with all hands.)

Some three-score in number were the four- and the five-masters. Many did valiant service in the first World War, braving gale and submarine in the western ocean, often manned by no more than half a dozen crew. Not a few volumes record their achievements, but for all that, most of them saw their last days in ignominious deterioration on a mudflat, a sad end for a noble fabric.

Thomaston was known as "The Town That Went To Sea" because so many of her sons took to that calling that, in the heyday of sail, it is said every other house in the lovely elm-shaded village could boast of a master or mate. Here the last American square-rigger, the term being permissible because the *Reine Marie Stewart*

[51]

was square-rigged on the foremast, though fore-and-aft on the other three, was built by the world-known firm of Dunn & Elliot. A year later, the last of the town's long line (more than five hundred through the eighteenth, nineteenth and into the twentieth centuries) was launched with the five-master *Edna Hoyt* sliding from the same yard. Thomaston's record of one hundred square-riggers built between 1860 and 1920, carried the name of the little village on the Georges River to every port of all the seas, and is, so far as can be gathered from the records, without parallel.

Convincing evidence of the unsurpassable excellence of Thomaston's shipbuilding lies in the fact that the *Reine*, after being laid up at a riverside wharf for ten years, was sold in 1937, to a Canadian firm. She was found in fine condition despite her long idleness, and operated in the Second War in transatlantic trade until sunk by a German sub off the West African coast in 1942.

A few of the older New England coasters are now used during the summer for short tourist cruises, gliding along in mild weather close to the coast, making overnight harbors at convenient points, thus giving city-dwelling vacationists the illusion that they are roughing it. But government restrictions are likely to put an end to this very profitable — for the operators — game, and one of the first to abandon it was the Baltimore-built schooner *Eva S. Collison* which, launched in 1888, operated for many years as a fruit-carrier to and from the Bahamas. She is a fine little vessel with yacht-like lines. At present she lies on the mud in Rockland harbor, having been offered without success to the famous Marine Museum at Mystic, Connecticut. It would be a great pity should this attractive little vessel disintegrate, as so many others have done and are doing, on the noisome mud of a Down East harbor.

CHAPTER VIII

Cargo of Dragon's Blood

TEDDY PARKER

IN the middle of the Indian Ocean — somewhere around 13°
N. 57° E. — the *Salamat Sawai*, an open boat of about forty feet
rolled rhythmically on a windless sea.

It was hot, blazing hot. The sun was directly overhead and the
sea, like polished brass reflected a fierce light into any open eye.
The lateen mainsail hung in useless folds from a great yard which
groaned dismally against the mast as the ship rolled.

Amidships, trying to get some shade from the swinging sail, the
dark-skinned, turbanned crew lay around in hopeless attitudes.
There were four of them: Hajji Ismail, the sailing master, who
proudly wore a green turban to show he had been to Mecca; Hajji's
brother Ali, the cook and bosun; Saleh Mohammed, Hajji's nephew
a sad thin man who was assistant navigator by virtue of his voyages
to Zanzibar in a trading dhow, and lastly Hajji's uncle, Ali Mohammed, who looked about a hundred and one, was nearly deaf and
partly paralyzed below the waist but was, nevertheless, a wonderful
helmsman.

Abaft the well of the ship, where the crew lay, was a great
cylindrical boiler lashed athwartships. Its contents sloshed with the
roll of the ship. Behind the boiler in the raised stern sheets were
two more rough looking characters, naked from the waist up, dark
brown, bearded and turbanned like the others. These two were
your correspondent, T. Parker, and his regimental buddy, Tom — the
charterers of this remarkable vessel.

The afterguard, crouching in the shade of a crazily rigged
piece of blanket, were navigating. We were twelve days out from
Karachi, bound for Aden, and thought we had covered about a
thousand miles but we were not sure. What we did know was we
had run out of wind and it was our own fault, too. Our original plan

had been to sail straight south from Karachi on the tail of the northeast monsoon, swing westwards in about latitude 8° N. then pick up the beginning of the southwest monsoon and have a reach up past Cape Guardafui, the easternmost end of Africa, into the Gulf of Aden where we should get easterly winds.

A week of good sailing at the beginning had lured us into throwing away our plan and our good resolutions. Fed up with sailing at right angles to the rhumb line, we had altered course to the westward and had, of course, run into the great flat spot which we had known all along lay in our track.

Now we had just turned in a noon-to-noon run of nineteen miles. The sea looked as if it lay under cellophane and we were about as comfortable as a celluloid cat in a coke oven.

I finished fiddling with the chart and the log book.

"There's no going back, Tom. We'll have to keep on going west and that's all there is to it. If we keep on this latitude and run it down we should pass to the north of Socotra and pitch up in the Gulf of Aden somewhere."

Tom had been turning the pages of the "Red Sea and Gulf of Aden Pilot," a fine nautical work whose text had been written about one hundred years ago for the benefit of masters of sailing vessels. He looked up.

"Do you want to know what it says here about Socotra?"

"All right, lets's have it," I answered.

"Socotra, an island of the Indian Ocean, is situated 150 miles from Cape Guardafui and 220 miles from the Arabian coast. It is seventy-one miles long and twenty-two miles wide. Owing to the barren and inhospitable nature of the island, the dangerous coastline, the lack of suitable anchorages and the unfriendly attitude of the natives, the island is seldom visited. The prudent mariner bound to the eastward from the Gulf of Aden is advised to pass at least ten miles to the northward of it."

"It sounds like a charming old world holiday resort — tell me more."

Tom skimmed through the book. "There is only the usual rock by rock description of the coast — ah, yes, here is something: 'The chief export of the island is Dragon's Blood'. What do you think of that?"

[54]

"What sort of a dragon does it say it is? If it's the kind that breathes fire down your neck I am having no part of it. I am hot enough as it is."

"It doesn't say anything more. I think we had better go and find out, don't you?"

It seemed just as sensible a thing to do as anything else we were doing so I agreed without much of a struggle. The chart was consulted, a plan was made to get on the right latitude and run it down and then we relapsed into our normal state of coma.

In the evening, just as the sun was going down, a light breeze came away from aft. The great yard was squared off, the mizzen was set and as the sails filled the groaning and rolling gradually died away. As the mauve sky turned to velvety purple and the stars came out, Ali dragged some pieces of firewood out of the forepeak, flung them on the sandbox in the well and got the fire going. Hajji ground up the curry powder with a stone pestle and mortar. Rice was brought from the bag by the mainmast, and dried fish carefully selected from the big tin beside the boiler tank. Soon our curry and rice was served to us piled high on two great tin plates, while the crew, seated near the fire, ate out of a common dish with their hands.

The flickering fire light shone on the rugged, bearded faces of the crew and lit up the curving foot of the great sail as it swelled to the growing breeze. There was quiet murmuring of water along the side as our speed increased. We were really on our way to Socotra in search of Dragon's Blood.

For a week, propelled by faint and fickle breezes we ran our westing down. Each day at noon we checked our position using all our old world navigational aids and a fair sprinkling of guess work. Saleh Mohammed's pocket sextant and an abstract of declination from an Indian nautical almanac gave us our latitude, more or less. Our longitude depended on our dead reckoning which in turn depended on an ancient Arab compass and on the "Bromo-Parker" speed indicator.

This latter was a complicated device of our own design. Its main components were: the ship's head, a square box with a hole in the bottom lashed against the flat transom; a fishing line with a silver spinner; the ship's clock, and a packet of that well known toilet paper called "Bromo". To operate this device the ship's master squatted in the head and hurled a crumpled piece of toilet paper into the wake shouting "Mark" as he did so. The mate watched the clock and the master shouted "Mark" again when the toilet paper passed the spinner — clearly visible in those tropical waters. Knowing the length of the fishing line, a simple calculation gave us our speed through the water. You can guess how this device originated.

At the end of this week of poor going we reckoned we were pretty near Socotra and should in theory be able to see its high eastern end. Alas, the visibility looked infinite, the horizon was clear cut and there was no sign of a break on it. The crew, except for Saleh Mohammed, were fishermen and longshoremen from Bhit Island in Karachi Harbour. They had never sailed out of sight of land before and were getting distinctly restive. We jollied them along cheerfully and promised them land tonight or tomorrow but secretly imagined all sorts of navigational errors and wondered if we had not sailed clear out of the known world and were doomed to go on and on till we sailed over the edge and fell into eternity.

In the evening as the sun gradually sank, a miracle was revealed. Socotra, hidden in a heat haze all day, was right alongside and its jagged peaks showed black and firm against the red disc of the setting sun. After nineteen days and fourteen-hundred miles of slow sailing, we were bang on. That was something to celebrate so we rooted out the bottle of brandy from the medicine chest and did so. Our prestige with the crew rose to a new high. Cheerfully they made a bigger and better curry than ever and everyone was happy.

A fair breeze blew all night and gradually increased. Before dawn the light mizzen was stowed and soon after there was a loud crack. It was the bowsprit as usual. Nobody bothered to comment — we struggled forward, got the jib aboard, lowered it, and threw the remains of the spar into the firewood heap.

The seas were building up and soon the steering became erratic. Sometimes the ship squatted on her flat stern, at others her nose went down in a curving dive. We debated getting the big sail off but as that involved getting the whole yard down, unlacing the sail, taking off a ten foot length of span fished on to the end of the main yard and lacing on the storm sail, we took the easier course and did nothing.

Tom was using his whole six feet, six inches of big bone and strong muscle on that tiller but could not keep her straight. Soon he let her run up. A quartering sea broke over the waist and the well was flooded. At this we dumped old Ali Mohammed in the stern, gave him the tiller and started to bail like mad before our rice and flour got ruined. The old man sat there cross-legged with a face like a half-dead turtle and steered with one hand. After he had asked for a fresh trim of the tack, the main sheet and the back stay and had got the weight to his liking, he had that old crate skimming along on its tail like a 14-foot dinghy. He had been sailing her since she was built fifty years before so knew what he was about.

By mid-morning the end of the island was abeam and we raced along past sheer black cliffs with great jagged pinnacles of rock behind them. Although we were going through the water fast, I was puzzled by the fact that the land was going by very slowly. At first I thought it was an adverse current, but then realized that I had got the whole island out of perspective. Without a sign of a tree, house, or patch of vegetation to gauge by, I had underestimated its shape and size hopelessly. The cliffs were not a couple of hundred feet high, but nearer a thousand. The jagged rock pinnacles were more like three or four thousand feet high than one, and in consequence we were not three miles off but ten or more. The whole scene was one of gloomy desolation, well suited to a dragon's lair.

The sea eased but the wind held and all day we sailed along the coast, passing one steep black headland after another, yet not seeing a trace of vegetation or life. We were making for Tamrida on the center of the north coast which the "Pilot" said was the only village of consequence on the island. As we rounded one point, we saw before us a bay with a beach at the far side — the only one so far — and behind it a low point beyond which we reckoned Tamrida lay. Just before we reached this point the breeze dropped, so we closed with the coast and dropped anchor off the beach, using the main sheet as an anchor rode in default of anything else.

Some natives soon appeared, launched a dugout canoe and came paddling out to us. Completely naked except for a small loin cloth, very small, black as a boot and of low negroid appearance, they looked about the bottom of the scale of human types. However, they were unarmed and appeared fairly friendly so we made signs that they were to take us ashore.

[57]

This they did willingly and we set our unsteady feet on the beach and were led off to some rough, ill-made grass huts. Squatting on the mud floor of the smoky interior, we were entertained by a tiny black witch with long strap-like bosoms hanging to her string belt, given a cup of some hot drink which appeared to have been made from quinine, ashes and muddy water and regaled with a variety of monkey talk and signs. Soon tiring of this, we took off in search of Dragon's Blood and fresh food, both of which we needed badly. There was no animal life, fresh water or cultivation to be seen anywhere — nothing but rocks, sand and a few stunted bushes. What the natives lived on was a mystery but the smell of the huts suggested that fish might be an answer.

Our sea legs soon tired on land, so summoning our hosts we got them to take us back on board. The *Salamat Sawai*, which we had long since decided was rock bottom of human living conditions, now seemed an oasis of luxury. Even dirty old Hajji Ismail with his half-dyed, unkempt beard we welcomed as a distinguished and civilized old friend.

Next morning we sailed around the point into Tamrida Bay where we were immediately surrounded by a cluster of canoes whose savage inhabitants clung to the side of the ship emitting animal cries of amazement. We gave them scraps of cloth, old nails and all forms of rubbish which they siezed eagerly and in return gave us fresh fish of all shapes and colours. Anchoring off the town, we were paddled ashore in canoes which gave us a wild exciting ride through the surf breaking on the beach.

The town was similar to an Arab village with square, single-storied, mud-walled buildings, roughly whitewashed. It had no paved streets, no wheeled vehicles and nothing except the crudest forms of the necessities of life. We wandered around followed by a large crowd and entered without ceremony various houses in search of Dragon's Blood or fresh food but found nothing of either.

In the center of the town we came across one quite presentable house, built as a hollow square with verandas arranged around a central courtyard. This belonged to an Arab trader who greeted us courteously and bid us enter. We explained to him, in a poor mixture of Arabic and Hindustani, our need for fresh food. He informed us that fresh fruit or vegetables were unobtainable but suggested a sheep. We settled for that and a nearby aboriginal was sent to fetch it. We then asked him for some of the red stuff for which the island was famous. This rattled him a little but after further discussion he produced a sack of red blobs like sealing wax. He explained it was the sap of a small tree and that he exported it to Zanzibar and Southern Arabia where it was used for making red lacquer. Its name in Arabic sounded as if it might well be Dragon's Blood, so we agreed. We had got it. Elated at our succeee I gave him a silver rupee for a handful of the stuff and took my leave politely. Tom followed leading a sad, thin sheep on a string.

As we reached the beach, Tom pleaded some tale about weight and balance and handed me the sheep. When we got into the canoe it was clear that the sheep and I had different ideas. I wanted to get back to the *Salamat Sawai* but the sheep was determined to stay in Socotra. We fought it out as the monkey man tried to drive the canoe through the breakers but there was only one possible result — we capsized. Fortunately I was a better swimmer than the sheep and got such a grip on him as we floundered to the shore that he had no chance to get away. I had him flat on his side and triced up with a lashing as soon as we hit the sand. The next time, stunned by the waves and subdued with string, he went quietly.

We all got on board, upped anchor and set sail without regrets on a northwesterly course towards the Arabian coast. In the evening as the desolate land of Socotra faded from view, the sheep had its throat cut with due Mohammedan decorum and we sat around in the fading light awaiting our first meat meal in three weeks. Even in death that animal fought back. The great sheep supper was a dismal failure. He was as tough as boots and tasted as if he had been brought up on a diet of seaweed and cough mixture. We kept the rest of him for bait.

For three days the wind held moderate and steady between southwest and west. We ambled along with all sail set — we had cut a supply of new bowsprits in Socotra — and made good an average of four knots. As soon as we picked up the coast of Arabia, the breeze faded and left us looking at a barren landscape of pale brown hills with a foreground of sandy beach on which here and there we could spot occasional patches of green — probably palm trees. We had been reluctant to get too close to this coast as it has a well documented reputation for piracy but by now we wanted to get on and to hell with the pirates. We gradually closed with the shore hoping to get an offshore breeze in the evening when the hot barren land cooled down.

In the late afternoon, we were drifting along at a half to one knot about a mile off the shore somewhere to the west of the port of Makalla when from nowhere in particular an Arab boy appeared in a canoe and circled our craft. We hailed him but he did not answer at all. He came fairly close, stood up in his canoe and looked us over for a long time without saying anything. He then paddled off at a great rate in an easterly direction. We looked the way he was going and saw through glasses that he was heading for a small village of brown huts which we had not previously noticed.

By now the light was going and it was difficult to see clearly what was going on but we could make out the boy's arrival, a .cene of activity in the village which included long rifles being slung over mens' backs and a great long boat being dragged down the beach to the water's edge. Men piled into it in considerable numbers and then we lost sight of them. It was clear they were after us.

Our main armament was a .25-caliber Colt automatic which we cleaned up and put a clip in but it looked a little light against the opposition which was coming our way. While we were considering what to do next, we felt the longed-for breeze on our cheeks coming off the shore. We altered course out to sea and gradually gathered way in the growing darkness. After twenty minutes we altered course again to the east — the opposite of our previous course — trimmed the sheets quietly and sat there like mice. Then we heard some talking and the noise of oars or paddles splashing in the water. It got louder, and passed inside us and faded away to the west. They had missed us. We held our breath for a little and then headed offshore again in the growing breeze.

All night we held off shore and remained nervously alert but dawn came and showed us an empty sea. The threat was over. In the next week we kept land in sight but despite light variable and contrary winds we did not go looking for any more land breezes.

At last the true Gulf of Aden easterly wind we had been hoping for set in. It blew strong and true and was very welcome for by this time the bottom carried such a collection of barnacles and general tropical fungus that we slipped through the water about as well as a hairbrush through thick cream.

We left the coast and headed across the great bay that sweeps round to the rock of Aden. The crew started to complain about leaving the land again but by the time they had really worked themselves into a frenzy, the rock of Aden was showing on the horizon. I told them to look around and if they could find land we would head for it. They looked around, and saw it dead ahead and piped down. The wind had by now breezed up to about thirty miles an hour and was still freshening.

The bowsprit had carried away as usual and we were alternatively squatting in the troughs and racing along on the crests of quite a sizeable sea, but Ali Mohammed at the helm seemed quietly confident so we cracked on. It was apparent that at the rate we were going we would arrive in Aden during the night. We had no harbor chart so what to do was the problem. We decided to reach across the harbor mouth until the lights of the town opend up clear in the harbor entrance, gybe over and come straight in on what looked like a reasonably safe bearing.

Soon after it was dark the lighthouse came up bright and clear — the first light we had seen since the Kheti Bandar Light vessel of Karachi — nineteen hundred miles and a century ago. Three hours later we were still tearing along and could make out the black mass of the rock and the light spotted all over it. Soon the harbor opened up and the time now came for our great gybe.

With a big sea running, this was quite an antic. First the main sheet was let go until the whole sail was flogging away out ahead. Then the great yard, all fifty-five feet of it, was maneuvered into a very unstable position vertically up and down on the fore side of the mast. The back stay was cast off and transferred to the other side. The yard was allowed to cant over on the new tack and the bitter end of the main sheet passed around forward of the mast and brought aft on the new leeward side. All hands tailed on and, to the accompaniment of Indian cries, the sheet was hove in until the sail was drawing.

So off we went rolling and lurching into the harbor mouth in the black night with not the slightest idea what was inside. The seas gradually smoothed out as we got into the shelter of the rock but the steady breeze changed to vicious gusts from all directions. Over-canvassed and with a foul bottom, we were quite unmaneuverable. Our first encounter was with a black object which gave out a loud clang and bobbed away astern. Next we got caught aback, re-

[61]

fused to come about and headed rapidly for the same breakers. We managed to gybe out of this but with little room to spare. Further up the harbor we got in among anchored vessels, failed to come about again and drove into the side of one of Her Majesty's ships. A round of good British abuse in the broad accents of Devon greeted us from the deck. Although delighted to hear the familiar accent once more, we felt the time was not quite appropriate to reveal our identity. We remained quiet and scraped down her side until the bow caught in the companion ladder and threw her head around. The time had come to stop this bashing around, so spotting some masts of small craft at anchor we made for them and dropped anchor among them.

Daylight showed us to be in among native coastal cruising and fishing craft off the main part of the town. Enquiry from our neighbors showed that the correct drill was to wait where we were until someone came out to clear us. When they said that "this might be today, tomorrow or the next day, who could tell," Tom got fed up and started hauling up the anchor. The thought of missing out on the British breakfast he had set his heart on was too much for him. Hajji let draw the sail and I took the helm and steered for a smart looking dock where naval pinnaces, liners, tenders and harbor masters' craft were coming and going.

I laid her slap across the end of the jetty against the most important looking steps and tied up. That certainly produced some action. Officials of all sorts rushed in the direction of our dirty looking craft with horror and astonishment on their faces. A British type in a white helmet led the rat race, abused us roundly in Hindustani, and asked us who the hell we were and where we had come from and what in the name of Vishna Krishna and somebody else we were doing tied up there.

I rose to my feet in the stern and told him clearly in my best Poona British accent.

"This is the *Salamat Sawai* from Socotra with a cargo of Dragon's Blood. We want the doctor, the harbor master and the immigration officer and we would be grateful if you would moderate your language, stop gaping at us and go and find them."

That rattled him. He went, and so ended the voyage of the *Salamat Sawai*.

[62]

CHAPTER IX

And Little Children Shall Lead Them

J. S. SCOTT

W HEN I saw the courier come up the gangway, I knew we were in for bad news. For one thing, I recognized the pasty-faced yeoman as the surly little squirt from Operations who seemed to have the power that generally goes with the flag rank and who delighted in originating sailing orders to tired crews. Also, good news seldom came from the Naval Base Operations Officer's sacro-sanct premises. News, like leaves, transfers or promotions, generally came from our own Coast Guard Flotilla Staff, and never, never by courier messenger. Furthermore, the scuttlebutt, that mysterious grapevine of intelligence, had had it for some time that we were slated to spend our first Christmas in England at sea.

Our ship, if she could be classified as such, was a lowly Land-ing Craft Infantry (L.C.I.) that was spawned on a mud flat in Orange, Texas, of all unlikely places, had crossed the Alantic under her own unorthodox power of eight diesel engines hooked up to two reversible pitch propellers through gear boxes. Together with twenty-three other sister-ships in our bob-tailed flotilla, she had logged over twenty thousand sea miles in this first year of her short but active service.

The year and date was 1943, the twenty-third of December, and since our launching in January of that same World War II year, we had pounded across the Gulf of Mexico, pitched and rolled our way up the Gulf Stream against a northeast gale to Bermuda, chugged from there to North Africa, and then spent the summer and fall taking part in landing and convoying operations during the invasions of Italy and Sicily. After the Italian surrender, our flotilla, which had been the guinea pig for many new concepts of amphibious war-fare, was withdrawn from the Mediterranean theatre and sent to England to train. We were destined to spearhead the U.S. forces being built up in the British Isles for the Normandy Invasion.

[63]

Despite being shadowed by Nazi aircraft off Spain and hunted by a pack of U-boats crossing Biscay on our unescorted passage from Gilbraltar to the English Channel, we were happy over our new assignment. For one thing, we were sick and tired of the smells, fleas, flies, dysentery, malaria, whores, gonorrhea, heat, Arabs, French, Jews, and the U.S. Navy in the Mediterranean bases. Besides, we were dead tired and homesick. England, to us, represented the last and final stop, the jumping off place for bringing about the end of the War in Europe and the achievement of our Holy Grail — returning Stateside to our families.

Aside from our typical reservist's distaste for war, regulations and the service life, our self-pity was further aggravated by the fact that we were in the difficult status of being U.S. Coast Guard personnel, manning a U.S. Naval craft and usually operating under an American or British Army command. Frequently, we missed getting paid because no pay officer could be found who would honor our pay vouchers. Our only medical attention came from the U.S. Public Health Service, which was sometimes hard to find in the European Theatre of Operations. For food, uniforms and canteen rations, we generally had to depend on handouts from the Army Quartermasters, when and if we could persuade them that we were fighting on the same team. In short, the crew of our little bucket felt as though we were being kicked about and we were very, very sorry for ourselves. That is, until we arrived at our base in Plymouth, England.

Steaming in past the Hoe after successfully piloting our way through the heavily mined and E-boat infested Channel, our crew was initially shocked at seeing first hand the terrific devastation that the town of Plymouth had taken in the blitz. Bizerte, Palermo and Naples, by comparison, were quickly forgotten when we stared at this tremendous area that had been literally flattened by high explosive and fire bombs. We began to feel less sorry for ourselves.

Then when we stepped ashore and had our first chance to talk to the stoic but destitute victims of the Nazi Luftwaffe raids, our self-pity turned to embarrassment that we had ever complained of our temporary discomforts. These quiet people had endured much greater hardships for a longer period than we had. Finally, our troubles disappeared like a morning mist when we were forcefully made aware of the high admiration that the British hold for the United States Coast Guard.

[64]

AND LITTLE CHILDREN SHALL LEAD THEM

Traditionally a seafaring nation, the British have always played favoritism to their Naval or "Senior Service", as they put it. But we were soon to learn that in Devon and Cornwall, at least, the Coast Guard was on an even higher pinnacle of public esteem. Whether or not we were confused with their National Life Saving Institute, which has so many heroic rescues to its credit, or because our cutters had become so world renowned for their ice patrol, rescue work and early World War II convoy duty, we never determined. Nor did we care to find out. All that mattered was we felt wanted and proud to be allied with such stalwart people.

Girls are the time honored target of opportunity for sailors throughout the world and it must be admitted that our crew did well for themselves on that score, judging from what could be observed around the friendly pubs of Plymouth. However, the American gob has another love that sometimes come before women and whisky and that is the love for little children. We had not been tied up to the commercial docks (there was "no room at the inn" for us at the Naval Base) for more than twenty-four hours before the mole was crowded with youngsters, attracted, of course, by the generosity on the part of the "Yanks" in passing out chewing gum and sweets to the sugar-starved little victims of wartime austerity. Unlike the little Arab, French, and Italian urchins in the Mediterranean who used to beg and steal everything that wasn't nailed down, these kids were orderly, beautifully mannered and just plain grateful. The fact that many of them had attractive, English speaking sisters at home also served to tighten the friendships. Anglo-Coast Guard relations were never better.

On that gloomy, rainy morning just two days before Christmas when the unwelcome messenger appeared with the fateful dispatch, I dreaded opening it, for I had an inkling of what was coming. At a flotilla meeting for commanding officers, the word had been passed that the brass hats at the U.S. Naval Operating Base, Plymouth, had threatened to order all U.S. floating units to sea for the two-day Christmas and Boxing Day holidays in order to keep the season-inspired sailors from depleting the spirit ration in Plymouth. Although we recognized the reasoning behind this contemplated official action, what rankled in our breasts was that the fat-bottomed base personnel who had thought up the scheme were reported to have conveniently neglected to prohibit their own men from roaming the city during the same period.

My worries were compounded by two other matters, both of which pointed toward a bad morale situation on the ship during the Christmas period. Word had gotten around that a Liberty ship loaded with turkeys had arrived in the ETO with their traditional Christmas fare. Having verified this bit of information, I had sent my Commissary Officer high-tailing overland by jeep to get our share. He returned with the sad news that the birds were consigned to the Army and Naval bases and that no persuasion or bribery on his part could obtain even one bird for a Coast Guard unit.

The other more serious problem was that our mail from home had been non-existent since we had left the Mediterranean more than a month before. It was obvious that there had been a foul-up on the part of the Fleet Post Office. Another of my officers had spent nearly a week ransacking mail rooms in naval installations all over the U.K. in an unsuccessful hunt for our lost Christmas packages and letters. So we were faced with mail-less, present-less, turkey-less Yuletide, in a blacked-out, bombed-out, foreign port.

When I opened the fateful dispatch, all of my worst fears were confirmed. In the usual impassionate language, it started out with "WHEN IN ALL RESPECTS READY FOR SEA YOU WILL PROCEED..." and ended with the terse "ALL LEAVE AND LIBERTY ARE HEREBY CANCELLED".

Sailing orders in those terms meant the ship must be sealed off from communication with shore immediately, so I passed the word to have the gangway closed and for all hands to muster in one of our below-deck troop compartments. Although I dreaded the prospect of facing the men. I thought it was up to me to try and explain the situation and break the news as gently as possible. The crew listened without a murmur or grumble but I could read their faces and it was easy to see that my pep talk had done nothing to improve their spirits.

Next day, Christmas Eve, we took on fuel, water and the few pitiful foods rations we could get from shore and made the ship ready for the tossing around we expected to get from the wintery English Channel. Shortly before we cast off, the gangway watch announced that there was an elderly civilian gentleman on the dock who had asked to see the captain. Going on deck, I was surprised to see the

[66]

old white-haired schoolmaster from the neighborhood bombed-out school, standing in front of a group of nearly fifty small children, many of whom I recognized as the tots who had been hanging around the ship.

When I greeted the old man, he apologetically explained that his children were too young to understand the necessity of keeping ship movements secret during wartime, but that "little children have big ears" and having learned that we "Yanks" were going to have to put to sea for Christmas, they wanted to give us a few presents as tokens of their "grateful friendship."

After mustering all hands on the quarter deck, a package was passed aboard and in it was a wrapped gift for every man in the crew. And to make it even more touching, each present was something practical like a warm pair of socks, a muffler, a pair of mittens, or a watch cap, things that we instantly realized represented not only a lot of thought and expense but also precious clothing ration coupons.

Up to that moment I thought our ship's company was a fairly tough, battle-seasoned bunch of sailors. And maybe they were. But never have I seen such an open display of tears on the part of so many grown men as there was on that dismal December day. When some composure was regained, a delegation came forward and asked for permission to pass out the ship's canteen rations, well knowing that to re-supply them could be a matter of weeks and would depend on finding the rarest of all birds — a soft hearted Supply Officer.

After the candy, gum, and cookies had been distributed amongst the little group of rosy-cheeked, tow-headed children clustered on the pier, the time for our scheduled departure had arrived. As we tossed off our shore lines and backed out into the stream, their squeaky little voices broke out in a familiar Christmas carol.

There is not a man alive in that crew today who doesn't recall that scene and get a lump in his throat when he hears "O Little Town of Bethlehem".

Chapter X

The Ledge

L. S. HALL

O N Christmas morning before sunup the fisherman em-
braced his warm wife and left his close bed. She did not want him to
go. It was Christmas morning. He was a big raw man, with too much
strength, whose delight in winter was to hunt the sea ducks that
flew in to feed by the outer ledges, bare at low tide.

As his feet touched the cold floor and the frosty air struck his
nude flesh, he might have changed his mind in the dark of this
special day. It was a home day, which made it seem natural to think
of the outer ledges merely as some place he had shot ducks in the
past. But he had promised his son, thirteen, and his nephew, fifteen,
who came from inland. That was why he had given them his present of an automatic shotgun each the night before, on Christmas
Eve. Rough man though he was known to be, and no spoiler of
boys, he kept his promises when he understood what they meant.
And to the boys, as to him, home meant where you came for rest
after you had had your Christmas fill of action and excitement.

His legs astride, his arms raised, the fisherman stretched as high
as he could in the dim privacy of his bedroom. Above the snug murmur of his wife's protest he heard the wind in the pines and knew
it was easterly as the boys had hoped and he had surmised the night
before. Conditions would be ideal, and when they were, anybody
ought to take advantage of them. The birds would be flying. The
boys would get a man's sport their first time outside on the ledges.

His son at thirteen, small but steady and experienced, was
fierce to grow up in hunting, to graduate from sheltered waters and
the blinds along the shores of the inner bay. His nephew at fifteen,
an overgrown farm boy, had a farm boy's love of the sea, though he
could not swim a stroke and was often sick in choppy weather. That
was the reason his father, the fisherman's brother, was a farmer and
chose to sleep in on the holiday morning at his brother's house.

[68]

Many of the ones the farmer had grown up with were regularly seasick and could not swim, but they were unafraid of the water. They could not have dreamed of being anything but fishermen. The fisherman himself could swim like a seal and was never sick, and he would sooner die than be anything else.

He dressed in the cold and dark, and woke the boys gruffly. They tumbled out of bed, their instincts instantly awake while their thoughts still fumbled slumbrously. The fisherman's wife in the adjacent bedroom heard them apparently trying to find their clothes, mumbling sleeply and happily to each other, while her husband went down to the hot kitchen to fry eggs — sunnyside up, she knew, because that was how they all liked them.

Always in winter she hated to have them go outside, the weather was so treacherous and there were so few others out in case of trouble. To the fisherman these were no more than woman's fears, to be taken for granted and laughed off. When they were first married they fought miserably every fall because she was after him constantly to put his boat up until spring. The fishing was all outside in winter, and though prices were high the storms made the rate of attrition high on gear. Nevertheless he did well. So she could do nothing with him.

People thought him a hard man, and gave him the reputation of being all out for himself because he was inclined to brag and be disdainful. If it was true, and his own brother was one of those who strongly felt it was, they lived better than others, and his brother had small right to criticize. There had been times when in her loneliness she had yearned to leave him for another man. But it would have been dangerous. So over the years she had learned to shut her mind to his hard-driving, and take what comfort she might from his unsympathetic competence. Only once or twice, perhaps, had she gone so far as to dwell guiltily on what it would be like to be a widow.

The thought that her boy, possibly because he was small, would not be insensitive like his father, and the rattle of dishes and smell of frying bacon downstairs in the kitchen shut off from the rest of the chilly house, restored the cozy feeling she had before she was alone in bed. She heard them after a while go out and shut the back door.

Under her window she heard the snow grind drily beneath their boots, and her husband's sharp, exasperated commands to the boys. She shivered slightly in the envelope of her own warmth. She listened to the noise of her son and nephew talking elatedly. Twice she caught the glimmer of their lights on the white ceiling above the window as they went down the path to the shore. There would be frost on the skiff and freezing suds at the water's edge. She herself used to go gunning when she was younger; now, it seemed to her, anyone going out like that on Christmas morning had to be incurably male. They would none of them think about her until they returned and piled the birds they had shot on top of the sink for her to dress.

Ripping into the quiet pre-dawn cold she heard the hot snarl of the outboard taking them out to the boat. It died as abruptly as it had burst into life. Two or three or four or five minutes later the big engine broke into a warm reassuring roar. He had the best equipment, and he kept it in the best of condition. She closed her eyes. It would not be too long before the others would be up for Christmas. The summer drone of the exhaust deepened. Then gradually it faded in the wind until lost at sea, or she slept.

The engine had started immediately in spite of the temperature. This put the fisherman in a good mood. He was proud of his boat. Together he and the two boys heaved the skiff and outboard onto the stern and secured it athwartships. His son went forward along the deck, iridescent in the ray of the light the nephew shone through the windshield, and cast the mooring pennant loose into darkness. The fisherman swung to starboard, glanced at his compass, and headed seaward down the obscure bay.

There would be just enough visibility by the time they reached the headland to navigate the crooked channel between the islands. It was the only nasty stretch of water. The fisherman had done it often in fog or at night — he always swore he could go anywhere in the bay blindfolded — but there was no sense in taking chances if you didn't have to. From the mouth of the channel he could lay a straight course for Brown Cow Island, anchor the boat out of sight behind it, and from the skiff set their tollers off Devils Hump three hundred yards to seaward. By then the tide would be clearing the ledge and they could land and be ready to shoot around half-tide.

It was early, it was Christmas, and it was farther out than most hunters cared to go in this season of the closing year, so that he felt sure no one would be taking possession ahead of them. He had shot thousands of ducks there in his day. The Hump was by far the best hunting. Only thing was you had to plan for the right conditions because you didn't have too much time. About four hours was all, and you had to get it before three in the afternoon when the birds left and went out to sea ahead of nightfall.

They had it figured exactly right for today. The ledge would not be going under until after the gunning was over, and they would be home for supper in good season. With a little luck the boys would have a skiff-load of birds to show for their first time outside. Well beyond the legal limit, which was no matter. You took what you could get in this life, or the next man made out and you didn't.

The fisherman had never failed to make out gunning from Devil's Hump. And this trip, he had a hunch, would be above ordinary. The easterly wind would come up just stiff enough, the tide was right, and it was going to storm by tomorrow morning so the birds would be moving. Things were perfect.

The old fierceness was in his bones. Keeping a weather eye to the murk out front and a hand on the wheel, he reached over and cuffed both boys playfully as they stood together close to the heat of the exhaust pipe running up through the center of the house. They poked back at him and shouted above the drumming engine, making bets as they always did on who would shoot the most birds. This trip they had the thrill of new guns, the best money could buy, and a man's hunting ground. The black retriever wagged at them and barked. He was too old and arthritic to be allowed in December water, but he was jaunty anyway at being brought along.

Groping in his pocket for his pipe, the fisherman suddenly had his high spirits rocked by the discovery that he had left his tobacco at home. He swore. Anticipation of a day out with nothing to smoke made him incredulous. He searched his clothes, and then he searched them again, unable to believe the tobacco was not somewhere. When the boys inquired what was wrong he spoke angrily to them, blaming them for being in some devious way at fault. They were instantly crestfallen and willing to put back after the tobacco, though they could appreciate what it meant only through his irritation. But he bitterly refused. That would throw everything out of phase. He was a man who did things the way he set out to do.

He clamped his pipe between his teeth, and twice more during the next few minutes he ransacked his clothes in disbelief. He was no stoic. For one relaxed moment he considered putting about and gunning somewhere near home. Instead he held his course and sucked the empty pipe, consoling himself with the reflection that at least he had whiskey enough if it got too uncomfortable on the ledge. Peremptorily he made the boys check to make certain the bottle was really in the knapsack with the lunches where he thought he had taken care to put it. When they reassured him he despised his fate a little less.

The fisherman's judgement was, as usual, accurate. By the time they were abreast of the headland there was sufficient light so that he could wind his way among the reefs without slackening speed. At last he turned his bow toward open ocean, and as the winter dawn filtered upward through long layers of smoky cloud on the eastern rim his spirits rose again with it.

He opened the throttle, steadied on his course, and settled down to the two hour run. The wind was stronger but seemed less cold coming from the sea. The boys had withdrawn from the fisherman and were talking together while they watched the sky through the windows. The boat churned solidly through a light chop, flinging spray off her flaring bow. Astern, the headland thinned rapidly till it lay like a blackened sill on the grey water. No other boats were abroad.

The boys fondled their new guns, sighted along the barrels, worked the mechanisms, compared notes, boasted, and gave each other contradictory advice. The fisherman got their attention once and pointed at the horizon. They peered through the windows and saw what looked like a black scum floating on top of gently agitated water. It wheeled and tilted, rippled, curled, then rose, strung itself out and became a huge raft of ducks escaping over the sea. A good sign.

The boys rushed out and leaned over the washboards in the wind and spray to see the flock curl below the horizon. Then they went and hovered around the hot engine, bewailing their lot. If only they had been already set out waiting. Maybe these ducks would be crazy enough to return later and be slaughtered. Ducks were known to be foolish.

In due course and right on schedule they anchored at mid-morning in the lee of Brown Cow Island. They put the skiff overboard and loaded it with guns, knapsacks, and tollers. The boys showed their eagerness by being clumsy. The fisherman showed his in bad temper and abuse which they silently accepted in the absorbed tolerance of being boys. No doubt they laid it to lack of tobacco.

By outboard they rounded the island and pointed due east in the direction of a ridge of foam which could be seen whitening the surface three hundred yards away. They set the decoys in a broad, straddling vee opening wide into the ocean. The fisherman warned them not to get their hands wet, and when they did he made them carry on with red and painful fingers, in order to teach them. Once the last toller was bobbing among his fellows, brisk and alluring, they got their numbed fingers inside their oilskins and hugged their warm crotches. In the meantime the fisherman had turned the skiff toward the patch of foam where as if by magic, like a black glossy rib of earth, the ledge had broken through the belly of the sea.

Carefully they inhabited their slippery nub of the North American continent, while the unresting Atlantic swelled and swirled as it had for eons round the indomitable ledges. They hauled the skiff after them, established themselves as comfortably as they could in a shallow sump on top, lay on their sides a foot above water, and waited, guns in hand.

Actually the day was relatively mild, and they were warm enough at present in their woolen clothes and socks underneath oilskins and hip boots. After a while, however , the boys began to feel cramped. Their nerves were agonized by inactivity. The nephew complained and was severely told by the fisherman — who pointed to the dog, crouched unmoving except for his white-rimmed eyes — that part of doing a man's hunting was learning how to wait. But he was beginning to have misgivings of his own. This could be one of those days where all the right conditions masked an incalculable flaw.

If the fisherman had been alone, as he often was, stopping off when the necessary coincidence of tide and time occurred on his way home from hauling trawls, and had plenty of tobacco, he would have not fidgeted. The boys' being nervous made him nervous. He growled at them again. When it came it was likely to come all at once, and then in a few moments be over. He warned them not to slack off, never to slack off, to be always ready. Under his rebuke they kept their tortured peace, though they could not help shifting and twisting until he lost what patience he had left and bullied them into lying still. A duck could see an eyelid twitch. If the dog could go without moving so could they.

"Here it comes!" the fisherman said tersely at last.

The boys quivered with quick relief. The flock came in downwind, quartering slightly, myriad, black, and swift.

"Beautiful —" breathed the fisherman's son.

"All right," said the fisherman, intense and precise. "Aim at singles in the thickest part of the flock. Wait for me to fire and then don't stop shooting till your gun's empty." The flock bore down, arrowy and vibrant, then a hundred yards beyond the decoys it veered off.

"They're going away!" the boys cried, sighting in.

"Not yet!" snapped the fisherman. "They're coming around."

The flock changed shape, folded over itself, and drove into the wind in a tight arc. "Thousands —" the boys hissed through their teeth. All at once a whistling storm of black and white broke over the decoys.

"Now!" the fisherman shouted. "Perfect!" And he opened fire at the flock just as it hung suspended in momentary chaos above the tollers. The three pulled at their triggers and the birds splashed into the water, until the last report went off unheard, the last smoking shell flew unheeded over their shoulders, and the last of the routed flock scattered diminishing, diminishing, diminishing in every direction.

Exultantly the boys dropped their guns and jumped for the skiff.

"I'll handle that skiff!" the fisherman shouted at them. They stopped. Gripping the painter and balancing himself he eased the skiff into the water stern first and held the bow hard against the side of the rock shelf the skiff had rested on. "You stay here," he said to his nephew. "No sense in all three of us going in the boat."

The boy on the reef gazed at the gray water rising and falling hypnotically along the glistening edge. It had dropped about a foot since their arrival. "I want to go with you," he said in a sullen tone.

"You want to do what I tell you if you want to gun with me," answered the fisherman harshly. The boy couldn't swim, and he wasn't going to have him climbing in and out of the skiff any more than necessary. Besides he was too big.

The fisherman took his son in the skiff and cruised round and round among the decoys picking up dead birds. Meanwhile the other boy stared unmoving after them from the highest part of the ledge. Before they had quite finished gathering the dead birds, the fisherman cut the outboard and dropped to his knees in the skiff. "Down!" he yelled. "Get down!" About a dozen birds came tolling in. "Shoot — shoot!" his son hollered from the bottom of the boat to the boy on the ledge.

The dog, who had been running back and forth whining, sank to his belly, his muzzle on his forepaws. But the boy on the ledge never stirred. The ducks took late alarm at the skiff, swerved aside and into the air, passing with a whirr no more than fifty feet over the head of the boy, who remained on the ledge like a statue, without his gun, watching the two crouching in the boat.

The fisherman's son climbed onto the ledge and held the painter. The bottom of the skiff was covered with feathery black and white bodies with feet upturned and necks lolling. He was jubilant. "We got twenty-seven!" he told his cousin. "How's that? Nine apiece. Boy," he added, "what a cool Christmas!"

The fisherman pulled the skiff onto its shelf and all three went and lay down again in anticipation of the next flight. The son, reloading, patted his shotgun affectionately. "I'm going to get me ten next time," he said. Then he asked his cousin, "Whatsamatter — didn't you see the strays?"

"Yeah," the boy said.

"How come you didn't shoot at 'em?"

"Didn't feel like it," replied the boy, still with a trace of sullenness.

"You stupid or something?" The fisherman's son was astounded. "What a highlander!" But the fisherman, though he said nothing, knew that the older boy had had an attack of ledge fever.

"Cripes!" his son kept at it. "I'd at least of tried."

"Shut up," the fisherman finally told him, "and leave him be."

At slack water three more flocks came in, one right after the other, and when it was over, the skiff was half full of clean, dead birds. During the subsequent lull they broke out the lunch and ate it all and finished the hot coffee. For a while the fisherman sucked away on his cold pipe. Then he had a swig of whiskey.

The boys passed the time contentedly jabbering about who shot the most — there were ninety-two all told — which of their friends they would show the biggest ones to, how much each could eat at a meal provided they didn't have to eat any vegetables. Now and then they heard a sporadic distant gunfire on the mainland, at its nearest point two miles north.

At length the fisherman got a hand inside his oilskins and produced his watch.

"Do we have to go now?" asked his son.

"Not just yet," he replied. "Pretty soon." Everything had been perfect. As good as he had ever had it. Because he was getting tired of the boys' chatter he got up, heavily in his hip boots, and stretched. The tide had turned and was coming in, the sky was more ashen, and the wind had freshened enough so that whitecaps were beginning to blossom. It would be a good hour before they had to leave the ledge and pick up the tollers. However, he guessed they would leave a little early. On account of the rising wind he doubted there would be much more shooting. He stepped carefully along the back of the ledge, to work his kinks out. It was also getting a little colder.

The whiskey had begun to warm him, but he was unprepared for the sudden blaze that flashed upward inside him from his belly to his head. He was standing looking at the shelf where the skiff was. Only the foolish skiff was not there!

For the second time that day the fisherman felt the deep vacuity of disbelief. He gaped, seeing nothing but the flat shelf of rock. He whirled, started toward the boys, slipped, recovered himself, fetched a complete circle, and stared at the unimaginably empty shelf. Its emptiness made him feel as if everything he had done that day so far, his life so far, he had dreamed. What could have happened? The tide was still nearly a foot below. There had been no sea to speak of. The skiff could hardly have slid off by itself. For the life of him, consciously careful as he inveterately was, he could not now remember hauling it up the last time.

"Christ —" he exclaimed loudly, without realizing it because he was so entranced by the invisible event.

"What's wrong, Dad?" asked his son, getting to his feet.

The fisherman went blind with uncontainable rage. "Get back down there where you belong!" he screamed. He scarcely noticed the boy sink back in amazement. In a frenzy he ran along the ledge thinking the skiff might have been drawn up at another place, though he knew better. There was no other place.

He stumbled, half falling, back to the boys who were gawking at him in consternation, as though he had gone insane. "God damn it!" he yelled savagely, grabbing both of them and yanking them to their knees. "Get on your feet!"

"What's wrong?" his son repeated in a stifled voice.

"Never mind what's wrong," he snarled. "Look for the skiff — it's adrift!" When they peered around he gripped their shoulders brutally facing them about. "Downwind —" He slammed his fist against his thigh. "Jesus!" he cried, struck to his madness at their stupidity.

At last he sighted the skiff himself, magically bobbing along the grim sea like a toller, a quarter of a mile to leeward on a direct course for home. The impulse to strip himself naked was succeeded instantly by a queer calm. He simply sat down on the ledge and forgot everything but the marvelous mystery.

As his awareness partially returned he glanced towards the boys. They were still observing the skiff speechlessly. Then he was gazing into the clear young eyes of his son.

"Dad," asked the boy steadily, "what do we do now?"

That brought the fisherman upright. "The first thing we have to do," he heard himself saying with infinite tenderness as if he were making love, "is think."

"Could you swim it?" asked his son.

He shook his head and smiled at them. They smiled quickly back, too quickly. "A hundred yards maybe, in this water. I wish I could," he added. It was the most intimate and pitiful thing he had ever said. He walked in circles round them, trying to break the stall his mind was left in.

He gauged the level of the water. To the eye it was quite stationary, six inches from the shelf at this second. The fisherman did not have to mark it on the side of the rock against the passing of time to prove to his reason that it was rising, always rising.

All his life the fisherman had tried to lick the element of time, by getting up earlier and going to bed later, owning a faster boat, planning more than the day would hold, and tackling just one other job before the deadline fell. If, as on rare occasions he had the grand illusion, he ever really had beaten the game, he would need to call on all his reserve of practice and cunning now.

He sized up the scant but unforgivable three hundred yards to

Brown Cow Island. Another hundred yards behind it his boat rode at anchor, where, had he been aboard, he could have cut in a fathometer to plumb the profound and occult seas, or a ship-to-shore radio on which in an interminably short time he would have his wife's voice talking about homecoming.

"Couldn't we wave something so somebody would see us-" his nephew suggested.

The fisherman spun around. "Load your guns!" he ordered. They looked as if the air had suddenly gone frantic with birds. I'll fire once and count to five. Then you fire. Count to five. That way they won't just think it's only somebody gunning ducks. We'll keep doing that."

"We've only got just two-and-a-half boxes left," said his son.

The fisherman nodded, understanding that from beginning to end their situation was purely mathematics, like the ticking of the alarm clock in his silent bedroom. Then he fired. The dog, who had been keeping watch over the decoys, leaped forward and yelped in confusion. They all counted off, fired the first five rounds by threes, and reloaded. The fisherman scanned first the horizon, then the contracting borders of the ledge, which was the sole place the water appeared to be climbing. Soon it would be over the shelf.

They counted off and fired the second five rounds. "We'll hold off a while on the last one," the fisherman told the boys.

His son tallied up the remaining shells, grouping them symmetrically in threes on the rock when the wet box fell apart. "Two short." he announced. They reloaded and laid the guns on their knees.

Behind thickening clouds they could not see the sun going down. The water coming up, was growing blacker. The fisherman thought he might have told his wife they would be home before dark since it was Christmas Day. He realized he had forgotten about its being any particular day. The tide would not be high until two hours after sunset. When they did not get in by nightfall, and could not be raised by radio, she might send somebody to hunt for them right away. He rejected this arithmetic immediately, with a sickening shock, recollecting it was a two-and-a-half hour run at best.

He rose and searched the shoreline, barely visible. Then his glance dropped to the toy shoreline at the edges of the reef. The shrinking ledge, so sinister from a boat, grew dearer minute by minute as though the whole wide world he gazed on from horizon to horizon balanced on its contracting rim. He checked the water level and found the shelf awash.

Some of what went through his mind the fisherman told to the boys. They accepted it without comment. If he caught their eyes they looked away to spare him or because they were not yet old enough to face what they saw. Mostly they watched the rising water. The fisherman was unable to initiate a word of encouragement. He wanted one of them to ask him whether somebody would reach them ahead of the tide. He would have found it possible to say yes. But they did not inquire.

The fisherman was not sure how much, at their age, they were able to imagine. Both of them had seen from the docks drowned bodies put ashore out of boats. Sometimes they grasped things, and sometimes not. He supposed they might be longing for the comfort of their mothers, and was astonished, as much as he was capable of any astonishment except the supreme one, to discover himself wishing he had not left his wife's dark, close, naked bed that morning.

"Is it time to shoot now?" asked his nephew.

"Pretty soon," he said, as if he were putting off making good on a promise. "Not yet."

His own boy cried softly for a brief moment, like a man, his face averted in an effort neither to give nor show pain.

"Before school starts," the fisherman said, wonderfully detached, "we'll go to town and I'll buy you boys anything you want."

With great difficulty, in a dull tone as though he did not in the least desire it, his son said after a pause, "I'd like one of those new thirty-horse outboards."

"All right," said the fisherman. And to his nephew, "How about you?"

The nephew shook his head desolately. "I don't want anything," he said.

"All right —" the fisherman said again, and said no more.

The dog whined in uncertainty and licked the boys faces where they sat together. Each threw an arm over his back and hugged him. Three strays flew in and sat companionably down among the stiff-necked decoys. The dog crouched obedient to his training. The boys observed them listlessly. Presently, sensing something untoward, the ducks took off, splashing the wave tops with feet and wingtips, into the dusky waste.

The sea began to make up in the mounting wind, and the wind bore a new and deathly chill. The fisherman, scouring the somber, dwindling shadow of the mainland for a sign, hoped it would not snow. But it did. First a few flakes, then a flurry, then storming past horizontally. The fisherman took one long, bewildered look at Brown Cow Island three hundred yards dead to leeward, and got up.

Then it shut in, as if what was happening on the ledge was too private even for the last wan light of expiring day.

"Last round," the fisherman said.

The boys rose and shouldered their tacit guns. The fisherman fired into the flying snow. He counted methodically to five. His son fired and counted. His nephew. All three fired and counted. Four rounds.

"You've got one left, Dad," his son said.

The fisherman hesitated another second, then he fired the final shell. Its pathetic report, like the spat of a popgun, whipped away on the wind and was instantly blanketed in falling snow.

Night fell all in a moment to meet the ascending sea. They were now barely able to make one another out through driving snowflakes, dim as ghosts in their yellow oilskins. The fisherman heard a sea break and glanced down where his feet were. They seemed to be wound in a snowy sheet. Gently he took the boys by the shoulders and pushed them in front of him, feeling with his feet along the shallow sump to the place where it triangulated into a sharp crevice at the highest point of the ledge. "Face ahead," he told them. "Put the guns down."

"I'd like to hold mine, Dad," begged his son.

"Put it down," said the fisherman. "The tide won't hurt it. Now brace your feet against both sides and stay there."

They felt the dog, who was pitch black, running up and down in perplexity between their straddled legs. "Dad," said his son, "what about the pooch?"

If he had called the dog by name it would have been too personal. The fisherman would have wept. As it was he had all he could do to keep from laughing. He bent his knees, and when he touched the dog hoisted him under one arm. The dog's belly was soaking wet.

So they waited, marooned in their consciousness, surrounded by a monstrous tidal space which was slowly, slowly closing them out. In the space the periwinkle beneath the fisherman's boots was king.

Snow, rocks, seas, wind, the fishermen had lived by all his life. Now he thought he had never comprehended what they were, and he hated them, though they had not changed. He was deadly chilled. He set out to ask the boys if they were cold. There was no sense. He thought of the whiskey, and sidled backward, still holding the awkward dog, till he located the bottle under the water with his toe. He picked it up squeamishly as though afraid of getting his sleeve wet, worked his way forward and bent over his son. "Drink it," he said, holding the bottle against the boy's ribs. The boy tipped his head back, drank, coughed hotly, then vomited.

"I can't," he told his father wretchedly.

"Try — try —" the fisherman pleaded.

The boy obediently drank, and again he vomited hotly. He shook his head against his father's chest and passed the bottle forward to his cousin, who drank and vomited also. Passing the bottle back, the boys dropped it in the frigid water between them.

When the waves reached his knees the fisherman set the warm dog loose and said to his son, "Turn around and get up on my shoulders." The boy obeyed. The fisherman opened his oilskin jacket and twisted his hands behind him through his suspenders, clamping the boy's booted ankles with his elbows.

"What about the dog?" the boy asked.

"He'll make his own way all right," the fisherman said. "He can take the cold water." His knees were trembling. Every instinct shrieked for gymnastics. He ground his teeth and braced like a colossus against the sides of the submerged crevice.

The dog, having lived faithfully as though one of them for eleven years, swam a few minutes in and out around the fisherman's legs, not knowing what was happening, and left them without a whimper. He would swim and swim at random by himself, round and round in the blinding night, and when he had swum routinely through the paralyzing water all he could, he would simply, in one

[81]

incomprehensible moment, drown. Almost the fisherman, waiting out infinity, envied him his pattern.

Freezing seas swept by, flooding inexorably up and up as the earth sank away imperceptibly beneath them. The boy called out once to his cousin. There was no answer. The fisherman, marveling on a terror without voice, was dumbly glad when the boy did not call again. His own boots were long full of water. With no sensation left in his straddling legs he dared not move them. So long as the seas came sidewise against his hips, and then sidewise against his shoulders, he might balance — no telling how long. The upper half of him was what felt frozen. His legs, disengaged from his nerves and his will, he came to regard quite scientifically. They were the absurd, precarious axis around which reeled the surged universal tumult. The waves would come on and on; he could not visualize how many tossing reinforcements lurked in the night beyond — inexhaustible numbers, and he wept in supernatural fury at each because it was higher, till he transcended hate and took them, swaying like a convert, one by one as they lunged against him and away aimlessly into their own wild realm.

From his hips upward the fisherman stretched to his utmost as a man does whose spirit reaches out of dead sleep. The boy's head, none too high, must be at least seven feet above the ledge. Though growing larger every minute, it was a small light life. The fisherman meant to hold it there, if need be, through a thousand tides.

By and by the boy, slumped on the head of his father, asked, "Is it over your boots, Dad?"

"Not yet." the fisherman said. Then through his teeth he added, "If I fall — kick your boots off — swim for it — downwind — to the island..."

"You . . . ?" the boy finally asked.

The fisherman nodded against the boy's belly. "Won't see each other," he said.

The boy did for the fisherman the greatest thing that can be done. He may have been too young for perfect terror, but he was old enough to know there were things beyond the power of any man. All he could do he did, by trusting his father to do all he could, and asking nothing more.

The fisherman, rocked to his soul by a sea, held his eyes shut upon the interminable night.

[82]

THE LEDGE

"Is it time now?" the boy said.

The fisherman could hardly speak. "Not yet," he said. "Not just yet . . ."

As the land mass pivoted toward sunlight the day after Christmas, a tiny fleet of small craft converged off shore like iron filings to a magnet. At daybreak they found the skiff floating unscathed off the headland, half full of ducks and snow. The shooting *had* been good, as someone hearing on the nearby mainland the previous afternoon had supposed. Two hours afterward they found the unharmed boat adrift five miles at sea. At high noon they found the fisherman at ebb tide, his right foot jammed cruelly into a glacial crevice of the ledge beside three shotguns, his hands tangled behind him in his suspenders, and under his right elbow a rubber boot with a sock and a live starfish in it. After dragging unlit depths all day for the boys, they towed the fisherman home in his own boat at sundown, and in the frost of evening, mute with discovering purgatory, laid him on his wharf for his wife to see.

She, somehow, standing on the dock as in her frequent dream, gazing at the fisherman pure as crystal on the icy boards, a small rubber boot still frozen under one clenched arm, saw him exaggerated beyond remorse or grief, absolved of his mortality.

CHAPTER XI

No More Guns Tonight

SCARRITT ADAMS

THE President of the United States was below decks with
Julia, his sweetheart, listening to a song fest when that third shot
went off. The time was precisely fixed by the shattered pocket
watch at twenty minutes before four o'clock. The ship's log fixed the
date at February 28, 1844, back in the stirring times of "Tippecanoe
and Tyler, Too" and "Fifty Four Forty or Fight."

At eleven o'clock that Wednesday morning the widower President John Tyler, his son John, Jr., Mrs. Robert Tyler and Miss
Cooper had left the White House accompanied by a small negro
servant. They drove off along Pennsylvania Avenue and then cut
south to the steamboat wharf at Greenleafs Point for a pleasant
day's excursion in the USS *Princeton*. It was a fine day, a little cool,
but bright and sunny without a cloud in the sky.

Julia Gardner, accompanied by her father Colonel David Gardner, drove off from Miss Peyton's boarding house at the corner of
Pennsylvania Avenue and Four-and-a-Half Street to join the presi-
dential party. Julia hoped to marry the President in June.

The senate adjourned for the day, after a brief early morning
session, to accept Captain Stockton's invitation for an excursion in
his new experimental ship *Princeton* with the fabulous Ericsson six-
bladed propeller, a retractable smoke stack and the experimental
gun named *Peacemaker*. It was their duty to improve their knowledge of technical advances in the Navy.

The heads of all the government departments, all except Mr.
Spencer, Secretary of the Treasury, closed up their offices for the
day to go along for the cruise of the Potomac. There were Abel Upshur, Secretary of State, and William Wilkins, Secretary of War.
Thomas Gilmer, Secretary of the Navy, brought his wife and children along. It was the thirteenth day of office for both Wilkins
and Gilmer.

NO MORE GUNS TONIGHT

It took nearly all the carriages in town to bring this crowd of four hundred guests to the wharf where a small steamboat, chartered by Captain Stockton, waited to take them the six miles to the *Princeton's* anchorage near Alexandria. At twenty after eleven, the boat shoved off and puffed down river on the calm Potomac.

Upon reaching Alexandria, the beautiful "fairy phantom ship" *Princeton* loomed in sight. The band struck up "Hail Columbia." Coming closer they could see the crew manning the yards and rigging in ceremonial array. The steamboat made a wide sweep around the *Princeton* to give the guests a better view of this amazing new kind of ship. At the bow the gun *Peacemaker* stood on its carriage in massive grandeur and at the stern Ericsson's gun *Oregon*, though slightly smaller, held its own. They dwarfed the twelve other old-fashioned 32-pounder conventional guns.

Peacemaker, especially, was a devilish big gun. Captain Stockton himself had it forged in the new manner out of ten tons of wrought iron, bored to fire a twelve-inch cannon ball. He modeled it after the great inventor Ericsson's gun *Oregon* but made it a foot thicker at the breech as an added safety factor because *Oregon* already had a little crack in it. When it was completed "This magnificent piece of ordnance was appropriately baptized *Peacemaker"* under a fountain of champagne. Stockton was mighty proud of that gun. If necessary, it would be the "fight" in "Fifty Four Forty or Fight" in case England had any notions about Oregon. Now here it was "bright as Aunt Peggy's pewter plates on Saturday evening" for the great of Washington to admire as their steamboat approached the *Princeton.*

Finally the crowded steamboat came alongside the *Princeton,* put a gangway across from her hurricane deck and disgorged her passengers who were out for a sea-going picnic. The band played the "Star Spangled Banner," the Marine guard presented arms, and the gunners fired a twenty-one-gun salute as the President and his Cabinet came on board.

Captain Robert Field Stockton, rich, handsome, successful, popular, the "observed of all observers," welcomed his friend, the President, aboard his dream ship that he himself had built. He greeted his immediate boss Secretary Gilmer and Mrs. Gilmer who, alone amongst all the happy guests, seemed preoccupied and stuck

[85]

close to her husband, and the famous Dolly Madison, eighty years old and raring to go.

At noon the *Princeton,* the very first warship in all the world to be propeller-driven, glided silently away, her hard coal showing no smoke, her speed augmented by sails set to the light but favorable breeze. The band played "Hail to the Chief" when she passed majestic Mount Vernon. Gaiety and song filled the air.

Some of the men remained on deck to watch the ship handling and to see *Peacemaker* fire its first shot, counting up to sixteen the number of times the shot skipped across the water. But most of the excursionists, hungry and cold, went below to eat and get warm.

They found that all the portable linen partitions between rooms, Stockton's own invention, had been removed to make one large dining and reception room, extending the whole length of the ship, with a long banquet table set up on one side. Even at that only half of them could sit down to the table at the same time.

The ladies dined first, on partridges, turkeys, hams, ducks, chickens, fruit and liqueurs, especially imported by the host from Philadelphia at his own expense. It was a great picnic. They heard *Peacemaker* fire its second shot, the last one for the day. The gunner made his regular post-firing inspection of the gun. Then, with the exhibition firing over, the band played "Home, Sweet Home," the ship turned around, furled her sails, and headed back for Washington, using her engines only against wind and tide.

It was time for the gentlemen to eat — the afternoon was wearing on — the ladies gathering on the other side of the room. Now men would take their eating and drinking seriously. The picnic became a banquet. Captain Stockton took his place at the head of the long table with President Tyler on his right and Senator Levy Woodbury on his left. Next to Woodbury sat the Secretary of State, and next William Wilkins, the Secretary of War, and so on. On the other side Postmaster General Charles Wickliffe sat next to the President and Commodore Charles Stewart, famed warrior of the old Navy, next.

They tackled the game and meat and "superior" champagne. Empty bottles piled up as the *Princeton* breasted the current homeward bound. By now it was three o'clock. All was "merry as a marriage bell." Captain Stockton arose at meal's end to toast "the President of the United States." There was vociferous response and "three times three" cheers.

The President responded with a toast to "the three big guns — the *Peacemaker*, the *Oregon* and Captain Stockton." Miss Wickliffe, the Postmaster General's daughter, talked one of the gentlemen into proposing a toast to "The American Flag, the only American which wears a star and the only one which bears a stripe." Everybody thought this was fine and everybody was feeling fine. Somebody thought that *Peacemaker* ought to be fired just one more time before they got home. But Captain Stockton said, "No more guns tonight." It was three thirty in the afternoon and time for the excursionists to get home.

Then the new Secretary of the Navy, on his thirteenth day in office, interceded on behalf of the popular demand for just one more shot. He wanted to see it, too. Captain Stockton naturally gave in to his boss and issued the order to Lieutenant William Hunt, who was in charge of the gun, to make preparations for firing another shot.

Those still on deck noticed that Lieutenant Hunt supervised this loading with particular personal attention to detail. He himself took the copper canister containing twenty-five pounds of flannel-wrapped Du Pont powder and inserted it in the muzzle of *Peacemaker*. Quarter Gunner Hugh Kelly and Seaman David Harrington followed it up with a ropeyarn wad and rammed the charge home. Mr. Robert King, the gunner, assisted by Seaman James Granger, stuck his priming wire in the touch-hole to feel when the charge was home. Next Kelly and Harrington rolled in the 212-pound hollow cannon ball, wadded it and ran it down with a graduated rammer so they could tell when it was home while King, with his priming wire, felt the powder charge compress. Then they rammed it again to make it absolutely secure in the gun. When these careful experts reported the full charge home, Lieutenant Hunt sent a midshipman down to the banquet to notify Captain Stockton that the gun was loaded and ready to fire.

Captain Stockton asked the Secretary of the Navy to make one final toast before they went up to watch *Peacemaker* fire its third shot. In real sea-going fashion Secretary Gilmer proposed "Fair Trade and Sailor's Rights." After this last toast the President and his Cabinet rose from the banquet to go topside. On his way out the

Secretary of the Navy, pointing at the stack of empty champagne bottles, suggested that somebody "remove all those dead men."

Peacemaker, ready for its third shot, was pointed over the port bow at the shores of Virginia. A chilly breeze came up. Captain Stockton took his place behind and to the left of *Peacemaker*, the nearest of anybody, propped his left foot on the bed of the gun carriage and called out his usual order "Stand clear of the gun." Lieutenant Hunt stood alongside his captain and Gunner King stood to the left of Hunt. William Wilkins, remarking that "though Secretary of War, I don't like this firing and believe that I shall run," took his place discreetly aft. The large-framed broad-shouldered Secretary of State and the forty-two-year old black-eyed, black-haired Secretary of the Navy, wrapped in his blue Spanish cloak, stood behind the gun beyond Stockton, with Julia Gardner's father just behind them. The President's little servant leaned his chest against a nearby 32-pounder.

The *Princeton*, steaming effortlessly along with its new propeller, was only four miles from Alexandria. Colonel Seaton, mayor of Washington, went back to look for his hat. *Peacemaker* was waiting for the President. But the President had stopped to talk to a friend at the cabin door. He heard a burst of song from the revellers below that reminded him of old times, so he went to join them, saying that he would rather hear the music than see the gun fired.

With no further reason to wait, Gunner King cocked the firing lock on the breech of *Peacemaker*. He set it to go off automatically when the ship rolled three degrees. But since there was no motion from the smooth Potomac, King would introduce an artificial "roll" by cranking the elevating mechanism. The cap would then burn and explode the charge the instant the mechanism reached three degrees of elevation.

Gunner King began cranking.

Down below nearly all the ladies had remained and at least half of the gentlemen. They didn't care what was going on up on that chilly old deck. *Peacemaker* could fire all it wanted to as far as they were concerned. But here it was cozy and warm, the ladies pretty, the gentlemen, gallant. There was good cheer with cognac and champagne, music and song. They hardly noticed, and little cared, when they heard the dull boom on the deck above them.

[88]

That was the business of the Secretary of War, the Secretary of the Navy, and the captain.

Up on deck though, the dull boom was *Peacemaker's* third shot, the shot that the Secretary of the Navy ordered to be fired after the captain had said "No more guns tonight." It was, in fact, a loud explosion. *Peacemaker* had blown up. A thick cloud of smoke enveloped the giant cannon and the little group around it. A huge hunk of *Peacemaker* hurtled out of the smoke, gashing the wooden deck and tearing through the bulwarks. When the smoke cleared, survivors saw that the whole breech of *Peacemaker* was blown out. They saw a little pile of motionless human beings on deck consisting of the Secretary of the Navy, Secretary of State and Julia Gardner's father. They were all dead. So was President Tyler's little colored boy. Strangely enough Lieutenant Hunt and his gun crew survived.

The piece of *Peacemaker* that stove in Secretary Upshur's chest stopped the hands of his pocket watch at precisely twenty minutes before four o'clock.

Captain Stockton, also knocked down as if dead, staggered up, shook himself out of a daze, and took charge to sail the *Princeton* back to Washington and to a most certain Court of Inquiry.

Back in the city, ebony-black John Sable, waiter in Gadsby's Hotel where Stockton lived, brought the startling report to hotel guests that "*Peacemaker* is bursted, the hack is just from the wharf with the news." The whole town was stunned. The State, Navy and War Departments went into mourning. President Tyler nearly lost his life on the way back from his Cabinet officers funeral in a runaway carriage.

Said the Court of Inquiry "No shadow of censure can be attached to any officer or any of the crew of the *Princeton*." But the Naval Affairs Committee in Congress found that "these large guns were purchased by Captain Robert F. Stockton without any express order from the Navy Department . . . as would seem to be the proper course."

Nevertheless, two weeks after the explosion in which two of his Cabinet officers were killed, President Tyler "ordered another gun of the size and dimensions of that lately destroyed to be made under the direct supervision of Captain Stockton." And in June he married Julia.

Chapter XII

The War's Best Kept Secret

H. K. RIGG

 He name Bloody Foreland, a point along the coast of Donegal in Northern Ireland, is alone enough to conjure up dreadful thoughts of disaster. Through a stroke of fate, and as if prophetically named, it will go down in naval annals as the scene of one of the most terrible tragedies of World War II. The incident, although involving the loss of hundreds of lives and a capital ship, and witnessed by thousands of Allied troops, never was known to the enemy.

The blanket of wartime security, drawn down quickly, has shrouded the tragedy from public knowledge ever since, so that today no more than a few people, other than those concerned, know the full story. It was one of the best kept secrets of the war.

The two ill-starred vessels in this great catastrophe were the Cunard-White Star liner *Queen Mary* and the British "C" Class Cruiser, H.M.S. *Curacoa*. The time and date of the accident was two o'clock in the afternoon of October 2, 1942.

The weather was fine and clear, there was a moderate breeze from the west but the sea was rough, with a heavy westerly swell running. The *Curacoa*, at the time, was acting as escort to the *Queen Mary*, and, except for a screen of destroyers some miles over the horizon, there were no other vessels in the vicinity.

The day had begun in routine fashion with the *Queen Mary* approaching the coast of Ireland toward the end of one of her transatlantic express runs carrying troops. On this particular trip she was loaded with between ten and eleven thousand American soldiers in addition to her crew of nine hundred and eight hands.

The huge ship — only her fleet sister the *Queen Elizabeth* exceeded her eighty-one-thousand-ton size — was rocketing along at an estimated twenty-eight-knots, but far below the flank speed of forty that she could do in a pinch. Neither of the *Queens*, in all of their

[90]

many thousand of miles of war service, ever traveled in convoy principally because they were faster than most escorts and able to outrun any submarine and most surface raiders. For security they relied on camouflage, speed, and, of course, zigzag maneuvers. Symbolically, they were code named "The Monsters." Far at sea the Monsters had little to fear but when approaching the shore they needed maximum protection because it was then that they came within range of the enemy's land-based aircraft, and they were large, fat, high priority targets for an aerial torpedo or bomb.

On this fateful voyage from New York to the Clyde, the Queen Mary had experienced a routine crossing without contacts or even alerts from enemy craft. On her last morning out at 8 A.M. she made a scheduled rendezvous with H.M.S. Curacoa and a screen of six British destroyers a little over a hundred miles off the Irish Coast.

The Curacoa was a forty-two-hundred-ton veteran of World War I, refitted as an anti-aircraft vessel, and only recently had come out of the repair yard following a particularly meritorious battle in the Norwegian campaign. She was bristling with "Chicago pianos" and other quick-firing guns, and her gun crews were eager to catch a glimpse of one of the Focke-Wulf Kondors that made a practice of pouncing on coastal shipping.

She had a ship's complement of four hundred and thirty officers and ratings and her skipper, Captain John Wilfrid Boutwood, D.S.O., Royal Navy, was an old hand at this duty, having escorted the Queen Mary on three previous crossings. He was well aware of his mission, which was to stay as near as possible to his charge to provide an umbrella of anti-aircraft fire in the event of attack, meanwhile deploying his destroyer screen just over the horizon for perimeter defense and patrol.

When the Queen's master, Captain Cyril Gordon Illingworth (no relation to the famous British yachtsman Captain John Illingworth) received the report that morning that his escort was in sight four or five miles ahead, he was noticeably relieved and signalled his course and speed which were 108 degrees and twenty-eight knots. The cruiser in turn reported that she was doing her best speed of twenty-five knots, on the same heading, and that she would maintain station ahead until the Queen Mary overhauled her and then would fall in her wake.

[91]

The watch officers on the *Curacoa* had correctly assumed that the big passenger liner was carrying out the maneuver known as zigzag Number Eight. This involved steaming for four minutes on the mean course, followed by a turn of 25 degrees to starboard. This starboard leg was pursued for eight minutes when a turn of 50 degrees to port was made. This leg was steered for another eight minutes, whereupon a turn of 25 degrees to starboard was ordered, which brought the vessel back to her main course. After proceeding for four minutes on the mean course, a turn of 25 degrees to port was made and the same procedure was followed on this port leg until the vessel returned once more to her mean course. The complete zigzag to starboard and port required forty minutes and was calculated to advance the vessel 93 per cent of the total distance run.

As the forenoon wore on, the *Queen Mary* due to her superior speed and ability to cope with the heavy swells, gradually overhauled the cruiser. After lunch, Captain Boutwood aboard the *Curacoa* observed that his course was holding the cruiser somewhat outside the limits of the *Queen Mary's* most southerly zigzag and, since they were then approaching the area where air attacks were most probable, he altered his course to port eight degrees for a short period to keep closer to his charge.

Aboard the *Queen Mary* the troops had been filing through the mess decks in orderly shifts for a typical American meal of steak and potatoes, pie and ice cream. On the bridge First Officer Robinson was due to be relieved for his lunch at three bells, but just before it struck, the *Queen Mary* reached the southern limit of her starboard zigzag which placed her on the cruiser's starboard quarter, and he ordered the course altered 50 degrees to port. When the Monster was about half-way through her swing he decided that if he followed the port leg pattern he would pass too close under the stern of the cruiser and he ordered the helm steadied. At that moment he was relieved by Junior First Officer Wright and, naturally, explained the course changes he had been making.

A few minutes later Mr. Wright again brought the *Queen Mary* left but he, too, judged that she would pass too near the escort and countered his order with one for hard a-starboard.

Captain Illingworth, who had been in the chartroom while meridian sights were being worked out, overheard the order and came out on the bridge to inquire what was happening. After sizing up the situation, he ordered Mr. Wright to bring the *Queen Mary* left to the port leg and observed:

"Carry on with the zigzag. These chaps are used to escorting. They will keep out of your way and won't interfere with you."

The Monster plowed across the wake of the *Curacoa* at less than two cables (1200 feet) and about the *Queen Mary's* own length under her stern.

Shortly before 2 P.M., First Officer Robinson returned to the bridge after finishing his lunch and as he relieved his junior was informed of the Captain's order to maintain the zigzag pattern and that the *Queen Mary* had just completed the port leg of her pattern and was presently steaming to starboard.

At that point the *Curacoa* bore about two points on the *Queen Mary's* bow at a distance of a little over two cables and the two ships were converging. Mr. Robinson waited a moment and when the cruiser did not seem to be altering her course, he ordered the helm to port and then hard aport as the Monster charged down on the wallowing cruiser.

The *Queen Mary* started to swing, but it was too late. Seconds later the cruiser all but disappeared under the Monster's house-high bow. There was a slight bump as she struck the cruiser about a quarter of the *Curacoa's* length forward of her fantail. The troops lining the *Queen's* rails watched horrified as the cruiser lay over on her beam's end then snapped in two. The two halves washed to each side and the *Queen* steamed cleanly between them. To starboard, the stern section of the *Curacoa* rolled her still turning propellers into the air and sank as the Queen's wake washed over. To port, the forward part of the ship belched smoke and steam, and bodies and bits of wreckage dribbled off as she slowly righted herself.

Captain Boutwood was clinging to the bridge rail. Later he commented:

"Within a minute or two I realized there was no hope of saving my ship, not even the forepart. The noise of escaping steam was deafening and after I had given up hope of saving the ship I instructed the officers to go down and take charge of what ratings they could lay their hands on to get the life-saving equipment cut down to use. In the space of about five minutes the cruiser sank."

It was that sudden.

Aboard the *Queen Mary*, the jar from the collison was so slight that those who were below decks could not believe what had happened. Captain Illingworth, who was in the chartroom at the time, snatched his steel helmet and rushed to the bridge under the impression that they had come under attack from airplanes. When, to his horror, he learned what had taken place, he first ordered the speed reduced, a damage control party forward to inspect the bow for damage, and a signal sent to the destroyer screen to start rescue operations.

The captain of the *Queen Mary* was in those moments to learn the true meaning of the old expression "the loneliness of command." As he stood on his bridge watching the pitiful flotsam from one of his country's proud warships bob to the surface in his wake, he remembered that his sailing orders made him responsible for his ship and the lives of the troops on board and that to stop would have placed his vessel in jeopardy.

When the damage control party reported to the bridge that the damage to the *Queen Mary's* bow had been remarkably light and that she was able to proceed, Captain Illingworth had no alternative but to continue on his course and leave his fellow countrymen to their fate in his wake.

On the *Curacoa* the death blow had been delivered so quickly and without warning that many of the crew never knew what had hit them. There had been no time to launch rafts or even don life jackets before they found themselves floundering in the icy cold, 45 degree, North Atlantic. Three hundred and twenty-nine sailors died in those awful moments and by the time the destroyers arrived on the scene there was only one officer and one hundred and one of the ship's company of four hundred and thirty left to save. That officer, by a strange quirk of fate was her captain, John Wilfrid Boutwood.

In subsequent court proceedings, Captain Boutwood testified that, like any captain, he depended on his watch officers for the routine of maintaining station, but when it was apparent that a dangerous situation was developing he had personally taken the con and had ordered the cruiser's helm to starboard fifteen degrees. The *Curacoa* was making heavy weather of it in the westerly swell and at the time of his order the Captain noticed she had yawed seven degrees to port and was slow to respond to her right rudder. Of his

[94]

subsequent orders in the moments of time before the collision Captain Boutwood wasn't certain, and there was no one to give corroborative evidence for the Captain because all the watch officers had gone down with the ship.

Our facts on this collision were gleaned from an obscure document brought to THE SKIPPER's attention by Dr. Cortez F. Enloe, fleet surgeon of the New York Yacht Club, who put us in touch with Commodore James B. Moore, Jr., of the Manhasset Bay Yacht Club. Commodore Moore, in turn, very kindly made available to us his privately printed copy of the findings of the Admiralty Court in a suit filed by England's Lord High Admiral against the Cunard Line for damages, which was heard early in 1947, almost five years after the collision.

All the principals in the collision were interrogated by the "Elder Brethren," as the justices so picturesquely refer to themselves, and the Brethren even observed tests with a sister ship to the *Curacoa* and model tests to determine if the forces of interaction, which come into play between two ships moving through the water in close proximity, had been the cause of the collision.

Their final decision was that interaction had not been the cause and that the sole blame lay on the *Curacoa*. Partly this was based on the wartime convoy doctrine, which had nothing to do with the Rules of the Road, that the *Queen Mary*, as the escorted ship, was the "stand on" vessel and was therefore entitled to the right of way from H.M.S. *Curacoa* which was judged to be the "give way" vessel. In addition, the justices found that "the *Curacoa* is seriously to blame for a bad lookout (and, presumably, a failure to keep a maneuvering plot); for failing to alter her course to starboard in due time or sufficiently, and for putting her wheel to port at the last."

On the last point of the indictment, Mr. Justice Pilcher, who rendered the decision, observed:

"Whether the wheel of the cruiser was put to port at the last as a result of a panic order, or as the result of a misinterpretation of some order given by Captain Boutwood, will never be known. I am satisfied that the wheel was in fact put to port at the last, that the putting of the wheel to port was negligent and that it was this action which immediately brought about the collision."

Which may be, but it is this writer's private opinion that the primary cause of the collision could have been due to the strange

[95]

design characteristic of British Men-of-War. Traditionally the helmsman steers from a position several decks below the bridge and is completely blind as far as being able to see where he is going. The compass card in front of him is the quartermaster's only reference to his ship's heading. Keeping a close station in a heavy following sea is a tricky situation even if you can see to meet and correct the yawing and sheering.

At any rate, later in 1947, an appeal was heard in the English Court of Appeal and the decision was modified. The *Queen Mary* was held liable for one-third of the damages.

Regardless of the post mortems, this incident was one of the saddest in the history of the British Navy and the best expressed sentiments are those of Mr. Justice Pilcher, who summed up his opinion with the remark:

"It is abundantly clear that the collision was one which never ought to have been permitted to occur."

There is one American who will never forget that awful day. He is the Reverend Francis Burke of Warwick, Virginia. Burke was chaplain of one of the American Army units aboard the *Queen* and was in his bunk on one of the lower berth decks when the collision occurred. He recalls noticing a slight bump but thought nothing of it, believing that it had been caused by a freak sea hitting the hull. Shortly afterwards the word was passed for him to report to the bridge. When he got topside, he was met by Captain Illingworth who quietly requested that he read the service for burial at sea, explaining that his ship had run over the escorting cruiser. For the American padre it was a rugged introduction to the horrors of war.

But the strangest thing of all was that this tragedy has gone so long so little known. At the time, of course, the proceedings of the Navy courts of enquiry and the courts-martial were classified and to date they have not been declassified. Undoubtedly the thousands of troops aboard, who knew what had happened within minutes via that mysterious grapevine — the ship's scuttlebutt — were enjoined to say nothing. Such admonitions have seldom been effective. There have been a few reports in English newspapers on the results of the Admiralty proceedings but apparently they died quietly in the back pages.

By some pattern of happenstance, it is a story that has, next to the atom bomb, been one of the war's best kept secrets.

CHAPTER XIII

On the Knees of the Gods

JOSEPH CONRAD

THE other year, looking through a newspaper of sound principles, but whose staff *will* persist in "casting" anchors and going to sea "on" a ship (ough!), I came across an article upon the season's yachting. And, behold! it was a good article. To a man who had but little to do with pleasure sailing (though all sailing is a pleasure), and certainly nothing whatever with racing in open waters, the writer's strictures upon the handicapping of yachts were just intelligible and no more. And I do not pretend to any interest in the enumeration of the great races of that year. As to the 52-foot linear raters, praised so much by the writer, I am warmed by his approval of their performances; but, as far as any clear conception goes, the descriptive phrase, so precise to the comprehension of a yachtsman, evokes no definite image in my mind.

The writer praises that class of pleasure vessels, and I am willing to endorse his words, as any man who loves every craft afloat would be ready to do. I am disposed to admire and respect the 52-foot linear raters on the word of a man who regrets in such a sympathetic and understanding spirit the threatened decay of yachting seamanship.

Of course, yacht racing is an organized pastime, a function of social idleness ministering to the vanity of certain wealthy inhabitants of these isles nearly as much as to their inborn love of the sea. But the writer of the article in question goes on to point out, with insight and justice, that for a great number of people (twenty thousand, I think he says) it is a means of livelihood — that it is, in his own words, an industry. Now, the moral side of an industry, productive or unproductive, the redeeming and ideal aspect of this bread-winning, is the attainment and preservation of the highest possible skill on the part of the craftsmen. Such skill, the skill of technique, is more than honesty; it is something wider, embracing

[97]

honesty and grace and rule in an elevated and clear sentiment, not altogether utilitarian, which may be called the honor of labor. It is made up of accumulated tradition, kept alive by individual pride, rendered exact by professional opinion, and, like the higher arts, it is spurred on and sustained by discriminating praise.

This is why the attainment of proficiency, the pushing of your skill with attention to the most delicate shades of excellence, is a matter of vital concern. Efficiency of a practically flawless kind may be reached naturally in the struggle for bread. But there is something beyond — a higher point, a subtle and unmistakable touch of love and pride beyond mere skill; almost an inspiration which gives to all work that finish which is almost art — which *is* art.

As men of scrupulous honor set up a high standard of public conscience above the dead-level of an honest community, so men of that skill which passes into art by ceaseless striving raise the dead-level of correct practice in the crafts of land and sea. The conditions fostering the growth of that supreme, alive excellence, as well in work as in play, ought to be preserved with a most careful regard lest the industry or the game should perish of an insidious and inward decay. Therefore I have read with profound regret, in that article upon the yachting season of a certain year, that the seamanship on board racing yachts is not now what it used to be only a few, very few, years ago.

For that was the gist of that article, written evidently by a man who not only knows but *understands* — a thing (let me remark in passing) much rarer than one would expect, because the sort of understanding I mean is inspired by love; and love, though in a sense it may be admitted to be stronger than death, is by no means so universal and so sure. In fact, love is rare — the love of men, of things, of ideas, the love of perfected skill. For love is the enemy of haste; it takes count of passing days, of men who pass away, of a fine art matured slowly in the course of years and doomed in a short time to pass away, too, and be no more. Love and regret go hand in hand in this world of changes swifter than the shifting of the clouds reflected in the mirror of the sea.

To penalize a yacht in proportion to the fineness of her performances is unfair to the craft and to her men. It is unfair to the perfection of her form and to the skill of her servants. For we men are, in fact, the servants of our creations. We remain in everlasting bondage to the productions of our brain and to the work of our hands. A man is born to serve his time on this earth, and there is something fine in the service being given on other grounds than that of utility. The bondage of art is very exacting. And, as the writer of the article which started this train of thought says with lovable warmth, the sailing of yachts is a fine art.

His contention is that racing, without time allowances for anything else but tonnage — that is, for size — has fostered the fine art of sailing to the pitch of perfection. Every sort of demand is made upon the master of a sailing yacht, and to be penalized in proportion to your success may be of advantage to the sport itself, but it has an obviously deteriorating effect upon the seamanship. The fine art is being lost.

The sailing and racing of yachts has developed a class of fore-and-aft sailors, men born and bred to the sea, fishing in winter and yachting in summer; men to whom the handling of that particular rig presents no mystery. It is their striving for victory that has elevated the sailing of pleasure craft to the dignity of a fine art in that special sense. As I have said, I know nothing of racing and but little of fore-and-aft rig; but the advantages of such a rig are obvious especially for purposes of pleasure, whether in cruising or racing. It requires less effort in handling; the trimming of the sailplanes to the wind can be done with speed and accuracy; and the greatest possible amount of canvas can be displayed upon the least possible quantity of spars. Lightness and concentrated power are the great qualities of fore-and-aft rig.

A fleet of fore-and-afters at anchor has its own slender graciousness. The setting of their sails resembles more than anything else the unfolding of a bird's wings; the facility of their evolutions is a pleasure to the eye. They are birds of the sea, whose swimming is like flying, and resembles more a natural function than the handling of man-invented appliances. The fore-and-aft rig in its simplicity and the beauty of its aspect under every angle of vision is, I believe, unapproachable. A schooner, yawl, or cutter in charge of a capable man seems to handle herself as if endowed with the power of reasoning and the gift of swift execution. One laughs with sheer pleasure at a smart piece of maneuvering, as at a manifestation of a living creature's quick wit and graceful precision.

Of those three varities of fore-and-aft rig, the cutter — the racing rig *par excellence* — is of an appearance the most imposing, from the fact that practically all her canvas is in one piece. The enormous mainsail of a cutter, as she draws slowly past a point of land or the end of a jetty under your admiring gaze, invests her with an air of lofty and silent majesty. At anchor a schooner looks better; she has an aspect of greater efficiency and a better balance to the eye, with her two masts distributed over the hull with a swaggering rake aft. The yawl rig one comes in time to love. It is, I should think, the easiest of all to manage.

For racing, a cutter; for a long pleasure voyage, a schooner; for cruising in home waters, the yawl; and the handling of them all is indeed a fine art. It requires not only the knowledge of the general principles of sailing, but a particular acquaintance with the character of the craft. All vessels are handled in the same way as far as theory goes, just as you may deal with all men on broad and rigid principles. But if you want that success in life which comes from the affection and confidence of your fellows, then with no two men, however similar they may appear in their nature, will you deal in the same way. There may be a rule of conduct; there is no rule of human fellowship. To deal with men is as fine an art as it is to deal with ships. Both men and ships live in an unstable element, are subject to subtle and powerful influences, and want to have their merits understood rather than their faults found out.

It is not what your ship will *not* do that you want to know to get on terms of successful partnership with her; it is, rather, that you ought to have a precise knowledge of what she *will* do for you when called upon to put forth what is in her by a sympathetic touch. At first sight the difference does not seem great in either line of dealing with the difficult problem of limitations. But the difference is great. The difference lies in the spirit in which the problem is approached. After all, the art of handling ships is finer, perhaps, than the art of handling men.

And, like all fine arts, it must be based upon a broad, solid sincerity, which, like a law of Nature, rules an infinity of different phenomena. Your endeavor must be single-minded. You would talk differently to a coal-heaver and to a professor. But is this duplicity? I deny it. The truth consists in the genuineness of the feeling, in the genuine recognition of the two men, so similar and so different, as your two partners in the hazard of life.

[100]

Obviously, a humbug, thinking only of winning his little race, would stand a chance of profiting by his artifices. Men, professors or coal-heavers, are easily deceived; they even have an extraordinary knack of lending themselves to deception, a sort of curious and inexplicable propensity to allow themselves to be led by the nose with their eyes open.

But a ship is a creature which we have brought into the world, as it were on purpose to keep us up to the mark. In her handling a ship will not put up with a mere pretender, as, for instance, the public will do with Mr. X, the popular statesman, Mr. Y, the popular scientist, or Mr. Z, the popular — what shall we say? — anything from a teacher of high morality to a bagman — who have won their little race. But I would like (though not accustomed to betting) to wager a large sum that not one of the few first-rate skippers of racing yachts has ever been a humbug. It would have been too difficult. The difficulty arises from the fact that one does not deal with ships in a mob, but with a ship as an individual. So we may have to with men. But in each of us there lurks some particle of the mob spirit, of the mob temperament. No matter how earnestly we strive against each other, we remain brothers on the lowest side of our intellect and in the instability of our feelings.

With ships it is not so. Much as they are to us they are nothing to each other. Those sensitive creatures have no ears for our blandishments. It takes something more than words to cajole them to do our will, to cover us with glory. Luckily, too, or else there would have been more shoddy reputations for first-rate seamanship.

Ships have no ears, I repeat, though, indeed, I think I have known ships who really seemed to have had eyes, or else I cannot understand on what ground a certain thousand-ton barque of my acquaintance on one particular occasion refused to answer her helm, thereby saving a frightful smash to two ships and to a very good man's reputation. I knew her intimately for two years, and in no other instance either before or since have I known her to do that thing. The man she had served so well (guessing, perhaps, at the depths of his affection for her) I have known much longer, and in bare justice to him I must say that this confidence-shattering experience (though so fortunate) only augmented his trust in her.

Yes, our ships have no ears, and thus they cannot be deceived. I would illustrate my idea of fidelity as between man and ship, be-

[101]

tween the master and his art, by a statement which, though it might appear shockingly sophisticated, is really very simple. I would say that a racing-yacht skipper who thought of nothing else but the glory of winning the race would never attain to any eminence of reputation. The genuine masters of their craft — I say this confidently from my experience of ships — have thought of nothing but of doing their very best by the vessel under their charge. To forget one's self, to surrender all personal feeling in the service of that fine art, is the only way for a seaman to the faithful discharge of his trust.

Such is the service of a fine art and of ships that sail the sea. And therein I think I can lay my finger upon the difference between the seamen of yesterday, who are still with us, and the seamen of tomorrow, already entered upon the possession of their inheritance. History repeats itself, but the special call of an art which has passed away is never reproduced. It is as utterly gone out of the world as the song of a destroyed wild bird. Nothing will awaken the same response of pleasurable emotion or conscientious endeavor. And the sailing of any vessel afloat is an art whose fine form seems already receding from us on its way to the over-shadowed valley of oblivion.

The taking of a modern steamship about the world (though one would not minimize its responsibilities) has not the same quality of intimacy with nature, which, after all, is an indispensable condition to the building up of an art. It is less personal and a more exact calling; less arduous, but also less gratifying in the lack of close communion between the artist and the medium of his art. It is, in short, less a matter of love. Its effects are measured exactly in time and space as no effect of an art can be. It is an occupation which a man not desperately subject to seasickness can be imagined to follow with content, without enthusiasm, with industry, without affection. Punctuality is its watchword. The incertitude which attends closely every artistic endeavor is absent from its regulated enterprise. It has no great moments of self-confidence, or moments not less great of doubt and heartsearching. It is an industry which, like other industries, has its romance, its honor, and its rewards, its bitter anxieties and its hours of ease. But such seagoing has not the artistic quality of a single-handed struggle with something much greater than yourself; it is not the laborious, absorbing practice of an art whose ultimate result remains on the knees of the gods. It is not an individual, temperamental achievement, but simply the skilled use of a captured force, merely another step forward upon the way of universal conquest.

Chapter XIV

The Day Grandad Quit the Sea

D. P. BARNHOUSE

ONE reason I remember that summer was because Toby Heaton suddenly stopped pushing me around and calling me tomboy, the way he had for sixteen years. It was hard to reconcile him with the boy who'd given me his tame gannet and my first black eye. But mostly I remember it as the summer Grandad was put on the spot, and the time we had the big party.

It was sort of a conspiracy, really, with the victim the last to know. Grandad had been promising for twenty years to quit the sea. He'd made and wriggled under more deadlines than even Gran could remember, and she'd had it — up to the gunwales! I think she hoped that a public capitulation might prove more binding and if a golden wedding wasn't the occasion to find out, she'd like to know what was.

Ordinarily, compared to Gran, a clam is a big blabbermouth, but this time she let herself go. It wasn't long before the whole town knew that Saturday was Captain Eph's anniversary party and the day he came ashore for good.

Grandad brought the *Susan* in from Boston on a Thursday. Ralph Petty, our customs officer, buttonholed him on the government wharf as he was checking off cargo.

"I hear tell you're retiring, Skipper."

"Yep," said Grandad — "one of these days." He and Mr. Petty had been feuding ever since Gran declined to become Mrs. Petty. It was a mild sort of conflict, but neither trusted the other farther than you could throw a walrus.

"Well, all I can say is, I wish it was me. You're lucky to have sons to take over." He looked over the growing pile of bales emitting from the hold. "Good cargo for your last trip."

This last remark may have caused Grandad some concern, but he wasn't going to let Ralph Petty get a rise out of him. However, when Miss Brushett in the post office wished him a happy life ashore and said she'd be seeing him at the party Saturday, he decided he'd best get up to the house and see what was going on.

For once Gran was almost too preoccupied to pay him much attention. She was busy turning the house upside down and scouring and polishing everything in sight. Grandad was a bit put out. After all, he'd been gone for more than a month. She kissed him absently and said she hoped he hadn't forgotten about their golden wedding anniversary.

"Will's coming home, too," she told him happily.

Will was the uncle we didn't mention too often in front of Grandad. To him, a landlubber was *persona non grata* even with a Ph. D. in ichthyology. He considered a captain's papers worth a dozen college degrees and he never quite forgave Gran for encouraging "queer notions" in their youngest.

"He's coming in on the steamer Saturday."

Grandad gave a noncommital "Humph," then . . . "What's this about me staying ashore?"

"Well, of course," said Gran. "You know very well you promised this would be your last trip."

"But we've a cargo for Oporto in a fortnight."

"One of the boys can take it. Come and give me a hand with the organ— there's a dear."

"Stop scrimshankin'," Grandad said, "and what's this I hear about a party? It's a pity a man doesn't know what's going on in his own house."

"Now, Eph," Gran soothed, "we've never had a really nice party . . . with candles and the good silver. I've never had a chance to use the Spode teacups that Aunt Bet gave us for a wedding present."

"Tea parties!" Grandad protested. "If there's anything makes me binicky, it's all those potted meat sandwiches washed down with switchel and female chitchat. No sir, you can count me out!"

"No potted meat," said Gran. "We're having lobster salad and the tea won't be cold. The Brushett girls have promised to do a reading from Tennyson. It won't hurt to do things up properly just this once."

"Proper!" snorted Grandad. "There's a word they should drop from the English language."

[105]

Toby and I were painting the rails on the upper balcony that faces the bay. We couldn't help hearing. Gran's voice was low but firm. Grandad's got louder and louder. After a while he came out on the balcony. His eyes had a trapped look.

"Why do you suppose your Grandmother is so set on this shindig?" He glared at me as though I'd put her up to it. I decided to play it cagey.

"Haven't you ever heard of sentiment, Grandad. It's not every day you have a golden wedding."

"Sentiment, my foot! She's got more than one hook to her line or I'm a shad. We never threw a party in all these years."

"You've scarcely been ashore long enough," Toby said dryly.

"Watch your tongue, young man," Grandad snapped. He looked out over the habor where the *Puffin* and the *Spindrift* lay at anchor and the *Susan* tugged at her dock lines.

"Well," he said at length, ruefully, "if we've got to have a party it needn't be a blasted pink tea. It's a cinch we've got to dig up something better than switchel to drink out of those dinky little cups of Aunt Bet's." He seemed to perk up a bit. "If only I had the makings, I'd whomp up a punch that might even scare off the Brushett sisters."

When we finished the railings, Gran had Toby and me do the woodwork in Uncle Will's old room. At least it saved me from all that baking and fixing that was going on in the kitchen.

"Can't we clear out some of these bottles?" Toby asked, eying the cluttered shelves.

"Heavens, no," I said. "Those are important specimens."

Uncle Will's work at the fisheries station had to do with the life cycles of cod parasites. The summer he was home I'd helped him cut up hundreds of fish, searching for those bottled horrors. He was lots of fun and not at all queer like Grandad said. He designated me "Junior Worm Watcher" and gave me a ten dollar bill when he left for the mainland.

The room looked pretty good when we'd finished. We checked with Grandad and found that he wasn't doing so well with the punch. His task was a tough one, seeing that our wine cellar was as empty as an apple barrel in April.

This situation had existed ever since Newfoundland had followed Canada into prohibition. In the old days, Grandad always brought home a few cases every time he went to Spain or Portugal, as well as a bottle of champagne for Gran. It was the only liquor she ever touched.

Prohibition didn't make much difference at first. There were still the French islands of St. Pierre and Miquelon a few miles off our coast where choice imported beverages could be bought at bargain prices. Local boats on short runs weren't scrutinized too carefully at first. Then a lot of "bankers" wakened to the fact that there was more money in contraband than in cod.

Grandad lost a lot of good crewmen to the rum trade. They thought he was crazy to keep his boats on the Banks when a bottle purchased in St. Pierre for fifty cents would fetch four dollars in Newfoundland and even more on the mainland. But he declared that the law was the law, even if it didn't make much sense.

After the reveuers caught Bob Marshall's *Nellie B* with a cargo of liquor hidden under a layer of cod bait, they scarcely took their eyes off our harbor. To make matters worse, Ralph Petty began checking up on every crewman who came ashore.

These recent developments didn't make Grandad's task any easier. A foraging trip through the village produced a case of stout and a bottle of elderberry wine.

"That drop won't make a ping in the bottom of the bucket," he mourned.

"We could take a run down to St. Pierre tomorrow and do some shopping," Toby suggested. Grandad wrestled with his conscience, but not for long.

"Don't see any help for it," he said, "but how are we going to get by the government cutters and old man Petty?"

They said I could go along. There was only a skeleton crew aboard and the *Susan* rode high with empty holds. She was the schooner Grandad's father had given him on his marriage. He named her after Gran. She was a lot like her, too — reliable and steady, but she could show her heels to the best of them in a stiff breeze.

We had a good beam wind all the way across. In St. Pierre I helped Grandad buy an anniversary gift for Gran while the "refreshments" were being stowed aboard.

"Should be something with gold," he said vaguely.

I chose a gorgeous sable muff with a gold chain shaped like a snake. It had two red rubies for eyes.

"Gran will just love this," I said. He looked a bit dubious but added some expensive French perfume. Inside the muff he tucked a bottle of the best champagne he could buy.

It was a stiff beat to windward all the way home, so it was nearly dusk by the time we rounded our headland. Through the glasses I spotted a government cutter just off the embankment.

"Keep your eye on her," Grandad yelled. "The rest of you get those cases up from the cabin and bait those lobster pots. Make sure the buoy ropes are sound.

The men scurried about like shiners in a bait bucket. They broke open the cases and stowed bottles away in the lobster pots which were laid ready by the rail. Grandad brought the *Susan* about just as we passed over the sandbar running out from Bishops Point. With the sails screening us from ashore, they dropped the pots over the rail one by one. The buoys bobbed up in our wake.

"You s'pose they'll notice them from shore?" Grandad was worried.

"Not likely," Toby reassured him, "with the bay full of white horses. Anyway, what's wrong with setting out pots?"

"Here?" Grandad snorted contemptuously . . . "Any fisherman in his right mind knows this isn't good lobster ground."

"Don't worry," Toby said. "Revenuers aren't fishermen. If they were, they wouldn't be revenuers."

"You boys can pick the pots up later when the cutter's gone. Toby, you rig the dinghy so you can land at our own pier and stay clear of old man Petty."

When we tied up to the government wharf, there was Ralph Petty on hand to greet us. "Been up to St. Pierre?" he inquired.

"Well . . . yes," Grandad admitted, a bit taken aback.

"Anything to declare?"

"Some French perfume." He offered it grudgingly for inspection. Mr. Petty looked it over curiously.

"Let it go," he said magnanimously. "I reckon it's for Susan. You're having a big party tomorrow, I hear." Grandad nodded without rising to the bait.

"Any alcohol on board?" My heart did a couple of back flips.

[108]

I'd forgotten about the bottle of champagne. I could tell by his face that Grandad had, too, but he recovered quickly.

"Now Ralph," he said, in a tone of injured innocence, "you know me better than that. The *Susan's* clean as a whistle."

"Glad to hear it," old man Petty said. "Yessir, they tell me you're tossing over the anchor for good . . . what's that you got there?" He pointed to the blue box that Grandad held under his arm.

"Just another present for Sue," Grandad said. As he opened it to fish for the bill, the gold snake caught Mr. Petty's eye. He reached for it just as Grandad snatched away the box. The next moment, the muff was dangling from Mr. Petty's hand — swinging slowly, heavily, like a pendulem of doom, and gurgling gently at every swing.

". . . Well now," said old man Petty, "if that ain't a clever notion!"

We were all pretty gloomy about Mr Petty confiscating Gran's muff and her bottle of champagne. At least we still had the perfume, and the makings for the punch were safely stashed out on the sandbar in clear sight of land. The cutter hung around the harbor all evening. With darkness the wind came up suddenly and it was too rough to take the dinghy out.

The next day was Saturday. It dawned clear and fine but the wind hadn't gone down any. The cutter was still in the harbor. Uncle Will was due in about ten. Gran was as excited as I was at the prospect of seeing him after two years. If Grandad shared our feelings, he didn't show it. Perhaps he was too worried about all that good cognac lying out there in twenty feet of water. He prowled around, checking the barometer every five minutes, getting in everyone's way. Gran had filled every bowl in the house with flowers and their scent mingled with the delicious smell of freshly baked rolls and pound cake. I helped the aunts fix lashings of lobster salad. We took turns running to the balcony to see if the steamer was in sight. When it was an hour overdue, Grandad walked down to the dock. He brought back disquieting news. They'd had a wireless message from Bellow's Arm.

"The steamer's got a cracked propeller shaft," he said. They're holding her up there for repairs."

"My land, Eph" Gran exclaimed in dismay "Will mustn't miss the party. You'll have to go down and pick him up." In those days there was no way to reach Bellow's Arm except by sea.

"I've already sent a message back," Grandad told her. "Toby's rounding up the crew."

"You are a duck!" Gran cried, and gave him a quick little hug. Grandad was never the demonstrative type. He looked a bit startled, but not in the least displeased.

I took my bucket of lobster out to the balcony and glumly watched the *Susan* tack out of the harbor, her lee rail buried all the way. Out by the sandbar she seemed slow coming about. I couldn't see much except the sails flapping as she luffed up into the wind.

The rest of the day Gran kept me busier than a capelin on a cod bank. It was a three to four hour run to the Arm with the wind the way it was. About eight that evening, Gran told me to hitch up the pony cart and go down to the wharf. I was just passing Penny's Pond when I heard the *Susan's* signal. By the time I got there, she was warped in and tied. Uncle Will was already in the customs office with Grandad and Toby. He'd grown a mustache and looked more dignified and mature, but when he looked at me, his eyes had the same old twinkle.

"You've quite grown up, missy," he said. "We'll have to promote you to Senior Worm Watcher."

Old man Petty was checking Uncle Will's luggage. I saw Gran's muff sitting there on his desk beside the bottle of champagne. It made me mad.

"Any alcohol?" he asked.

"About three gallons," Uncle Will said, pointing to a slatted crate done up with yards of twine and baling wire. I thought I'd faint on the spot.

"Aha!" said old man Petty and pounced on the crate. It had a mess of really tough knots and he got pretty fussed up fighting with them and snapping his fingernails.

"Here, let me help you," Uncle Will said when he'd got down to the last one, and sliced through it with his jackknife. He lifted out a glass jar. Old man Petty grabbed it and then I thought he was going to faint. It was full of long, grayish, stringy things. The label on the jar read "DIPHYLOBOTHRIUM LATUM (BIO-LOGICAL SPECIMENS)." He shuddered and put it back quick.

"Why didn't you say it was *that* kind of alcohol?" he said sourly.

"You never asked me," Uncle Will said.

[110]

Back at the house, I helped empty all the bottles into a strainer held over our big copper kettle.

"Fetch me the decanters," Uncle Will said, "and a funnel."

"You going to drink that stuff?" I asked incredulously, eying the gooey mass in the strainer, "with all those worms!"

"Worms, my eye!" Grandad chortled. He picked up one of the long grayish ribbons and swallowed it with relish.

"This is the best darn spaghetti I ever tasted." He smacked his lips . . . "Spaghetti a la cognac you might call it."

"Noodles," Toby corrected him, "and if we don't get some more for the galley and give the cook back his mason jars, he's going to skin me alive."

So that's what you were doing out on the bar," I said . . . "the lobster pots . . ."

"Raised 'em on the way down," Grandad said. "Didn't know what in heck to do with them till Will came up with this notion. A regular brain storm!" He could hardly speak for laughing. "You should've seen Ralph Petty's face!" He slapped Uncle Will on the back — hard. "I guess an education comes in handy sometimes, at that," he roared. Then he turned to Gran. "I'm sorry you won't have your champagne, Susy."

If she had any misgivings about the way things were shaping up or about the Spode teacups, she didn't let on. "Don't you worry yourself, Eph. It's going to be the best party we ever had." Her pale blue eyes had that faraway look — the look they'd held so often when they gazed out to sea, searching for a sail. "My land!" she exclaimed. "If we don't stop this jawing, our guests will be arriving."

Well, as parties go, I dare say Gran's set some sort of record. Perhaps the guests were not exactly the ones she'd expected. In our village you didn't invite people; you just spread the word around and let them make up their own minds. Everyone knew what the occasion was. Maybe it got around about the cognac, too. Anyway, the whole village turned out. Gran looked almost like a girl again with her pearls over her best poplin. All the men argued about who got to dance with her next. Grandad didn't look too pleased. His feet were far more nimble on a heaving deck than they were on a dance floor. He looked even less pleased when Ralph

Petty breezed in looking like the cat that ate the canary and handed Gran a big blue box that gurgled ever so faintly.

"Eph left this in my office," he said. "I reckon it's a surprise." Gran beamed on him and let him have two dances in a row. After some coaxing and a few visits to the punch bowl, he sang five verses of "Never Marry a Sailor." The Brushett sisters surprised everyone by reciting "The Shooting of Dan McGrew" instead of the usual "Lady of Shalott." Supper was served at midnight, but nobody seemed to feel like going home.

Toby and I sat in the kitchen drinking coffee and watching the last embers wink out. He held my hand for a while. I began to think the change in him might turn out to be an improvement after all.

"Do you think Gran can do it this time?" I asked him.

"Do what?"

"Hold Grandad to his promise."

Toby shrugged. "Anyway, it was a fine party," he said.

The last guests finally left. The house seemed strangely silent after all the noise and merriment. I tried to imagine what it must be like being a sailor's wife — watching for storm signals — listening for foghorns.

"I'd best be going," Toby said. "It's pretty late."

Suddenly there was a pop and a light tinkling sound from the parlor. We tiptoed across to the swinging door and opened it a tiny crack. The big oak table was cluttered with empty plates, wine glasses and crumpled linen napkins. Gran and Grandad sat close together, right arms linked, glances locked. The open champagne bottle emitted a tiny wisp of fog. Their glasses clicked together in the Baltic toast so popular on the island. (Unless the gaze is unbroken while the drink is downed it is said the wine will go flat, and along with it, any romantic attachment that may exist.)

Toby and I linked arms. "Prosit!" we echoed softly. It's a bit tricky that holding of the eyes. I spilled some coffee on the front of my new dress and Toby wiped it off carefully.

"I'll bet she makes it stick this time," I predicted. Toby took another quick look into the parlor and closed the door quietly. "No takers," he said.

CHAPTER XV

The Bottoms Up Riddle

FRANK BARCUS

EACH life lost on the Great Lakes in the Storm of 1913, which has come down through the years as the worst disaster in Lake history, brought sorrow to someone. To those who mourned, it made no difference whether the seaman had been lost from the deck of a modern five-thousand-ton freighter or from an ancient wooden barge. To the world at large, however, realization of the extent and force of the storm's fury and of the toll it had demanded in human life came only after many days had passed and boats not mentioned in dispatches began to loom among the missing.

The first report of an absolute loss was so unusual that it immediately focussed the attention of the nation. The entire marine world, even more than the man in the street, was astounded and shocked, for it was forced to believe what it had always thought impossible, that a modern steel freighter could be and had been capsized by the force of a freshwater gale. Somehow — and to this day nobody can tell exactly how — a vessel had been overturned and, stranger still, had been left floating with only her keel exposed to the air.

The news was first reported by radio on Monday. A ship was floating upside down about eleven miles northeast of Fort Gratiot Light near Port Huron. There she remained, apparently transfixed until she sank completely out of sight ten days later.

In that period she became the center of as wild and grisly a comedy of errors as the imagination can conceive. Because of her position, she could not be positively identified, and marine experts guessed every name missing from shipping lists. Her size was guessed at by everyone competent or incompetent to do so, and the cause of her plight gave rise to some weird speculations.

While she held the front pages of the nation as "the mystery ship," she meant heartache and sorrow to hundreds of people. The lost ships were beginning to be counted; now a body washed ashore was identified; now a piece of wreckage told of a sinking. But many still hoped that some way, somehow, a life might have been spared from one of the lost vessels. The name of the "mystery ship" was not a sensational question to them. They wanted to learn her name so they would know if their loved ones had been lost aboard her.

For more than a week the ship lay in international waters between the United States and Canada. These waters are under the joint supervision of the federal authorities of both countries, yet no attempt was made by either to discover the ship's identity. Either could have taken on the work of investigating the wreck and determining the name of the ship. Some investigation was especially urgent as the wreck's position endangered navigation.

In spite of the many reasons for taking action, the Canadian government did nothing about the ship and the United States government did just enough to botch things up.

The U. S. revenue cutter *Morrill* was sent to the scene of the wreck and when she got there, was immediately ordered to return to Lake Erie. The reason given for this second order was that the *Morrill* was needed to assist the steamer *G. J. Grammer,* which was driven offshore one-half mile east of the harbor mouth at Lorain, Ohio. Actually the *Grammer* was resting easily on a sandy bottom, was in no danger herself, and menaced no one else; thus she seemed to need assistance the least.

To say that the transfer of the *Morrill* to Lake Erie shocked the marine world is putting it mildly. The cutter was desperately needed in Lake Huron. She was the only craft available for work at the scene of the wreckage. And there was much necessary work to be done — collision with sunken wrecks to be prevented, bodies to be recovered, possibly even lives to be saved.

When William Livingstone, president of the Lake Carriers' Association, learned of the government's action, he became a one-man storm in himself. He initiated furious efforts to uncover the cause of this action, and immediately dispatched the tug *Sarnia City* to the overturned hull. This was the first real attempt to learn the identity of the mystery ship.

When Captain Ely of the *Sarnia City* returned from his inspection, he said he had "found it impossible to make out the name of the ship because of the high seas and the fact that the vessel was lying keel upward." However, because he knew how anxiously the maritime world awaited any word at all, he started the great guessing game. "I think it's one of the big fellows," he said. "That's the way it looks to me I think she was headed back toward the river (St. Clair) running for shelter, when she must have been caught in the trough of a sea and bowled over."

This was on Tuesday, November 11. That same day, ten frozen bodies were found strewn along the Canadian shore of Lake Huron, along with a lifeboat containing two more bodies. All of the bodies were wearing life preservers. The lifeboat, and its crew, which were discovered farther along the shore, both bore the name of the steamer *Regina*. This was thought to solve the mystery of the overturned freighter.

Several other reasons seemed to establish the mystery ship as the *Regina*, one of the large freighters that disappeared with her entire crew. When the *Regina* had passed into Sunday's storm, Danny Lynn of the Lynn Marine Reporting Company remarked that "the deck load the *Regina* was carrying looked dangerous. She appeared top heavy with a load of sewer and gas pipe which stuck way above the rail."

Although this conclusion was generally believed, some doubts were still expressed among the mariners. It was said that "the *Regina's* bottom was painted green and the bottom of the overturned freighter was black."

Superintendent Dugan of the Merchant's Mutual Line Company, owners of the *Regina*, visited the wreck along with Captain Thomas Reid of the Reid Wrecking Company and said that "the mystery ship was not the *Regina*." This further complicated the mystery. Captain Reid stated that never before in his life had he seen a ship upside down. "Its almighty hard to tell anything from a boat's bottom," he said

President Livingston was in perhaps the best position to judge the ship's identity. His efforts to trace her identity were continually bringing in reports and rumors for him to sift. From his information he concluded that reports that the ship was a "big fellow," a five- to six-hundred-footer, were probably exaggerated.

"I am informed by Captain Reid," said Livingstone, "that there are eight plates around the vessel, not exceeding five feet each in width, which would indicate the breadth of the ship to be perhaps from forty to forty-three feet. The length of the plates visible on the sides of the vessel might afford a basis for concluding that the vessel's length does not exceed from two hundred and fifty to three hundred feet. Of course, I may be in error, but I feel almost certain the vessel's length will be found not to exceed three hundred feet."

On Tuesday night Livingstone said: "The fact that practically all boats of the Lake Carriers' Association have been accounted for lends strength to the belief that the vessel is Canadian."

The Canadian ownership postulate gained strength with another discovery made earlier Tuesday. Three bodies had come ashore near St. Joseph on the Canadian shore of Lake Huron, all wearing life preservers with the name *Wexford*. The *Wexford* was a Canadian ship, and since she was only 270 feet over-all, according to Livingstone's guess, she might well have been the overturned ship.

On Wednesday, eight more bodies were washed ashore in a lifeboat near Port Franks, Ontario, and it was announced that of the ten bodies found along the Canadian shore the day before, seven wore life preservers with the name of the steamer *Charles S. Price* on them and three wore *Regina* preservers. But on Thursday an even grimmer harvest was reaped, and it was soon evident that the overturned vessel could be any one of many. Three bodies lashed to a life raft stamped with the name *John A. McGean* came ashore five miles south of Goderich, Ontario. This was the first report that this steamer was definitely lost.

The same day, twenty more from the same vessel washed ashore near the same spot, with wreckage from the most modern 550-foot steel freighter, *Carruthers*. More wreckage and bodies from the *Wexford* appeared at the same spot, followed by jetsam from the steamer *Argus*.

On Thursday a representative of the owners of the *Regina, James Carruthers,* and *Turret Chief* — all missing — informed Livingstone by long distance telephone from Sarnia that the little tug *Sport* and the services of a professional diver could be obtained on Friday morning.

"For God's sake, get them if you can," cried Livingstone. "If the weather is at all favorable, have the tug and diver go out and send the bill to me. You cannot be any more anxious than I to learn the identity of the vessel."

[116]

THE BOTTOMS UP RIDDLE

Sending down a diver to discover the name of the mystery ship was one of the hardest problems that confronted the marine men. For one thing, there was nothing that the tug could tie to on the overturned hull, and yet the boat from which the diver would be lowered would have to anchor alongside the wrecked boat. A heavy sea would make the whole attempt dangerous.

While the preparations for diving were being made, the rumor and theory factory was going full blast, producing some strange and wonderful material. One of the most astounding notions was brought forth by one Captain Wescott, who believed that the crew caught in the overturned ship might have lived for two or three days under the hull, as in a giant diving bell. Curiously enough, he had superficial backing for his theory in an actual case: the capsizing of the schooner *New Connecticut* on Lake Erie in the early 1860's. When wreckers arrived at the ship three days after the capsizing, she lay on her side with her hatches under water. Yet, within her there was still one person alive — a woman, wife of one of the crew — who was rescued and survived her terrible experience.

Many technical marine experts were attempting to account for the condition of the vessel. While it is exceedingly rare for a freighter to turn turtle, there are many ways in which it might happen, according to shipbuilders. Earnest Ketchum, secretary-treasurer of the Detroit Shipbuilding Company, voiced the general technical opinion in a statement to the Detroit "News":

"If the boat had been loaded," said Ketchum, "the upsetting would have been simple enough. She was not loaded, however, because if she had been, her forward end would not float at all. She would have gone down instantly. Since she could not have been loaded, the only possible theory is that the high seas, which must have been running twenty or twenty-one feet, got under her and sent her over.

"Going out in a gale like that her master undoubtedly let water into her to be used as ballast. Rolling as she was in the trough of the heavy seas, the water ballast would rush from one side of the vessel to the other, and the more it rushed back and forth the farther over the vessel would list. With her rolling constantly increasing and gaining impetus each time she careened, a high wave getting under her would surely send her on over.

"Then the boilers would break away from their stands, smashing downward as she went over to rest on the inside of the deck. They would hold the after end of the vessel on the bottom, while the forward end, which would have air in it, would float; and the force of gravity would drive the water toward the after end. This would leave the vessel in the same position as the mystery ship now in Lake Huron, stern down and bow out, with an even keel showing."

Mr. Ketchum used the above observation to back his guess at the identity of the mystery ship. "It is hardly possible that she is the *Regina,* because she was loaded, and we all know from past wrecks and also as boat builders that no vessel will float with a cargo in her because any part of her is bound to be much heavier than the air that would be in her. A vessel navigating light, if she is watertight, is like a corked bottle. So long as the hatches of the vessel hold, the boat will remain afloat; when they give way, the boat will go down."

With all these theories given by so many experts in marine matters, anything sounded possible but probably none of the theories was right. Only one thing was definitely known: that a ship had turned turtle; that much was visible. How she came to turn will no doubt remain the great mystery of the Lakes.

Friday, the day set for divers to solve the mystery, brought more tension. Rough seas and added preparations delayed the attempt. More bodies were washed ashore near Point Clark lighthouse, twenty-five miles above Goderich, Ontario — eight men and a woman from the *James Carruthers,* one man from the *Argus,* and one unidentified — but nothing indicating the mystery vessel's name.

At last, on Saturday, six days after the storm, William Baker, a professional diver from Detroit, was ready to go down beside the hulk and clear up the mystery.

"We lay near the wreck all night on the tug *Sport,*" said Baker, "waiting for the dawn. We had everything arranged to make the descent at the earliest possible moment. I was ready at 5:30 and half an hour later I started down.

"As I went down I felt the ship's sides all the way for twenty feet. Then I lost contact but I kept on going down, expecting to run into the side again. When I discovered that I was too far down I started to come up and found the wreck once more.

"I ran into the pipe rail around the texas work and hung on

there until I found out where I was. There was a round railing on the edge of the bulwarks. I went around this railing until I ran across the name. There I stopped and took my time.

"I read the name twice and then once more to be absolutely sure. The name was painted in black letters on white bulwarks — *Charles S. Price.*"

History does not reveal how tasty the marine experts may have found their positive words once the true identity of the overturned vessel was learned. Not only were the men who had sworn she was the *Regina* sadly put out, but also all the boys who had flashed their superior mathematical abilities and expertness in measurement.

The American steamer *Charles S. Price* had an over-all length of 524 feet, leaving President Livingstone two hundred feet behind in his calculations; and he and other experts, in judging her beam to be 42 feet, were cheating her of twelve feet of her rightful width. But worst of all was the waste of shipbuilder Ketchum's thrilling romance — the one which had the ship teetering from side to side like a drunkard, her belly full of water ballast sloshing about — for the *Price* had left Ashtabula on Saturday, November 8, with a full load of soft coal.

Once her identity was known, however, the *Price* posed an even greater question — one which has never been answered. She had left Ashtabula with a crew of twenty-eight men. She was last seen above water by Captain May of the steamer *H. A. Hawgood,* bucking the storm north of Sand Beach at noon Sunday "heading into it and making bad weather." From that time until she overturned near Port Huron on Monday, no man can tell what happened to her.

The first theory of her actual fate was brought about by the testimony of her only "survivor," former first engineer Milton Smith, at a Canadian inquest on some of the bodies washed ashore.

Smith claimed he had a premonition of disaster when he left the *Price* at Cleveland on Saturday, the day before the storm. His shipmates had ridiculed him for leaving the ship with the end of the sailing season so near. Some laughed, some scoffed, and some made insulting remarks, but Smith had had visions of his wife pleading with him to leave, and of his family in Port Huron. Nothing could move him from his determination.

[119]

"My Gawd!" exclaimed Smith, "I might ha' been in her! I might ha' been in her! I was getting tired of sailing, anyway. I wanted to get away from it and I realized this was my best chance. I knew every boy on the *Price*. I am especially sorry for poor Arz McIntosh of St. Clair, our wheelsman. When Arz heard I was coming back to Port Huron, he came up to me and said: 'Milt, is it true that you are going to leave the ship?' I told him that it was and he said, 'Dammit! I wish I was going with you.'

"I can see poor Arz now. The boy was having trouble with his eyes and wanted to come home to have them operated on. He had practically made up his mind to come along with me but said that he guessed he could stick it out for just one more trip. Poor fellow."

Smith went to Thedford, Ontario, to help establish the identity of bodies in the morgue there. The first body he looked at was that of John Groundwater, chief engineer of the *Price*.

"That's him," said Smith to Coroner Clarke. "That's big, good-natured John. How the boys all liked him."

"Are you sure that is him?" asked the coroner.

"As sure as I know my own name is Smith," he replied.

"Well, this man had one of the *Regina's* life preservers wrapped about his body," said the coroner.

Smith was dumfounded. The mystery was more than he could fathom. Then the obvious answer dawned upon him — the *Regina* and the *Price* must have collided.

Groundwater's body was not the only one from the *Price* found with a *Regina* life preserver. Every additional body added its testimony to the belief that the two vessels had collided near Port Huron. Perhaps when the ships struck, the seamen had grasped the first belts at hand, thrown to them when they landed in the water. One theory was that some of the *Price's* crew had jumped to the deck of the *Regina* when the accident occurred. This theory was strengthened by the finding of two men, one from each ship, with their arms clasped about each other.

However, the testimony of the diver tended to refute this theory: "After making sure that the boat was the *Charles S. Price*," said Baker on his ascent, "I went farther forward to the stem to see if there were any damaged plates that would indicate a collision or any other damage to the boat. From there I pulled myself along the

[120]

rail to the after side of the forward house and found nothing that showed any signs of collision.

"By then the sea was coming up and began to toss me about. I had to give it up. I was under water an hour in all, and I investigated about forty-three feet of the starboard bow. I had no chance to go any farther on the wreck and didn't get inside her at all.

"The bow of the *Price* is being buoyed up by the air that was imprisoned in her when she went over. There are now two streams of bubbles coming out of the bow and there seems to be no doubt that the boat will continue to settle down as soon as all the air leaks out of her."

While the diver's story produced strong evidence against the collision theory, it could not be accepted as conclusive because of the limited area he had searched. Many marine experts still believe that the *Regina* will some day be found close to the vessel she struck, although Captain Thompson of the tug *Sport*, before going back to port with the diver, dragged his anchor around the wreck and met no obstacle. He told Livingstone that he "believed the washing away of the *Price's* hatches and the storm-tossed shifting of the cargo combined to throw the vessel on her side, capsizing her without warning to the crew."

If it had not been a collision, what were the other possibilities? The two vessels, when last seen by Captain May of the *Hawgood*, were many miles apart, the *Price* just north of Sand Beach, the *Regina* fifteen miles south of the same spot. Captain Dan McKay, of a D & C passenger steamer, had also seen the *Price,* turning around into the trough of the seas about ten miles south of Harbor Beach and heading back for the St. Clair River. All this made for another confusing clue in the mystery of the *Regina* and the *Price* — they were sighted at about the same time going in opposite directions. How then were the *Regina's* life preservers on *Price* bodies, and what about that battered and frozen couple clasped together on the icy Canadian Beach?

In discussing the wreck of the *Price* the day her name was learned, Captain Carmine of the *Morrill* said, "It is my opinion that the *Price's* crew abandoned her at least thirty-five miles up the lake, or at a point opposite Harbor Beach. The finding of several of her crew near Port Frank would seem to refute entirely the theory of a collision between her and the *Regina.*" The inference was that several of the crew might have been picked up by the *Regina* later on.

Against this theory of abandonment, however, was proof of how swiftly the *Price* had met her fate, as established by Milton Smith in his identification of the steward, Herbert Jones:

"There he was," said Smith "lying there with his apron on just as he looked hundreds of times when he was about to prepare a meal or just after he he had prepared it. Evidently the poor fellow didn't even have time to look after his wife's welfare, which shows how quickly the boat must have gone down."

With no time allowed to abandon the *Price*, with no other vessel close enough to have collided with her, there seemed but one other possible answer to the riddle — that the *Regina* had seen the *Price* turn turtle, had run to her assistance, and had thrown over lifebelts and started to lower boats, when the sea finally overcame her in turn.

None of the bodies could give more than the mute evidence of a common death somewhere in the icy waste of black water. Their effects were only those things a man generally has about him at his work. The body of William McInnis, twenty, wheelsman on the *Price*, carried a letter from his mother, a diary showing his daily expenses and a small parcel of money order receipts for the money he had sent his mother during the season — just what you might expect a decent fellow from a frugal Canadian farm family to keep about him. There were no hurried notes of terror, no fragments to tell of their last moments. They had been struck in the midst of life — it was mercifully quick.

CHAPTER XVI

Nowhere Is Too Far

CARLETON MITCHELL

AFTER the remorseless efficiency of steam ended the era of commercial sail, there was a span of years when white wings of canvas all but disappeared from the oceans of the world. A few men, like Captains Joshua Slocum and John Voss, made long passages, often alone, but they were professional seamen braving the elements in small vessels for profit or glory, marine *curiosa* gaped at by landsmen with the same awe accorded beached whales.

Now landsmen go down to the sea in their own little ships. Sails dot distant waters. The Cruising Club of America recently published a book chronicling voyages by its members; it was entitled "Nowhere Is Too Far," which accurately sums up a phenomenon of the mid-twentieth century. No longer are such ventures stunts; they are part of a way of life.

Last year (1960) a fleet of 135 small sailing yachts — limited by rule to between thirty-five and seventy-three feet on deck — raced across 635 nautical miles of open ocean from Newport to Bermuda. Immediately after, seventeen continued on across the North Atlantic to a finish line off Marstrand, Sweden. At the same time, others were driving from England to New York against prevailing westerly winds, a fleet somewhat more newsworthy because the skipper of each vessel raced alone — singlehanded, in the parlance of sailing.

Meanwhile, other little ships were cruising, moving as wind and the inclination of the owner directed. In Naples for the Olympic Games, I received a letter congratulating me on *Finisterre's* Bermuda Race victory from a friend last seen in Tahiti aboard his thirty-eight-foot ketch, now in New Caledonia by way of the Society Islands and Fiji. After reading the letter, I walked past Castel del' Ovo to greet another skipper who had sailed over from New York for the Olympic Games, with stops at the Azores and Gibraltar.

And simultaneously similar little boats — in size down to

cockleshells barely twenty feet on deck — were scattered across the waters of the Aegean, the Baltic, the Caribbean, and all other seas except perhaps the polar, an armada involving uncounted hundreds of boats crewed by thousands of men and women of every nationality, background and financial status.

Why do they do it? Every small vessel venturing offshore is on its own, a lonely entity, face to face with the most elemental force on planet Earth. There is discomfort, even danger. Distance and duration of a voyage alter these facts only in a matter of degree. No gallery rises to applaud an act of skill or bravery on the slippery foredeck of an ocean racer; no rescuer is likely to be standing by the cruiser drifting toward a remote reef.

In a cabin scarcely larger than a telephone booth laid on its side, usually pitching and rolling like a howdah on a rampaging elephant, the crew must perform the chores of living, for perhaps weeks on end. Sail must be trimmed to each vagary of breeze, each dark squall must be watched against disaster. When it rains, everything aboard is wet; when it is glassy calm those on deck broil in the sun.

There are blistered palms, and cold beans spooned directly from the can, and the misery of being unable to sleep in a tossing bunk. And always in the back of the mind lurks the threat of the falling barometer, the gathering gale, the sullen insenate building of waves, primordial and pitiless. Sailors still die within sight of the shore.

Few of the people braving wide waters in small boats are professional seamen. Many begin sailing Sunday afternoons on a sheltered estuary, lengthen their cruises to a weekend, and then are overwhelmed by an irresistible urge to go farther, beyond the horizon. Some have studied navigation in libraries and apprenticed themselves as unpaid crew to learn the rudiments of the sailor's ancient arts — to "reef, hand, and steer." Others, with less patience and perhaps more money, simply buy a boat and take off, trusting to Providence and the Coast Guard.

Nor are all intent on voyaging to distant and exotic shores. Most are tethered by the unseverable complications of civilization — a job, a family, a mortgage on a house. For them cruising can occupy only a few weeks of any given year, perhaps a voyage out around Cape Cod to the coast of Maine or Nova Scotia, maybe a beat across the Gulf Stream to the Bahamas or islands beyond, perhaps the race to Bermuda or Honolulu.

Why, when most urbanites remain home rather than seek a taxi on a drizzly night, will others don oilskins to crouch in the cockpit of a plunging little vessel somewhere offshore — cold, hungry, perhaps ill, uncertain even of their exact whereabouts in relation to known dangers? As scientists probe space and talk in terms of mach speeds, pressing toward the ultimate frontier, why should anyone be so anachronistic as to feel a challenge in exploring charted waters in an wholly outmoded conveyance, plodding along at four knots?

For many years it has been a question with particular meaning for me, because I am one of the plodders. Perhaps the first time it came into clear focus was shortly after midnight on July 6, 1952, when my 58-foot yawl *Caribbee* was approximately three hundred miles south of Cape Race, Newfoundland, the nearest land. We had been four days at sea, racing from Bermuda to Plymouth, England, a voyage destined to slant across the chill wastes of the North Atlantic for twenty-two days.

When my watch came on deck at eleven it was black dark, a heavy overcast blanketing even a glimmer from the moon. There was a fresh reaching breeze, and we lugged sail: spinnaker, balloon forestaysail, main, mizzen, and mizzen staysail — everything that could be hung from the masts. Seas burst over the counter. *Caribbee* was shooting down the crests, pausing, shooting again, sometimes taking wild sheers, spinnaker collapsing and filling with crashes that shook the whole boat.

Good seamanship dictated a reduction of sail. We had gone beyond the boundary of rational judgment into that heady realm of deliberate acceptance of danger. But we were racing, and it occurred to no one on board to lower a square foot of canvas.

When our eyes became fully adjusted to the gloom, the lights of a steamer were sighted astern. She slowly overtook us; her running lights became visible, then a row of ports along her side. Suddenly her searchlight flared. *Caribbee* was as sharply etched as the carving on a cameo, each line standing out against the black background of the night, each drop of the bow wave sparkling like a diamond. Fore and aft, we were a smother of breaking water, while overhead soared a literal cloud of sail.

[125]

In the eerie glare I was somehow aware of how we must appear in the eyes of others, driving a fragile creation of wood and cordage through the night, far offshore. Why? must have asked the cynical professional seamen on the bridge, and why? I echoed, a question which has frequently recurred during my sailing career, sometimes while I was sitting in the cockpit watching the sunset burnish the water of a placid gunkhole; sometimes while wrestling with flogging sails during a screaming squall at sea (when I usually added under my breath: "And what the hell am I doing here?").

Escape would seem to be the most obvious explanation — escape from the crowded shore, where the cities have become unbearable cauldrons of noise and fumes, the countryside ravaged by creeping suburbia and above the stalled lines of automobiles linking the two, twang the electronic voices of the hucksters. In its simplest sense, going to sea is getting away from it all.

Yet it is more than that, for nowhere is there truly escape for the intelligent twentieth-century man. Then, I have asked myself, is it the fulfillment of a compulsion, a basic inner hunger for the sea as other men can exist only through the tranquillity of tilled land?

The same ineffable need in earlier ages must have created the navigators who pushed back the known horizons, and then the rovers, the buckoes who drove clippers through the Roaring Forties. Now that there is no longer beauty or romance in professional seafaring, such men must sail to satisfy the hunger.

Akin to this is the urge that drives others to climb distant, difficult mountains. Here also is a compulsion hard for the outsider to understand, and perhaps in many ways similar. Far from the plaudits of the crowd, dedicated individuals come to grips with nature on its own terms, voluntarily undergoing hardships, exertion, even physical danger, purely for the satisfaction of personal accomplishment.

Perhaps the practitioners of both sports are unconsciously rejecting the insulation of our button-pushing civilization, seeking a return to the elemental, when the human species depended for survival on strength and courage, virtues essential in earlier cultures. Often, I think, the sense of snugness and security in the tiny cabin of a small vessel anchored in a safe harbor after a long voyage — a feeling like no other in the world — could only stem from a heritage of crouching before the fire in a long-forgotten cave, a stone sealing the entrance, the day's kill on the floor.

Like mountain climbing, too, is the sense of mutual dependence which binds shipmates. As Alpinists rope themselves together on dangerous slopes, yachtsmen offshore in heavy weather lash themselves to the boat. It is literally sink or swim together. A crew muzzling a flailing jib on the foredeck must have confidence in the helmsman, the man aloft repairing a broken spreader trusts his life to those below tending the lines. From such moments comes a sense of group identification — a team spirit, a closeness — hard to experience elsewhere.

Yet through every approach there seems to run one thread: the rewards of sailing are mostly personal. It is all I have written and much besides — it is drifting into a quiet cove at dusk; it is the exhilaration of a brisk beat to windward, spray like flung jewels in the sun and the taste of salt on the lips; it is moonlight across water and a helmsman's satisfaction at having eased through a sequence of towering crests; it is tension in driving past shoals and pride in a well-turned splice.

A small boat allows opportunity for reflection, for the formulation of perspective and a philosophy, rare things indeed in this age. Like a contented turtle, the cruiser carries his house wherever he goes. A little yacht is man's portable castle, home in the most distant land. "Nowhere is too far," and nowhere need the sailor be lost — around him may be his books, his pictures, his links with the past.

Away from a familiar shore it is even possible to lose the time consciousness goading modern man. Once I asked an inveterate cruiser why he always seemed so relaxed when we met. "I throw away the calendar," he answered. "I not only throw away the calendar but the clock. It keeps me from ever being in a hurry."

But sailors defy exact classification. The next may get his reward from driving a boat to the utmost, savoring the tension of competition. To a racing skipper, the most important thing aboard is the scurrying second hand of a watch, and life is regulated by it. Sails are changed to each shift and strength of breeze as a golfer matches clubs to distance and terrain and woe betide him who wanders from course.

Thus perhaps the ultimate answer to "Why?" is the infinite

[127]

variety of sailing. Always there is another challenge. Learn coastwise pilotage and there is celestial navigation; fashion a splice in rope and next it is wire; turn out scrambled eggs and someone suggests soufflé.

Compressed into a space having a cubic content less than that of a good closet must be stowed the items of a well stocked house: food, beverages, linen, clothes, pots, pans, dishes, fuel, medicine, books, writing paper — no running to the corner drugstore or supermarket at sea!

But a boat is more complicated than any edifice ashore. There must be sails, rigging, and the myriad items needed for propulsion, for repair, for communication, for ascertaining position, even for survival in the event of disaster.

But above all there must be the skills to bind everything together. A small vessel is wholly on its own, a microcosm, an outpost of civilization wherever it may be. Those aboard must not only know the way of a ship with the sea, but possess the skills to cope with every phase of modern life and the operation of their craft — must be doctor, plumber, carpenter, sailmaker, rigger, electrician, cook, astronomer, radio technician, meteorologist.

A lifetime is much too short to learn everything — much too short. Yet with each increase in ability and knowledge there comes a sense of achievement to the individual. The endless challenge and the personal rewards — these are why enough for sailing the byways and the oceans.

CHAPTER XVII

The Cave of Doom

GEOFFREY W. FIELDING

DOWN at the end of the earth, forever circling the frigid lands of the Antarctic, the racing westerlies and Roaring Forties chase each other in violent mayhem, a ceaseless tempest — like a dog condemned forever to chase its tail. Unhindered, unimpeded by alien land, the raging winds scourge the slate-gray barren waters, scooping and scouring the hissing seas into gigantic waves.

Countless sailing ships went missing in these hostile waters of the South Pacific, their graves marked only by the flotsam and jetsam of the foundering. A few small islands — Bounty, Chatham, Campbell, Auckland — mere specks in the ocean vastness, stand athwart the great circle route from the Antipodes to Cape Horn, additional handicaps for the hard men who sailed the handsome clippers.

Captain William Kerby Loughlin paced the poop of the ship *General Grant*, a fine-lined clipper recently from the shipyards of Boston. Since leaving Port Philip, Melbourne, on May 4, just nine days before, he'd seen little of the sun. Fortunately the glass had dropped only after he had safely navigated Bass Strait, Flinders Island and the Tasman Coast. Now just one more hurdle faced him before he began the long five-thousand-mile easting down to the waste of Cape Horn.

Not that the Auckland Islands worried him. Far from it, for the crow's feet around his eyes marked the many years spent at sea. He knew his own capabilities and was satisfied. So were his owners. Otherwise what would explain the valuable cargo below deck insured for some one hundred and sixty-five thousand pounds sterling. Screwed down in the holds was the new wool clip from Australian sheep stations. There was zinc spelter, too, though some said that this was gold; and hides and skins, while two ironbound strong boxes, safely stowed away in the captain's cabin, contained over a ton of gold, consigned to England by the Bank of New South Wales.

"La-a-a-and, ho!" From the masthead the lookout's cry could barely be heard over the wail of the wind in the shrouds. Captain Loughlin moved to the lee rail and scanned the horizon off the port bow. His hand reached for the telescope tucked under the chief officer's arm and there, on the ill-defined line where the dull overcast reached down to the clawing waves, he could just make out the mist-veiled islands.

"Yes, that's it, Mr. Brown," he said, turning to the mate. "Y'can just see it when it clears a bit. Auckland's the big one, I think that small one must be Disappointment Island. Looks miserable, don't it?"

Without waiting for an answer he clumped down the ladder to his cabin and gazed at the chart. He was pretty pleased with himself. Not for nothing had he earned a reputation as a navigator. Dead reckoning for almost a week and here he was, right on course.

He joined the mate on deck again. "Think some of those diggers want to see it?" he asked. In the primitive but warm accommodations of the ship were sixty-eight miners, each rich from the gold fields of Ballarat and Bendigo. "Call Mrs. Jewell, too; she might want to take a look."

A seaman went below and a bunch of hard cases tumbled out on deck to get their last look at land for the next few weeks. But it was soon dark and they left the cold deck for the snug quarters below.

Gradually throughout the night the wind dropped away. Watches changed at the end of each four hours, and time passed to the strike of the ship's bell. A heavy haze settled over the ship and water, though the sea was still rough and an occasional rain squall hissed across the waves.

"Land, land, dead ahead." The sudden yell from the bow shattered the silent night.

There was a mad scramble on deck, the watch below burst from the fo'c's'le. Loughlin tumbled from his cabin to find the mate desperately trying to wear ship. But she wouldn't answer.

A huge wave curled, caught the *General Grant,* and hurled her forward with gathering momentum until she crashed into the base of a towering cliff. She pulled off as the seas recoiled for another punch, the wreckage of a jib-boom and bowsprit trailing alongside, and slid along the foot of the cliff for almost half a mile. Then the waves picked her up once more and rammed her past the line of breakers and deep into the blackness of a towering cave.

The clipper slowly jammed to a stop. Her heavy royals, top-gallants and yards punched into the cave's ceiling and tumbled to the deck. Her shrouds and backstays snapped explosively under the strain, while the waves shoved and pushed. Pandemonium raged, passengers screamed and cried, running this way and that up and down the dark, sea-swept deck while nervous fingers buckled on the weighty gold-filled money belts. That bullion meant more to them, almost, than life itself.

The night turned to the grayness of dawn and still the waves surged under the ship so that the stump of her mainmast drummed on the unyielding rock roof. A wave larger than the others, carried forward on the rising tide, creamed into the cave and picked the ship up for the last time, for the force of the mast hitting the roof drove the heel through the bottom and forced the keel. Through the huge splintered holes the gray-green seas poured into the hulk.

The passengers felt the ship rapidly settling beneath their feet and some jumped over the side into the boiling waves. Three men lowered one of the boats and pulled out of the cave to reconnoiter. They were never seen again.

Provisions were hurriedly tossed into another boat and it was lowered the few feet into the rising water. Strong arms of the sea-men pulled it out of the cave. Another boat followed, then the long-boat floated off the deck, loaded down to the gunwales with forty people.

Sluggish in the rough and tumbling seas the longboat drifted for about fifty yards out of the cave, but unable to ride over the breakers, it was caught by a particularly viscious wave and capsized, casting its unfortunate passengers into the surf.

Those in the two other boats, watched in horror. One of them, catching sight of long auburn hair churned by the waters, screamed, and dived over the side of the pinnace. It was Joe Jewell, a sailor, who knew that the hair was that of his wife, Mary Ann, a passenger on the ill-fated craft.

Gasping and struggling he managed to grab the woman and slowly hauled her back to the boat where strong arms dragged them aboard. Only three others, all of them particularly strong swimmers, were pulled from the water.

Desperately, for the rising tide was slowly dragging them back to the cragged rocks at the foot of the cliffs, all hands pulled on the long oars and slowly but gradually forced the boats to the relatively calmer waters beyond the breakers.

There the mate took tally of the survivors. His heart sank. Nine crewmen and six passengers . . . fifteen in all. Captain Loughlin was not there. He looked at the menacing mouth of the grim cavern and at the bits of wreckage still surging from it, and then at the towering twelve-hundred-foot cliffs. He waited with sinking heart for more survivors. He waited to hear an anguished cry of distress so that he might save more. And he waited. Then he turned to the others. "I'm sorry," he said, "but we can't go back in, we'll be lost if we do."

The others gazed at him with almost unseeing eyes and just nodded. He looked around for a place of calm, a beach, or the mouth of a stream, but the inhospitable cliffs stretched to the north and south as far as the eye could see and offered no refuge. The only likely spot appeared to be an island some miles distant, and Bart Brown slowly turned his boats.

Auckland Island had claimed another victim.

The island group was getting quite a reputation. Discovered in 1806 by Captain Abraham B. Bristow of the whaler *Ocean*, it lies approximately 190 miles south-south-west of Stewart Island, off the south island of New Zealand, at latitude 50 degrees, 32 minutes south.

Roughly shaped in the form of a gourd, with the bulbous part to the south, three-quarters of the group consists of Auckland Island itself, which measures twenty-five miles long, north and south, and seventeen miles wide. To the south of it, and following generally the contours of the southern coast, is Adams Island, fifteen miles east to west and two miles wide.

Between them is one of the two most important anchorages of the group, Carnley Harbor. The other, Port Ross (or Sarah's Bosom) is at the northeast corner. Off the rugged west coast, with its high cliffs and tumultuous waves, lies Disappointment Island, to which Brown was now heading, while Enderby Island, named after the

Ocean's owners, is close to Port Ross and the northeast corner. A number of smaller islands complete the group.

Vegetation, stunted from the constant westerly blast, is mainly ironwood, or rata trees. The almost impenetrable rata forest furnishes cover for lush undergrowth which feeds numerous types of domestic animals left by visitors to the island — the whalers, sealers, colonists, scientific expeditions, and rescuers of others wrecked there.

For the *General Grant* was not the first ship to go on Auckland Island, nor was she to be the last. Ten known ships were wrecked on the group between 1864 and 1907, and by the time the *General Grant* went on the rocks in 1866 three others, the *Grafton, Minerva,* and *Invercauld,* had found an end on the rugged coastline.

Bart Brown couldn't have cared less. All he was interested in was getting his people ashore. But landing was impossible on Disappointment Island. The smaller boat was swamped when it tried and almost all the provisions were lost. However, the boat and its occupants were recovered by the other boat without much additional damage being done. As night was falling, the only alternative was to stand off the island and spend the night in the boats and hope to find a landing place on the mainland the following day.

The exhausted sailors and passengers rocked in the boats all night long, taking catnaps periodically, though a gale sprung up and continued half the night. Occasionally someone would fall over in complete and utter exhaustion and lie in the bottom of the boat until awakened by the buffeting. They huddled together for warmth, yet constantly tried to be alert to the danger of the boats drifting too far apart or crashing together. Finally the sky lightened in the east and a new day broke.

When the wind calmed down the chief mate checked the mainland coast for a landing place. All he could see was the same gray sight, tossing waves crashed onto cliffs, leaden sky overhead, a depressive, soul wearying aspect. The boats swung around at his command and headed toward the northern coast, where supplies and equipment might be found at the abandoned settlement at Port Ross.

It was another long, exhausting day, but by evening the boats came to a beach near Port Ross and managed to land. Things looked desolate for everyone was cold, hungry and wet. There appeared to be nothing to help them, but one of the men found an unused match

[133]

in his pocket and after it had been dried out, twigs, dry grass, and sticks were collected and a small fire started.

There was not much to do that night except sleep and try to regain strength for the following day, so Brown set two-hour watches to keep the fire burning and the castaways dropped off into the dreamless sleep of the utterly weary.

The next day some of the remaining supplies from the boats were brought up and a small meal was eaten before they started to explore. Little of significance was found, except a dilapidated hut opposite Port Ross, but this meant shelter and so the camp was moved.

The fire, too, was taken to the new site, care being taken to keep the old fire going until the new one was established. Then the boats were moved closer.

Fortunately the seals had been coming back to Auckland in recent years, after almost a half century of slaughter by British and Yankee sealers, and thus the survivors had a ready source of food at hand. Daily a party went out in the boats to bash a few on the head and bring them back to the camp where they were skinned and cleaned.

The seals provided a steady if montonous diet. A few sea birds were caught and some eggs found among the rocks, and now and then a sheep or goat was brought in. Fishing was less successful, for the few they caught were riddled with worms.

A constant lookout was kept for passing sail, a fruitless vigil so it seemed as the days stretched into weeks and the weeks became months. However, they patched up the hut and set to making small wooden boats, about three feet long, on which they cut messages of their plight. These "Auckland Messengers" were launched into waves with the hope that some might be picked up by ships on the trade routes, or on distant shores, but none ever was.

The harsh southern winter months passed, and late in the year the chief officer decided that there was little future in waiting for the chance call of a ship at the Aucklands. The two boats were still serviceable and he broached the idea of fitting one out and heading for New Zealand. Three sailors volunteered to join him on the two-hundred-mile journey and so preparations were made.

The 22-foot pinnace was selected as the better of the two craft, and this they decked over with the skins of seals they had slaughtered. Canvas, used to line the hut, was cut for sail. Provisions for the four men included seven cans of soup . . . the remnants of what they had saved from the ship . . . dried seal meat, a few eggs, one goat and two kids, and a supply of water stored in seals' gullets, which they had saved.

Full summer, such as it was, had arrived at Auckland when they headed out of Port Ross on January 22, 1867. It was a risky business, for not only was the craft a mere cockleshell in those waters, but they had nothing with which to navigate. By guess and by God they planned to steer generally east-northeast in the hope of reaching civilization.

Meanwhile the remaining eleven survivors sought means to improve their lot. They continued to search the island in the vicinity of their camp and came across another hut. In it was a barrel stave noting the loss of the ship *Minerva* three years before and the rescue of its crew, but that didn't help them much, except to raise their hopes that they, too, might be saved.

They had saved little from the wreck and the clothes they wore were fast disintegrating. There were still plenty of sealskins around the camp so all hands set to and fashioned garments from these. The combination of seamen, accustomed to working with canvas, and Mrs. Jewell, accustomed, as were most women of her day, to making her own clothes, finally resulted in a new wardrobe for every one of them, though not in the latest Bond Street fashions. But they were more than adequate to keep out the biting cold. For needles they used sharpened bird bones; strips of sealskin and unroven canvas were used as thread.

A careful combing of the trash dump at the former settlement at Port Ross yielded some more useful things. They found a couple of axe heads, some nails and scraps of iron and, best of all, two old ovens. One improved their culinary efforts, while the second served to extract salt from the sea water. The occasional trapping of a rabbit or a goat still helped to supplement their seal-food diet, though no record gives the fate of a bulldog that had had its ears clipped, which wandered into the camp one day. It probably ended up in the cookpot, too.

While life was made somewhat more endurable, tragedy hit during August when one of the seamen, David McLellan, fell ill. The others just stood by helplessly, for not only was the nature of

[135]

his sickness a mystery, but even if it weren't they had no medicine. In September he died.

McLellan may have been a Jonah, for less than a month after his death a sail was sighted far on the rim of the horizon, too far away, actually, for the ship to make out the beacon fires of the castaways. She was the first ship seen since being wrecked sixteen months before. The remaining boat was launched to attract her, but she sailed steadily on.

One thing was very evident, however, and that was that their camp was not a good observation point, so they moved to Enderby Island where a constant lookout was established on the highest spot, which commanded a view along the full length of the island's north and east coasts.

More weeks went by when suddenly, those working around the camp heard the far-off cry of the lookout and turned to see him waving his arms and jumping up and down. They ran as fast as they could to the station and saw, as he pointed it out to them, another sail almost hull down on the horizon.

The fires were lit once more but while light remained the ship appeared to stay on her course. There was a chance, however, that the long columns of rising smoke had been seen and that night they eagerly anticipated dawn which would surely reveal a ship standing off the island. But daybreak found an empty ocean, as far as they could see, and once more the camp was smothered in gloom.

Next day, November 21, was a different story, for as soon as the first lookout went to the station with daylight, he saw a vessel running up the east coast towards Enderby Island. This time there was no mistake. Hurriedly the boat was launched and manned to intercept the ship.

She was the whaling brig *Amherst* out of Bluff, and never did a more motley bunch of humans climb aboard a ship than the ten survivors of the *General Grant*, with Mrs. Jewell a real gem in her original Auckland Island fur fashions.

Captain Gilroy, master of the brig, couldn't have been more generous. He dug deep into his provisions to give the castaways their first decent meal in eighteen months. Better still, he dug into his bonded stores and produced tobacco and rum. While the survivors smoked and drank he listened to their harrowing tale.

[136]

When they told him that Bart Brown and three men had left the island almost a year before to get help, Gilroy immediately cancelled his sealing voyage to search for the men for there had been no report of them landing anywhere in New Zealand or Australia. Pitt, Campbell, Antipodes, Bounty, Chatham, all were systematically searched in turn, but no sign of them was ever found, and they could only conclude that the small boat had gone down.

Before landing the survivors at Bluff, Gilroy went back to Port Ross where a slate was nailed to a dead tree. It carried the inscription:

SACRED TO THE MEMORY OF

BART BROWN, CHIEF OFFICER   ANDREW MORISON, A.B.

WILLIAM N. SCOTT, A.B.   PETER McNEVIN, A.B.

WHO STARTED IN A BOAT ON 22ND JANUARY, 1867 FOR NEW

ZEALAND WITHOUT CHART, COMPASS, OR NAUTICAL

INSTRUMENTS

Blessed are they that die in the Lord

As for the gold? For all that is known it still lies in the cave, or in the deep waters west of Auckland Island. Two of the passengers and one of the crew of the *General Grant* were drawn back to Auckland Island by its magnetism. A passenger, James Teer, was the first, in 1869. With the chartered paddle tug *Southland* he located the cavern but found no gold.

Next was David Ashworth, another passenger, who went in the *Daphne* under a Captain Wallace in 1870. Six men lost their lives in this attempt, including Ashworth and Wallace, and another failure was marked up. Last of the survivors to return was Cornelius Drew, an A.B. who chartered the 47-ton *Gazelle* in another fruitless attempt to get at the strong boxes in 1877. Constant bad weather, combined with primitive equipment, aborted the endeavor.

The most recent try was in 1954 when Bill Havens of Sydney, Australia, secured a permit from the New Zealand government to try for the gold. His two attempts ended in failure, for the two small ships he had purchased were wrecked long before he was anywhere near Auckland, one in the Red Sea and the other in the Timor Sea.

Modern day treasure hunters still rate the *General Grant* as one of the most likely spots in the world of valuable wrecks, and it is especially recommended as being "interesting." If gold is interesting then it should be, for if all the loot were found it would be worth some several hundred thousand dollars.

But even if the fortune is never found, the way the *General Grant* met her doom in a cave will no doubt go down in the history of the sea as one of the most bizarre tragedies in a long list which is no stranger to the unexpected, the odd, the incongruous.

CHAPTER XVIII

Fourteen Days Later

HUGH WHALL

IT was a warm muggy day with a white sun shining shadowlessly through a patina of haze. The yellow waters of the East China Sea heaved sullenly, unruffled by a light breeze blowing off the rocky China Coast. Two tung-oil blackened coasting junks moved northward out of sight of the coast, slipping over the glassy swells with incongruous ease in the fitful airs. It was August 20, 1945.

Just fourteen days before, the face of war had changed when Hiroshima was carried into the blue on a roiling mushroom cloud. Eleven days before, Nagasaki had disappeared in a great hole in the ground when the second atom bomb had dropped from the skies. Six days before, World War II had ended. The cease fire orders had been passed, and the beribboned, bemedaled, polished admirals, generals, and diplomats were gathering for the formal ceremonies of surrender.

The world at large was slowly being fed the long secret details of the bombs and there was an almost universal reaction of uncomprehending, horrified wonder. In the matter of days, one observation became a cliché.

"If there is ever another war," it was said on every hand, "it will end with sticks and stones."

Strangely enough, that cliché was to have a dress rehearsal... or the next thing to it... on this hazy August day on the East China Sea, for the stage was being set for the final naval battle of World War II. It was to be fought, not with bombs and planes, aircraft carriers and battleships, but in motorless sailing junks armed with a non-descript array of side arms, light machine guns, an antique field piece and — as almost the only concession to modernity — a bazooka with five rockets. It wasn't quite sticks and stones but it was a near cousin.

Aboard the two junks, outward bound from the village of

[139]

Haimen on the China Coast for Shanghai, was a motley collection of Chinese guerrillas, fishermen and smugglers, led by a handful of Americans belonging to the Sino-American Cooperative Organization's Unit Eight. This Unit, known as "Socko" from its SACO initials, comprised a group of American specialists who had been flown behind the Japanese lines midway in the war to organize and train the local Chinese in guerrilla tactics and in the use of modern weapons. When the signal went out to cease hostilities, two of this group, First Lieutanent Stewart Pitmann, USMCR, and Lieutenant Livingston "Swede" Swentzel, USNR, were ordered to transport a group of air-ground rescue men by junk to Shanghai to relieve the soon-to-be released allied prisoners.

Pittman, a twenty-five-year-old Yale graduate with a fondness for the unusual and long-time sailing enthusiast, was a tall, lean and wiry man with a hairline that appeared to be receding (but wasn't) and a certain intensity of manner. From an old Maryland family, he believed there was a correct way of doings things and an incorrect way, and the right way was the Pittman way. He had been with the Chinese guerrillas for over a year-and-a-half and well knew the sound of close combat. He was to get the first of two Silver Stars awarded for the coming fight.

Aside from the hand-picked guerrillas and a handful of Chinese fishermen, Pittman had three other Americans aboard with him, two of them Navy gunner's mates. The first was Floyd Rose, Gunner's Mate, Third Class, USNR. Hailing from North Carolina, Rose hated walking, and ever since he'd been in China he'd done nothing but walk, walk, walk, and walk some more. The junk trip for him, then, was pure pleasure and he looked forward to resting his weary and very sore feet. Pittman put him in charge of a fifty-caliber machine gun salvaged from a crashed American bomber.

Keith Barratt, the second gunner's mate, was a slight, introspective type. He seldom talked but those who knew him had come to appreciate the fact that he was a good man in a pinch and did the necessary without fuss and bother. Hit in the hip during a skirmish on the China mainland, he had carried a mortally wounded guerrilla on his back to save him from the coming Japanese. He was to win the second Silver Star.

The third man, David A. Baker, Fireman, Second Class,

USNR, was charged by Pittman with watching over the Chinese who were armed with submachine guns.

Swentzel, in command of the second junk, was cut from a different, if just as tough, cloth as Pittman. A good-natured hulk of a man with corn-colored hair, slow speech and shy mannerisms, he had a pair of hands for which any fighter would pay dearly. Before the war the foreman of a Brooklyn chemical plant, he was a reservist and had commanded the camp out of which Pittman operated in the hills back of Wenchow on the China Coast. He won the Navy Cross for his part in the fight.

Aboard his junk was one American sailor, James Reid, Seaman Second Class, USNR, who had a few lessons in the use of a bazooka from Pittman but had never fired one in battle and, now the war was over, never expected to. He was wrong and wound up with the Navy Cross for his marksmanship.

Also on Swentzel's junk were two passengers, members of an air-ground detachment. One was a marine, the other was Captain Austin B. Cox, United States Army, who was to learn how to use a Lewis machine gun, circa 1914, in a matter of seconds.

Sailing along on the starboard tack, Swentzel's Foochow deep-sea fishing junk was in the van and slightly to windward with Pittman astern, when the little fleet raised one of the tiny groups of rocky islands that are strung along the shores of China. They were eighty miles south of Shanghai with roughly a quarter of the voyage behind them.

As the islands rose out of the haze, a third coasting junk slipped from behind a headland and, rolling slightly, slid up the brown backs of the swells and then dipped down behind them until only the peaks of her variegated sails showed across the water. She was on the port tack and laying a converging course.

The two Americans turned to their walkie talkies — one other bit of modern equipment the fleet boasted, but one they had learned was inclined to die in the pinches.

"What do you make of her, Swede?" Pittman queried.

"Probably a fisherman." Swentzel's hands were big enough to cradle the WT and at the same time hold his binoculars.

"There seems to be one hell of a lot of men on her though."

The strange black junk approached slowly. She would pass slightly ahead of them if she kept her heading.

"You see the white shirts, Swede?"

"I see them."

"You see the uniforms, too?"

"Yes. Come back."

"What do you think?"

"I think they're Japs, Pitt. I see helmets."

"What's that up in the bow?" Pittman came back with a slight note of tenseness in his voice. "It looks like a field gun."

"No, you're right," answered Swentzel in his own way. "The war's over, but it looks like he wants . . ."

At that moment, the radio went dead.

Swentzel's last word that Pittman never heard was "fight" but he hoped there wouldn't be one. Their job was to deliver the passengers to Shanghai and it would only foul up the progress of peace if they were to be blown out of the water at that juncture. Also, he had only five rockets for the bazooka; the rest were on Pittman's junk. He ran over his ordnance in his mind: he had the Lewis gun . . . that was a good piece, reliable, and it could do a lot of damage. The old drum-type magazine mounted on top never jammed. But he had only a couple of spare drums. There were a few tommy guns and rifles aboard, plus a handful of grenades. He supposed he had enough, but certainly not too much.

From his junk, Pittman watched the Japanese wrestle with the antique looking field piece on the foredeck. It was difficult to make out the details because, as the Japanese junk rolled, her big foresail would drop across the scene like a huge window blind. But as the junks closed, he saw clearly that they were bringing the wheeled field gun to bear on Swentzel, blocking it off ready for firing.

Pittman called to one of his Chinese crewmen who spoke a smattering of Japanese.

"Yell over to them," he ordered, "that the fighting is over and we're Americans."

The interpreter shouted something that Pittman didn't understand and apparently the Japanese didn't either because they went right on fussing around the gun without raising a head. The Jap's foresail was still rising and falling over the gun but as Pittman and Swenztel watched, the junk started to turn and her varicolored patched and battened sail spilled the wind and began to flap. They both knew what was coming.

There was a puff of smoke from the Jap's foredeck followed by the thrump and splash of the shell and then the bark of the detonation. But even as the smoke rose from the Japanese gun, the rattle of small arms fire mingled with the chatter of the excited Chinese guerrillas aboard the American junks and the peace of a pleasant sailing day evaporated into the noise and confusion of battle.

With the first round from the enemy junk there was no doubt that Swentzel, being in the vanguard, was to be the initial target for the old 75 millimeter mountain gun. Even though the Japanese craft was rolling horribly now that it was hove to, the first shot was close, if short. It smacked into the water to starboard, sending up a geyser, and even as it did Swentzel could see the Japanese gun crew clearing the breech and reloading their weapon. The range was about a hundred and fifty yards, practically point-blank.

There seemed to be Japs everywhere aboard the enemy junk... tin helmets, white shirts, heads bobbing up and down, the blinking of small arms, but most discouraging of all, the field gun perched on the bow. Swentzel saw the second flash and then his foremast disintegrated into a web of flying splinters, tattered cloth, and broken battens.

Now he was in proper trouble. Both Swentzel and Pittman had found the sixty-odd foot junks to be amazingly handy in a respectable breeze, but in light air they needed every square inch of sail to maneuver, especially on the wind. The most important sail of all going to weather was the foresail . . . and his had gone by the board.

For an endless second there was quiet, then Swentzel shouted: "Give it to 'em!"

Young Jim Reid, who just had time to think what poor shots the Japs were when their first shell missed, leveled his awkward bazooka over the rail and, as the junk rolled, he fired. Where his first missile went, he never discovered. He cursed. There were four rockets left.

A little farther forward, Captain Cox, the army passenger who had garnered his share of ancient Chinese splinters when the fore-mast exploded, had picked up the Lewis gun at Swentzel's shout. He didn't know how to use it and pulled and jerked at every likely looking knob and lever. The junk rolled and his feet shot out from under him as he stepped into a pool of blood oozing from one of the Chinese crewman slumped on the deck. He sat down solidly on the black teak and at the same moment the gun stuttered. He had found the combination. He hefted the gun's sewer-pipe-like barrel to the rail, braced himself and happily listened as the staccato voice of the Lewis drowned out the other noise of war for him.

"Fire short bursts," he told himself. "Fire short bursts . . . the bastards."

The business-like chatter of the Lewis steadied young Reid and as he leveled the bazooka for his second shot he carefully waited, gauging the roll of the junk beneath him. The second rocket burst on deck amidships on the enemy junk.

"Got him . . . got him . . . got him . . . got him," he chanted to himself and put the remaining three rockets into the Jap junk in quick succession. He watched with a satisfied grin as the dust of ages, shaken loose by his hits, rose from the enemy's deck and enveloped the hull.

With her foremost and foresail lying in a tangled heap on deck, Swentzel's junk began to lose way and he hurried aft, ordering the helmsman to bear away and cross close under the Jap's stern. His course took him between Pittman and the enemy and the circle of battle closed to a little more than a hundred yards with the Japanese junk on one edge, Pittman's junk on the opposite, and Swentzel's crossing the middle. Over the circle rose the dust knocked loose by the rockets mixed with the smoke of burned gun powder and from it came the continued crackle of rifle fire and small arms fire drowning out the moaning of the wounded and the creaking and thrumming of the three ancient junks. It was a scene that would have been no stranger to Nelson or Howe, but one that Nimitz or Halsey would have sworn had long since disappeared into history books.

Although spared the direct wrath of the field gun, Pittman's junk was taking the full brunt form the Japanese anti-aircraft machine guns and her rifles. The vicious rattle came downwind and the smack of bullets as they plowed into the junk and her crew was everywhere.

Pittman crouched in the eyes of his ship, quietly directing the fire of the Chinese guerrillas as he had done in innumerable skirmishes during the year and a half on the China mainland. In that time the handful of Americans and the Chinese had become a well-knit, battle-tested unit.

Before the battle had joined, Pittman had helped Rose lash to the rail the tripod they had fitted to the fifty-caliber machine gun and had said:

"You try and nail that field gun if they start anything. If we don't get it, they'll hammer hell out of us."

And Rose had settled down behind the heavy gun with a sigh of pleasure. Now its authoritative pounding overlaid the lighter chatter of the submachine guns. The fifty's belts were loaded with both armor-piercing and tracer shells that were dotting a line across the intervening water. Carefully he swung the gun until the stream of shells winked around the field gun and flared off. In a matter of a few minutes the bobbing heads disappeared from the Jap's foredeck and the mountain gun fell silent — the second round that had sent Swentzel's mast overside was its last.

"Good boy, Rose," Pittman yelled above the din. "Good boy. Keep it up!"

At that moment Pittman felt the junk slowing beneath him and looking up saw the foresail begin to luff. He turned aft to shout at the helmsmen. There had been three Chinese fishermen on the exposed poop, two of them on the helm and the third handling the mainsheet. They weren't there. They were dead, cut down by the first burst from the enemy junk.

But before Pittman could move, he saw Keith Barratt racing across the main deck, weaving and dodging like a broken field runner. He vaulted to the poop, tackled the tiller that had begun to flail from side to side and steadied the junk on her course as the bullets whacked into the woodwork around him.

The battle was still fluid although the Japanese junk was now definitely at a disadvantage. His field gun had been knocked out, his ship was dead in the water with a tangle of wire and sails cluttering the deck.

It was possible that her commander had been as much surprised by the action as had the Americans. He might easily have mistaken them for a pair of fishing junks and he may have decided to commandeer them to relieve the crowding aboard his own vessel. Pittman learned later that the commander was a Japanese Imperial Army major and that the junk was jammed with eighty-four soldiers, five

Chinese crewmen, and mounds of equipment that had come from an airfield installation on Hainan Island off the coast of Indo-China. The junk was bound for Shanghai. At any rate, he had taken a pounding for his trouble and more was to come.

Swentzel, in bearing off, had gained speed and was rapidly crossing a line between the enemy and Pittman. His helmsman eased her up until she was on a course that would carry her something under thirty yards from the Jap's stern or well within grenade range.

The enemy junk had fallen completely silent though she was still being raked by American fire. The crew had taken refuge in her hold from the withering stream of bullets. But Reid, who had been so deadly with the bazooka, had another shot in his locker.

As Swentzel's junk glided along under the pressure of the warm land breeze, picking up momentum all the time, Reid hefted a grenade, waiting until the Japanese junk's range closed. Then he pulled the pin and lofted the grenade into the cloud of smoke and dust that hung over the Jap's deck. The grenade bounced on the deck, rolled over the lip of the hatch, dropped into the hold, packed with cowering Japanese, and exploded. The force of the explosion, compounded by the confines of the musty teak hull and deck of the junk, was horrific. Swentzel's junk swept on.

Aboard Pittman's junk, the shooting stopped as Swentzel crossed in front of the enemy and Pittman realized that the Japanese junk had stopped firing. But he, like anyone who had come to grips with the Japanese, recognized their love for and ability in the tactics of ambush. He wasn't to be caught napping. As the junk, with Barratt still at the helm, turned and followed in Swentzel's wake a bedraggled figure, holding what looked like a white Tee shirt tied to a bayonet, appeared out of the smoke on the Jap's deck. Pittman called to his interpreter:

"Tell them to jump overboard," he ordered. "Tell them I want every man in the water. Hurry up."

He turned to Barrett and directed:

"Bring her into the wind alongside but well off."

As the junk slipped beneath the Jap's stern, a few of the enemy began to jump into the muddy water. But only a few. There weren't enough of them when Pittman thought back to the crowded deck at the start of the battle and he wondered where the rest were. Below? Waiting for the Americans to come alongside? Then suddenly he realized that his Chinese guerrillas were still firing at the few hapless Japs who had dropped into the water.

"Christ! Stop it!" he shouted. "Stop it!"

The firing continued and growing slashes of red began to streak the brown water like snakes in the swell. He reverted to the special brand of Pidgin he used with the guerrillas:

"Ting! Ting!" he sounded like a bell. "Quit it! Ting!"

The guerrillas paid no attention, so quickly he clubbed his rifle and swung on the nearest Chinese. The man looked pained and held his head. He swung the rifle again at the next man. A swell of chattering broke out from the Chinese and, other than a desultory shot or two, the firing stopped. Some of the Chinese looked sheepish. Others just chattered, but finally only the slap of water on the hull, the creaking of the junk's gear and flapping of her sails as she came into the wind broke the silence.

The junk stopped, and Pitman's vessel began to drift down on the battered enemy. The junks bumped. They scraped flanks and separated slightly. They rolled back together again with a hollow thump.

Aboard the Jap junk there was splintered holes and tangled wreckage from one end of the deck to the other. There were bits of flesh and blood sprayed everywhere and lines and wire and torn sail lay in an incredible tangle. In the bow, vaguely visible through the mixture of smoke and dust which followed the vessel like a cloud of insects, was the field gun, its breech neatly drilled and locked by one of Rose's armor-piercing shells, its muzzle pointing aimlessly first into the water and then into the brassy Chinese sky as it followed the arc of the junk's roll. Even the Chinese, apparently mollified by the sight, gaped in bland wonder. There was no sign of movement.

"Come on, Barratt, let's take a look," Pittman said, turning to the gunner's mate who had left the tiller.

And just as centuries before men had scrambled from rail to rail, Barratt and Pittman boarded the Japanese junk, followed by several guerrillas. Her layout was similar to their own craft and they headed toward the after hatch. While Barratt and the Chinese stayed on deck to cover him, Pittman dropped through the hatch into the hold.

[147]

Down below the smell was beyond belief as Pittman waited for his eyes to adjust to the half light. The usual smell of junks and the odor of sour rice was overlaid by the stench of human excrement and the rankness of fresh blood. War in the open was one thing. This was another. The face of death was everywhere. Pittman began to make his way forward in the gloom, trying not to slip on the hold's blood-slimed deck.

Across from him and forward there was a slight movement. It was the Japanese major, commanding, lying on the deck mortally wounded but still able to follow out the code of the Japanese Imperials. As he watched Pittman pass, he grasped his sword in his left hand and shakily raised his pistol in his right.

At that moment, the moon-like face of one of the Chinese guerrillas appeared in the hatch forward, unnoticed. Behind it the barrel of a submachine gun was shoveled quietly over the hatch's lip. The safety snicked off and the staccato crashes reverberated through the dark hold as the bullets stitched their way aft over Pittman's shoulder until they found the major. The pistol dropped from his hand and he died, murmuring something in the language of his home islands. The battle was over. It had lasted a little more than twenty minutes.

Forty-nine Japanese were dead. Only four of the survivors were untouched while Americans, aside from a few splinters, were unscathed. Among the Chinese guerrillas, though, the Japanese bullets had taken a toll of eight dead and fifteen wounded. The Japanese junk was jury rigged and sailed back to Haimen accompanied by the American junks which were in sore need of repairs. Some time later Swentzel managed to get his passengers to Shanghai.

And so, even as the radioactive dust settled over the Pacific, and as the carriers went home to mothballs and the battleships to the scrap yards, the final battle of World War II was fought with a smattering of Twentieth Century weapons, using the tactics of the Sixteenth Century, in sailing craft that date back two thousand years. Thus ended what well may have been the last naval engagement fought under sail the world will ever see, or . . . the harbinger of sea battles to come.

CHAPTER XIX

A Bird In A Golden High

WALTER GLASER

NINE days uphill and more than twelve hundred miles northeast of the island of Kauai, the trimaran *Typee* came slowly to a silent halt and stood motionless on the sea in the warm early morning sun. According to our wind chart we were right on the edge of the Pacific High Pressure Area. Albert, our albatross, who had picked us up on the second day out and had tagged and dogged us ever since, plopped down, too, and drifted unconcernedly about a quarter mile astern.

The Northeast Trades had been steady, powerful and regular, and we had busted, knifed, and struck our way into them and the oncoming seas for over a week now. We were wrung out, salt encrusted, and burned black by wind and sun. And even though we all hoped for a swift and uninterrupted return passage, the prospect of a brief respite was not disagreeable. There hardly had been a watch where the helmsman had not gotten a solid dousing, but the water and air temperature were warm and it was not as unpleasant as it might sound. We still wore only shorts and, sometimes, parkas.

The sails hung limp and dead, and everywhere the gleaming cobalt sea was a smooth, water wasteland. Way out on the distant perimeter of the horizon, the cloud formations were static and airless and promising nothing. Yet it was not without charm. It was September, and the early morning ocean smelled good.

Typee now began slowly to turn the full compass. Her bows moved quietly onto San Francisco and then down lower towards South America. Back to the Hawaiian Islands from where we had come, and then over to Japan. On up to Alaska and, finally, around again so that way astern the small gray dot that was Albert fell back into the original position where he had plopped down into the sea.

Once again back on course I sat at the wheel and tried to steer the wayless boat. After a few minutes I gave up and went forward to

[149]

lower the sails — if for no other reason than to finally acknowledge the fact that we were truly becalmed.

The decks were still cool and wet from the morning dew, and here and there over the great expanse of *Typee's* twenty-foot beam, lay tiny flying fish that had come aboard in the darkness. Some were hardly bigger than overgrown mosquitoes. It never ceased to amaze me that flying fish could be so small. Somehow it seemed they should have all been at least eight to twelve inches long. But they weren't. I had gathered several of the miniature ones on the trip over and had thumbtacked them to the galley bulkhead to show everybody, and to show myself, too.

It seemed incredible that anything that size could suddenly whir up and out of the sea and beat its wings in a mad and frantic flight across the wave tops. But the thumbtacked one-inchers had dried out during their three months on the bulkhead and now were in the process of getting little mildewy furry sweaters which were obscuring them and making it difficult to tell what they were. I promised myself to collect some more and figure out some better way of preserving them. But not this day. This day I had to think about the calm, and what it meant, and might mean, and how much drinking water we had aboard and how long we could sit here on this beautiful blue plateau of empty ocean a thousand miles and more from land.

There was something else I had to think about, too.

I had to think about Albert.

He was beginning to get to me and I wasn't sure why. He was just a bird. An albatross. Yet somehow, I think he knew, and I knew, and maybe even Dick and Philo also knew, that Albert was more than what all the other albatross were. Well, way out here in the middle of this blue windless emptiness I could think anything I liked.

I lit a cigarette and popped out a smoke ring which hung there stationary in the still quiet. And then I impatiently kicked it out of shape with my bare foot and went below to make a cup of coffee.

Philo was snoring gently and peacefully in the starboard wing-bunk and Dick was asleep in the stern cabin. I got the alcohol stove primed and going, and while I waited for the pot to whistle I looked at the fuzzy little fish tacked on the bulkhead in front of me.

But I couldn't focus on much of anything because I was wondering what Albert was doing.

So I went back up the hatchway and looked astern and all around and he was gone.

Good riddance, I thought. Stay away. I don't trust you, Albert. I never have.

Below decks the kettle was whistling.

Wow, I thought. I'm thinking like some superstitious, omen-ridden sailor of the past. So far, we had had a good trip and how could a man born of the twentieth century suddenly abandon all reason and good sense and attempt to establish some causality between an albatross and the fact that we were becalmed? I wasn't the Ancient Mariner and Albert wasn't *that* albatross. This was the day of science and the intellect, of fiberglass and astronauts, and silicones and synthetics; of stainless steel and computers and polyethylene and plywood. And *Typee* was a light, and swift-sailing multi-hull. If we were destined to sit here for awhile, well so what? I had not trod out on the high seas armed with superstition instead of knowledge. I was braced and reinforced with all kinds of survival techniques. I knew how to get food out of the sea and I knew ways to get water too. And by God if it came right down to it, and we did lay here too long for comfort, then we'd build a set of oars and row her on out to the wind.

We were all right. I knew that.

I started back down through the hatchway to make the cup of coffee and then I saw him. Way out there up ahead. Too far to see the strange black mark on the underside of his right wing. But I didn't need that mark anymore anyway.

I could tell him from the rest.

I knew his glide and his soar and his sweep. And my heart sank because somehow I now began to feel that he had led us, rather than followed us, and that we were captives in a domain, a world that was truly his — the great lonely vastness of the Pacific High.

I still had a half hour to go before my watch was up. I turned the stove off and immediately heard Philo's rhythmical contented snore, and somehow the sound of it was reassuring.

As I sipped the steaming hot brew I had made, the panicky feeling began to subside.

[151]

It is important, I thought, that these guys never get wind of what I've been thinking. This is all between me and Albert and *Typee*.

"*Typee!*" I exclaimed aloud. How the devil could I have forgotten *Typee*? She had taken us to Hawaii. She would bring us back to California. The hell with Albert. *Typee* would handle everything.

On the following day at noon, we got our position and it was exactly where it had been the day before. The needle on the speed indicator of the Sum-log was lifeless and it was hard to imagine it would ever move again. Everything was the same, and nothing about this second day promised to offer anything more than the first.

We sat around on deck that afternoon reading and talking and taking it easy, but an edge of tenseness had developed — though nobody tried to give it words. Albert, though pointedly conspicuous by his absence in our conversations, was nevertheless out there in full view performing fantastic and incredible aerial acrobatics while we stayed rooted and motionless in the hot, sweltering sun. He was superb in a fiendish way. For without the wind, we, as a unit, had lost our potency, and I was certain Albert knew this and was rubbing it in. Sometimes he would glide on in at maybe thirty miles an hour and we could see the outermost edge of a wing tip curl down like a sensitive antenna and feel, yet never touch, the surface of the water. As he swept past us his eyeballs would roll over and take us in and I'm sure the look he gave us was one of contempt.

Up, then, he would zoom, stall out and, depending upon what he felt like at that moment, either fold his wings and come spinning down to crash on some luckless fish, or maybe just tie a few figure eights in the sky and polish it all off with a pirouette.

He could do anything and we could do nothing — nothing except sit there and pretend we weren't watching and envying and hating.

But then around four in the afternoon I got fed up and I did do something. I went below and noisily started dragging out all our two-and-a-half-gallon water jugs. Dick peered down the hatchway and asked me what I was doing.

"Never mind what I'm doing," I snapped, "I'll let you know what I'm doing when I'm through doing it."

He disappeared from the hatchway and I could hear Philo ask him what I was doing.

"He's flipping his lid," I heard Dick say.

We had fourteen jugs of water; eight twelve ounce bottles of Hawaiian beer; thirteen small cans of tomato juice. I came back up on deck then and stood there in the silence while they watched me and waited. Then I solemnly announced that I wanted them to take it easy on the water. Not in a true rationing sense but easy nevertheless. I needn't have told them that and communicated any of my anxiety or concern. They were both bright, intelligent guys. Good shipmates. I really shouldn't have insulted them that way. But I had to.

It was that lousy Albert. That blasted bird with those magnificent wings. And what about *Typee?* Why wasn't she doing anything about this? Why was she just sitting there absorbing it all? Why was she behaving like some silent, withholding female?

Dick was right. Only a day and a half of being becalmed and I was flipping my lid. I was determined now to forget that insidious bird and to get a good tight grip on myself.

So I clamped off my edginess and fear as best I could and withdrew into the role of sullen captain. And when, that night, Philo asked me why the hell we couldn't have a full night's sleep instead of standing our usual watches since there wasn't anything to do anyway, I said no, we were still a ship, or a boat, or whatever you wanted to call it, and there was plenty to do even if it looked like there was nothing to do. He could holler if a breeze stirred, and he could keep an eye peeled for a ship because it would be ludicrous to get run down in a flat calm on a clear night just because everybody was asleep. And no, anyway, if only just for the sake of "no" separating me from them. But that I didn't say.

At one o'clock in the morning of the third day of the calm I relieved Dick for my watch.

"Anything?" I asked.

"Nothing," he said.

In the darkness I couldn't see his face well. But I could hear it in his voice. He was sore at me. Well that was too bad, I thought.

[153]

He was lucky. All he had to be was sore at me. What did I have to be? I had to be sore at a mindless bird.

It was a fantastic watch I stood that night. It was awesome; it was beautiful; and it was frightening. There were no clouds, and the blue-black heavens capped us like a gigantic glass dome. Entrapped inside were billions of glittering, blinking diamonds. Every once in a while one of them would explode in a rocketing trail of fire and track and arch its way across the dome. Sometimes it would burn out in mid-flight, but sometimes, too, it would ride the circle of the dome until at last it would plummet in a great flaming radius down into the sea.

On the horizon, new stars would suddenly make their appearance, igniting like silent fireworks. Once, when Venus emerged above the level of the sea, I thought surely it was the masthead light of some massive ocean liner. For it stayed there glowing steady and even with a fierce and terrible brilliance. And it seemed a long time before it finally started to climb the circle of the sky.

Although *Typee* stood windless in the warm luminescent night, the water seemed to be surging by while phosphorescent illuminations of all shapes and sizes moved past her and on their way. Some were huge conglomerates or masses, and their green neon blinked on and off with an eerie and uncanny regularity.

Once a fish broke the surface nearby and a shower and spray of green sparkles tumbled and cascaded in the dark. And then, a few minutes before I was to wake Philo, I heard a great rushing in the air and I crouched instinctively while the tremendous dark-winged shadow that I knew *was* he soared past *Typee,* and I felt frightened and alone and helpless.

I waited until almost noon of the third day before I let it all out.

Philo and Dick were below sitting at the dinette table studying the charts and drinking coffee. The mileage indicator on the Sum-log still showed four zeros, and the needle was still dead, and there was no wind. Albert was up ahead dipping and gliding and occasionally zooming in and buzzing *Typee.*

I could have gotten the rifle and ammunition myself but I needed Dick and Philo to be part of it. So I called down the hatchway.

"What is it?" I heard Dick call back up.

"Bring me the rifle and a box of shells."

[154]

I heard them talking to each other in lowered voices.

"What do you want the rifle for?" Dick finally said.

"Never mind what I want it for. Just bring it."

They came up through the hatchway after a minute or two and Dick handed me the rifle and the box of shells. He looked puzzled and worried.

"What are you going to do?" Dick said, as he watched me feed the shells into the tube.

"You know what I'm going to do," I said. "I'm going to finish that bird off. That's what I'm going to do."

"Hell," Philo said, "He's just a bird. Why kill him?"

"Because," I said, straightening up after loading the gun and looking both of them in the face. "Because you two guys believe in him. That's why."

"We what!" Dick said, in disbelief.

"You believe in him and I don't," I said. "That's why you don't want me to kill him. But I'll tell you something. It doesn't really matter whether you believe in him or not. You both feel, and I feel, too, that if I do kill him something will happen. And because something will happen its the same as believing. We're sitting here useless on the ocean in the middle of nowhere and the only thing that could possibly happen which would make our situation different is to get wind. And that's what we want and that's why I'm going to kill him."

Albert was a few hundred yards off the stern coming in on a zig-zagging course. As fast as I could pump the twenty-two I showered a hail of bullets at him. I never touched him, and the racket and the lead flying past didn't seem to bother him a bit. As a matter of fact, it seemed to stimulate and arouse his curiosity.

Dick and Philo had suddenly given up criticizing and judging me and were watching intently.

I got the rifle re-loaded just as Albert was making a turn to come back on a new run. And now as he swept on in I had him in my sights, good and full and big and sure. For Albert and me the moment of truth had arrived. Behind me, to my amazement, I heard Dick and Philo shrieking:

"Get him! Kill him! Finish him!"

They were in it now with me. All of us. *Typee,* Albert, everybody.

[155]

The albatross kept himself centered perfectly in the sights and I knew in a second he would be floating dead on the surface of the sea. Dead on the rim of the Pacific High.

My finger was squeezing on the trigger but it wasn't squeezing all the way. I couldn't seem to make the trigger go all the way. And it wouldn't either. Because at last I felt the complete absurdity of what I was doing. I put the rifle down and my hands were shaking and I felt dizzy and sweaty and foolish. For a moment I had been truly lost in the wondrous magic power I had given him.

And then, as you would have it, a coincidence occurred. But it came after the fact and though the necessary stuff out of which superstition emerges may have been there, I needed no part of it.

The wind had come up. It was there. I could feel it on my face and arms and legs and all over. And in back of me I could hear Dick and Philo whooping and cheering.

"Wind!" they cried. "Wind! Wind! Wind!"

I stood where I was and I watched *him* out there gliding and sweeping the sea, and I thought to myself what a close call it had been. And how fortunate that a bullet had not complicated and confused and bound all of us together into a memory that would have been mystical and hard to forget.

We got sail on *Typee* then, and she responded and came alive after her three day sleep. We felt new and excited and confident. We trimmed the sheets and got her going, and we stowed all the loose gear and got her squared away.

When all was ship-shape and in order, we listened and heard the sound of the sea running and raging past her hulls and we looked up and watched the orange telltales streaming from her shrouds.

And in proper fashion too, the albatross took up his old familiar station, and he tailed and crisscrossed our wake until we were within a day of the coast.

CHAPTER XX

There's Something Out There

JACK BRYSON

USUALLY, Sunday afternoons were uneventful — even boring — for those of us attached to the United States Naval Amphibious Training Command Afloat at Cornfield Harbor on Chesapeake Bay. Those who were not stuck with the duty were ashore. And those who had to stay aboard wrote letters or read — or more likely just sat and stared, glumly wishing they were elsewhere.

But this particular Sunday there was suppressed excitement on the LST 915. It was a fall day during World War II. There was a nip in the air in spite of the warm sun, low in the western sky. It was a big day for a dozen of us on the 915 because it was launching day for one of the most unusual craft ever to disgrace the United States Navy. After four months of building, we were ready to launch the only sailboat in the "LST Navy" — a 15½-foot Snipe — fittingly named the *Wharf Rat*.

A few hours later our homemade Snipe would be involved in one of those inexplicable things that happen from time to time to remind us there is a mystery and an unknown element about the sea that perhaps accounts for some of the fascination it has for some men.

It was . . . well, you explain it if you can.

The *Rat* had been pieced together from whatever materials we could beg, borrow, or "midnight requisition" around the various naval docks and wharves. And she looked every bit as disreputable as a wharf rat, too!

But secretly we were proud of her because she stood for the joint efforts of most of the hundred and thirty men of the crew. Painstakingly we had built her from some yellowed, stained plans I found in a Norfolk bookstore. We spent long tedious hours below decks working on her. As the building progressed, more and more members of the crew pitched in with necessary talents of carpentry,

[157]

shipfitting, and marlinspike seamanship. And now our executive officer had just whipped the last stitch in the sail he had made for us.

Apprehensively, we lowered the sailboat the twenty feet from the main deck to the water, with fenders carefully placed to avoid bruising her tender sides. When at last she plopped into the water with a gentle splash, there was an audible sigh of relief from the crew gathered above.

As the young ensign who had ramrodded the project, I was more excited than the day we had commissioned our ship because the *Rat* had more of me in her than the impersonal 330-foot ship that I called my home. I could hardly wait to get aboard her.

I had heard about letting the hull soak and swell for a few days before sailing, but who could say when we would get another day like today. And the boat was dry as a bone, too . . . except for a few drops of water along the centerboard trunk that nobody paid much attention to just then.

By previous agreement my crew was to be the two men who had spent the next greatest number of hours on the chore of building her.

There was Lescomi, seaman second class, who had yet to see seventeen. I had often wondered how Lescomi had passed the recruiting officer. As I watched him come down the ship's ladder I could not help thinking I had looked older in sixth grade than he did that day.

Burgher was older. Blond, husky, and in his twenties, he was a good man to have with you in a tight spot. He was a second class radarman — and a damn good one, too. On watch he would stare into his radar scope as if it were a peep show, and never miss a contact; but at the same time he could keep a running commentary going on subjects far removed from radar.

In fact they were far removed from anything. Like one of his classics to his helper Lescomi: "Hey, Lescomi, ever catch yourself not thinkin' about girls?"

As my two stalwarts settled down in the boat I surveyed the scene. We were bobbing gently against a rope fender slung from the ship, and headed into the wind with sail flapping. Cornfield Harbor lay at the junction of Chesapeake Bay and the Potomac River. Our flotilla of LST's swung and tossed at their anchors like tethered, grazing elephants. It was a peaceful scene and the only activity was the gentle movement of the ships.

At the tip of the Maryland peninsula, to the southeast, was Point Lookout. The Potomac flowed into the Chesapeake from the west from where we had a strong breeze. To the east was the broad expanse of the Chesapeake Bay.

My plan was to sail with the wind as far as Point Lookout and then tack back to the ship for another pair of riders. It was now mid-afternoon and I thought we would surely have time to sail two more men around the anchorage before dark.

As we cleared the side of the ship the wind caught us astern, and with our sail full out we pranced toward the Chesapeake like a gay young filly. All the hours of blood, sweat and tears were wiped away in the joy of that moment. Looking at the gleam in the eyes of Burgher and Lescomi, I knew the boat was paid for right then and there.

My first intimation of trouble was when we cleared Point Lookout and came about in order to tack back west to the anchorage. There was quite a bit of water sloshing in the bottom under the floorboards. It was well we were heading back. Lescomi had started bailing.

We had a badly formed sail and sloppy rigging so I did not expect her to sail very close to the wind. I deliberately took broad reaches. But she made no headway.

Burgher, true to form, said, "Mr. Bryson, you're sailing backwards." I was annoyed, but he was right. We were, but why?

The centerboard was down, the sail was live, and the rudder was biting in hard. I called Burgher, "Are you sure that centerboard is all the way down?"

"Yeah, but it feels like it's stuck."

"Stuck?"

I leaned far over the side trying to see the bottom. I could see trouble. The centerboard was folded flat against the bottom of the boat like a big wet blanket. We now had all the sailing characteristics of a lost beachball. Where the wind blew, we would go; and that was out into the bay.

Our hindsight was twenty-twenty; we all then remembered that there had been some specification about the gauge required for the thickness of the centerboard. With a twinge of guilt I remembered

[159]

having said that the galvanized sheet metal I had found at Portsmouth looked good enough to me, even though it did seem a little bit flimsy.

To make it worse, instead of a five o'clock calm, the wind actually was picking up in force. The waves coming out of the Potomac were commencing to roll, and some of them were even showing white caps.

Fortunately, we had brought an Aldis lamp with us; I intended to waste no further time before using it. I knew we were being watched from the bridge, and I was the only one that knew Morse code.

I flashed our ship's call letters and followed with, "Trouble. Send boat."

The ship's twelve inch light signaled back, "Boat ashore picking up captain. Will contact shore."

Vainly I looked for a buoy or stake to which we could tie up before we were blown farther into the Chesapeake — where there was nothing but nearly twenty miles of open water to the other shore of Maryland. But there were none. We were well downwind of the last of them and now well past Point Lookout. Nothing but the open bay.

Hastily I rigged a sea anchor from a pail and the line we had aboard. Some of our yaws had been a little scary, and I was afraid we might broach, but unhappily the sea anchor threw us with our stern to the wind. And we found ourselves sailing out into the bay.

I reasoned we had to drop our sail and just drag our sea anchor in order to slow our departure from Point Lookout so that the ship's forty-foot LCVP would have time to catch us before dark. With the Aldis lamp to guide the LCVP to us, I felt sure we would be all right.

Looking at my gallant crew huddled around the centerboard and then at the gathering darkness, I felt compelled to say something cheerful.

"Well, we know she's built rugged and can take it."

"You mean like the centerboard, huh?" Burgher broke the tension. We all laughed.

When the ship called, I was so eager to stand up and answer that I nearly capsized us. Because now we were really rolling and tossing.

The ship's instructions were clear:

"Boat has returned. Conserve your light and give us one long flash every fifteen seconds. We will direct ship's boat from Con."

Thank God. I could tell the captain was aboard. This was obviously the way to do it. By giving the Navy's standard instructions to small boats, they could direct the LCVP right to us . . . and even after dark with the ship's radar to locate us.

I now debated if the sea anchor pail would serve us better as a sea anchor or as a radar target up in the rigging. Fortunately, I decided the former.

And still the wind picked up and the waves grew longer and deeper. The sun was down now, and the wind had turned raw cold. As we dipped down on some of the waves, the ship would actually drop out of sight momentarily in the fading light of the western sky. But then as we were borne upwards we could see all the ships of the flotilla silhouetted. They looked so serene and comfortable . . . and warm.

Then a joyous sight. As we crested on a large sea we saw the LCVP round the ship with a bone in her teeth and roar out into the bay after us.

I said, "Lescomi, they're on their way. It won't be long now." He grinned, but his lips were quivering. Was it the cold, or fear?

The wind was still picking up strength and on bad rolls we took water over the side. Burgher and Lescomi had been bailing steadily since we had cleared Point Lookout, but it seemed to me that the water was gaining on them. I was balancing on the foredeck making the long flashes every fifteen seconds.

The ship's boat was closer now, but it was only showing its starboard running light. If they were headed directly for us, they should be showing their red light too.

Burgher had noticed too and whispered, "Mr. Bryson, the boat's heading north of us."

I heard Lescomi sobbing; Burgher was doing his best to cheer him up. Quickly, I told them both to lie flat in the bottom of the boat so we would have as much stability as possible while I stood on the foredeck in order to raise my line of sight to the ship and increase the visibility of my Aldis lamp flashes.

I spread my legs wide, back to the mast, and flashed "SOS's" to the LCVP between my long flashes to the ship. But still we saw only the green running light. What was the matter? Couldn't they see me flashing?

To make it worse, I could read the ship's signals to them, and the LCVP wasn't following the ship's directions. The ship's messages to us were clear and visible. They knew exactly where we were and no doubt had us on radar besides.

Then I saw it. To the north of us was a flickering light on the stern of a fishing boat headed north to Baltimore. The ship's LCVP was following the fishing boat to Baltimore. We learned later that they had read's the ship's signals, too, but disregarded them because they thought *they* knew better than the ship where we were.

Desperately, I signaled the LCVP, "SOS . . . SOS . . . SOS . . .SOS . . ."

"Mr. Bryson, Mr. Bryson! The ship's calling." Burgher shouted. I watched.

"Sailboat why don't you flash? Are your batteries okay?"

Now we were in real trouble. I had never missed a fifteen second long flash. The ship evidently could no longer see our light. I reached higher with my light, but the water-laden boat lurched over sickeningly. Burgher leaped to the opposite side and barely righted us in time.

I could not chance standing on the foredeck again. I would have to flash from the cockpit of the boat and forget about visibility. Maybe an occasional high wave would momentarily hold us high enough for our light to be seen by the ship. Maybe . . .

In the cockpit I suddenly became aware that I was sitting in water. To avoid attracting Lescomi's attention, Burgher grabbed my wrist. He pointed to the base of the centerboard trunk. In the darkness I couldn't see what he was pointing out. .

Flashing the Aldis lamp there, I saw something that made me gasp. The bed logs of the centerboard trunk had pulled away from the keel. It was the pounding we were taking from the waves that had caused it. Burgher had been stuffing rags and strands of rope into the crevice to slow the leak.

I winced as I recalled that the plans had called for bronze quarter-inch bolts. We had substituted large brass wood screws.

Lescomi had simmered down and was now quietly bailing. Burgher and I were caulking the leak with all that was available, but we were all devoting most of our energy to just keeping the boat upright. Because of the violence of the wind and the waves, we could no longer see land, lights, or boats.

It was now far too late for the LST to get underway and find us. The delay caused by the error of the small boat would not now give them sufficient time to warm up the engines. Besides, they would never find us now. The water action was too rough to pick up a small radar echo like us.

I doubted if we could keep her upright much longer because as she filled with water her rolls became drunken wallows like a water-soaked log. I thought we had just about had it.

Suddenly the heavens lit up! We were blinded by the whitest light I had ever seen. Shielding our eyes, we were all trying to see where it was coming from.

At the same time, I heard the deep-throated roar of diesel engines As my eyes became accustomed to the light I could make out the beautiful, Navy grey of the sides of an LCI — the whole glorious one hundred and sixty feet of her.

"Identify yourselves", a powered megaphone blared while the ship's searchlights plied us up and down. And then I realized the reason for their concern. German submarines had been suspected of landing persons on the coast at night, and I had to admit we did look suspicious.

The explanations took a while because the captain was not readily willing to accept my story of a Snipe on an LST. But finally we were taken aboard and the *Wharf Rat* was taken in tow.

As we steamed back to Point Lookout I sipped hot coffee through chattering teeth and grinned down from the bridge at two of the happiest, wettest sailors I had ever seen. As I mulled over the merits of craftmanship and the necessity of quality in boatbuilding, the ship's executive officer came up to me.

"Your guardian angel was working tonight — more than you'll ever know," he said.

"Sure was," I agreed. "We sure were lucky."

"Lucky hell!"

"What do you mean?" I asked.

"That was the dumbest thing I've ever seen," he said thoughtfully. "We were just figuring our estimated time of arrival in Baltimore when suddenly the skipper jumped out of that conning tower chair of his and yelled to reverse all engines. The night was just as

[163]

black as you see it now. Then the captain pointed off the bow and said, 'There's something out there!' But nobody could see anything."

Another chill rolled up my spine, but it wasn't the cold night wind. It was the wonderment and awe that had given this captain the sixth sense — in the true tradition of the sea — to stop his ship in the dead of night, point his finger at the sea ahead, and say — "There's something out there!"

Chapter XXI

Spirit of Adventure

EUGENE CONNETT

Y OUNG feller, if someone can't or won't buy you a boat —
a decent one, that is — get anything you can, if you have to make it.

My first "boat" was a canvas job with ribs and stem made from
sections of barrel hoops, a keelson and two pieces of wood which
held the tops of the ribs more or less in place. It leaked, but I
managed to paddle her around on nearby waters. I loved that vessel
which I made all by myself at the age of ten. When I invited a
young friend for a cruise, her plimsoll mark was depressed too
much and water pressure caused her skeleton to collapse. But that
canoe filled me with a love for the water and started me on a life-
long career of sailing.

Several years later I latched on to a leaky old sharpie. She was
too much for my youthful physique with heavy oak oars, and I became inflamed with a desire to make her sail. So I fashioned a mast
from a pole on which a rug had been rolled, made a sail with my
mother's help on a sewing machine, assembled pieces of cord from
various bundles and other sources for running rigging, purloined a
coil of picture wire for shrouds, and, by golly, I actually sailed from
the town dock to Fireplace Creek before a gentle southwest breeze.
I didn't prove the earth was round, but I did prove I could make a
boat sail. I kept on trying to prove it for over a half-century.

I also proved that my sharpie wouldn't go windward, and I
had to tow her home, wading along the shore.

I won't tell all the gradual steps I climbed as I slowly but surely
acquired boats that would sail better and go to windward.

Now I sometimes wonder if many fortunate children today,
with junior sailing instruction, real sailboats in which to practice
and race — all supervised and carefully protected — aren't missing
something that kids sixty years ago were forced to enjoy the hard
way. It does seem to me that today's youngsters don't get the chance

to extemporize, experiment, struggle, and grope for a knowledge of boats and watermanship; to find out first hand what will work and what won't, and sometimes, even *why* it will or won't work.

When an instructor is at hand to teach everything from tying a knot to steering a boat, there isn't much opportunity to use one's own brains and imagination. One simply tries to carry out the instructions and struggles to remember them. This, of course, produces some first-class young sailors, trained to race around buoys, clean up their boats, and develop a desire to win. If that's our aim, we are succeeding.

I suspect however, that this method delays the full development of that valuable inquisitiveness, that desire to know the why and wherefore, that willingness to venture, which simply cannot result from class instruction. I doubt whether Harold Vanderbilt or Rod Stephens commenced their yachting careers in a junior sailing class. I imagine that it is quite a long time before the young well-trained sailor begins to wonder whether his competent instructor really knew and taught him everything he should know about boat, water, and weather.

For some years I watched junior sailing classes in action, and never ceased to marvel at the self-control and patience of the instructors who tried to maintain discipline and hold the attention of a large percentage of the class who, to my mind, would be learning more in their own leaky old tubs out on the water.

The four generations of my family that I knew personally never had the benefit of junior sailing classes. As one came along he first sailed on the family boat and just naturally began to pick up knowledge as he carried out simple orders. If he tied a knot that let go, he was liable to get the devil, and made it his business to learn how to tie a knot that wouldn't let go. Although I wasn't present during my grandfather's and my father's youths, I have been given to understand that they built rafts or other vessels in which they risked their lives and enjoyed themselves, and learned about boats and watermanship by *doing*, rather than listening. I know the next two generations did, and even managed to win some races. They also learned a great many things that racing couldn't teach them.

It is perfectly evident that today we must rely on junior sailing classes to take care of the hordes of youngsters who want to and should learn to sail. But here and there we will find a lad who would rather be a lone wolf and learn the hard way. I feel that such a one should be encouraged, rather than forced to take lessons. I don't mean that he should be presented with a new Snipe or a Lightning, but it might be wise to put him in the way of acquiring some sort of thing that will float. Don't worry about his drowning; he will learn to swim faster than in a class when he finds himself faced with the problem.

Believe it or not, I was taught to swim at a very early age by being chucked off the end of a dock. I swam all right, even if it was a dog paddle instead of the Australian crawl. I merely mention this to show that it is natural for a kid to stay afloat if he has to and it isn't made into a big deal — especially if he is engaged in something he enjoys and wants to continue — which didn't happen to be the case when I went off the dock. I suppose I must have felt that my father wouldn't throw me into water over my depth if I couldn't swim, so I swam. It was that easy, just sixty-six years ago.

I like to recall the two young boys I met in the middle of the Great South Bay some years ago, sailing in some sort of a nondescript cat boat. They told me they were on a cruise to Mattituck. When I gently inquired whether they were familiar with the Shinnecock Canal and Plum Gut, through both of which they would have to pass, they never heard of either. I am confident that they never reached Mattituck, not because of shipwreck, but because they found plenty of adventure before they even got as far as Shinnecock. Those boys were really learning the hard way and I am sure that they became *real sailors*. I often wonder who they were so that I could prove my point. They were probably in the last Bermuda Race.

What am I trying to prove? I suppose it boils down to this: learning more or less by rote to race around buoys should not be the sole objective in the making of a sailor. True, he will learn the Rules of the Road, how to trim a sheet, set a spinnaker, and perhaps win the championship of his class. He may develop those qualities which will make a real seaman of him later on; but he will develop them sooner if he is on his own, solving his problems by doing — even doing wrong. (The only way I ever learned anything was by not making the same mistake twice.) He will develop a self-confidence and proper pride in himself of far more value than by merely beating Nancy and Willie in a race.

The youngsters learning in their class will appear to develop faster, but a boy learning the hard way will learn his lessons more thoroughly and with much deeper understanding, and will be better able to handle himself in emergencies. In the long run he will be in more intimate harmony with water and weather, and he will have an opportunity to become closer to the type of seaman who started out as a boy on a square-rigged ship, *doing* things and learning that mistakes can mean far more than losing a race.

We must keep and encourage our junior sailing classes; but let's try to give some youngsters the chance to develop on their own if they show an inclination to do it that way. You won't have to make it too easy for them if they have this inclination. Some will come through, and some may not. The latter can always join the class. But those who come through on their own will be valuable citizens, and — incidentally — have priceless memories of their youthful days on the water.

CHAPTER XXII

A City Of Ice

PATRICK SHANNON

IN the annals of sailing one may encounter the name of a vessel that seems to have passed through every experience known to the maritime world, every adventure, every misfortune, and triumph.

Such a vessel was the *Loch Inver, a* four-masted barque, carrying double topgallants and hailing from the Clyde. She had been dismasted, wrecked, abandoned, salvaged and outfitted, and put into commission again. She had been a tea ship in the China trade and also a North Atlantic emigrant packet, a gun-runner in the Gulf of Guayaquil and a supply ship for a Hudson Bay geographical expedition. Then in her later years, in the early part of the century, she had been bought by a Greenock firm, overhauled from truck to keel and sent out to become a prize ship in the grain race, running between Australia and Europe by way of Cape Horn.

Once, however, there came a miracle, a phenomenon that was to put all her maneuverings and previous triumphs into the background. It was a moment to try one's reason, a marvelous absurdity, a mathematical impossibility. It was against all the laws of chance, and enough to drive one man insane, and send another into his last convulsion.

She had sailed from Spencer Gulf, South Australia, with a cargo of grain, bound for Falmouth for orders. She made her departure under topsails, foresail and jibs, and after leaving Kangaroo Island astern she steered due south so as to get below Tasmania and into the Fifties where the parallels of latitude are shorter. Then later, below New Zealand, picking up the westerly gales of those zones, she began to crack on sail and run her easting down.

Everything looked bright for a smart, clean passage across the South Pacific, once she was east of the Snares. If the westerly winds continued, the men reasoned, they might not have to haul a single yard around or trim a sail until they were well past the Horn — a matter of about six thousand miles.

And so they reasoned.

They were a mixed crew as usual, signed on and herded aboard in Wallaroo. The captain was an old pottering gnome with chin whiskers who seldom showed himself on deck. But when he did, he always appeared to be fussing around with bits of twine, pieces of sailcloth, cans of paint and putty, while the second mate Mr. Hawkins, stood by in a brassbound overcoat and eyed him with distaste, muttering something about these old scurrying twerps being a disgrace to the quarterdeck.

It was the new first mate, rather, who was in command of the ship. And it was this splendid specimen of humanity who held the crew's attention more than anybody else aboard. They had never seen such a man as this mate. They had always sensed that there were certain superior beings in the world, certain outstanding figures, forceful personalities who exuded confidence wherever they went, but they had never dreamed of anything like this. Always accustomed to seeing some muscle-bound, snuff-chewing gorilla pacing the poop, they now saw a tall, curly-haired apparition that brought up reminiscences of Grecian gods, men in shining armor, gladiators, field marshals, having the same classical bearing, the same erect magnetic manner, ever aloof, firm and infallible.

Consequently, with this impressive leadership nothing could go wrong. The sails would furl themselves, the gaskets bend themselves, the ship would bound along as though endowed with a new spark of life. The men went about their work in an enthusiastic daze. An exhilarating climate had been created, and there was no skulking, no hesitation now. One word was sufficient, a lifted finger maybe, a nod... and everybody jumped. Then the mate would pirouette and march slowly away, his braided cap lending the proper touch, the final mark of authority.

And such was the impeccable figure of the mate: a trimly pointed black beard, a devilish mustache twirling up, a proud cavalier look — and the man became a symbol, an heroic image, an epic in the living flesh.

If it weren't for the man's ability and seamanship a cynic might have put him down as a fraud, so perfect was this facade. Even his name was picturesque. Tresilian — Mr. Roger Llewelyn Tresilian, a Cornishman from Penzance, descendent of the wreckers and the last of the Cornish corsairs. When he spoke, his words were clear, brusque and to the point. In a commanding rich baritone his perfect white teeth would bite each word off, precisely, distinctly. Then he would turn his back, as if knowing without question that his order would be carried out to the letter.

Also, when he took a sight at noon, if the sails were blocking the sun from view, instead of going to the forecastle head to make his observation, he would motion to the man at the wheel to bring her off a point or two so he could get the sun. Then the order was given quietly, with dignity, a slight motion of a finger, an expressive look. There was going to be no mistake, no misunderstanding whatever. He intended to remain aft on the poopdeck where he belonged, and nowhere else. With him every order was made this way, with significance, either a suggestive motion — the flicker of an eye, the snap of a finger — or a forcible word. If a word, it would be in the tone of voice of one saying, "Get what I tell you, mister. I shall not repeat myself."

Altogether Mr. Tresilian was a direct individual, and a law unto himself. Nevertheless, as is usually the case aboard ship, there was sure to be someone who was left unimpressed.

One morning during the mate's watch, Mr. Hawkins sat below in the saloon at the cabin table, scowling over his morning tea. He was making it evident to the captain, in no uncertain terms, how he felt about supermen in general. Things had come to such a pitch that Mr. Hawkins could contain himself no longer. He leaned over the table confidentially, tapped the captain's hand and said in a fierce undertone:

"I don't give a damn, sir. I've yet to see the day I can't run a ship. No man's telling me my job. Let alone a tailor's dummy with fancy curls . . ."

He tightened his lips, pointing with his chin to the skylight, to where the mate was striding about, slapping his gloved hands together, sniffing in the morning air.

The second mate had always been a man who had longed for better days, and who felt that he had been imposed upon from the time he was born. His angry red face and small belligerent eyes were now turned to the mild unassuming captain, and at the moment his whole countenance — his heavy, quivering jowls and bristling

[171]

mustache, dripping with tea — appeared ferocious. His tea was cold. Everything was cold, bitterly cold. And at this time of the day, before going on deck, he was never in the best of humor. So it was in a fine raging mood that he faced the four o'clock dawn and the fury of another watch.

"A tops'l, for God's sake! Can you imagine it? If it was me, I'd damned soon bend on the fore and main tops'ls, and break out the fores'l, and get out of this goddam freezing hole. I'd do some sailing, believe me. I'd show those bastards for'ard what sailing is."

He raised his mug and drank hurriedly. The captain gazed gloomily down at his early morning cocoa, murmuring that the ship seemed to be acting sluggish. He'd have to see about sounding the tanks.

"Steward!" roared the second mate. "Bring me some tea. This bloody stuff's cold." Then turning to the captain, he said, "There's a limit, sir, a limit to what a man puts up with. Soon we'll be clawing off the frigging Shetlands with not so much as a dishrag out. But mark my words, sir, this'll be taken care of. Don't worry. I'll see the Board of Trade, if it's the last thing I do."

He inhaled deeply. The captain said dismally, as though to himself, "I'll have to speak to the mate. It's no use veering too far south."

The second mate drank a fresh mug of tea and stood up. "And another thing," he said. "When it comes to a bit of heavy work, who does it? A second-rate stumblebum. But don't mind me. I'm just an old tosspot. Don't let the fact that I've had two hours sleep in six weeks stand in the way of youth and beauty. Never mind that. Just so long as Mister Tresilian doesn't have to step for'ard, or soil himself down the hold . . . Pah! You'd think he was an old man with heart trouble the way he acts . . . Calls himself a sailor, does he? . . . Ha, Ha. . . More like a damn woman, if you ask me. You'd think he had on a bloody corset, the way he holds himself . . . Ha." He stepped away with a bitter, snarling laugh.

The captain mumbled something about it being eight bells.

Mr. Hawkins buttoned up his reefer. "Yes, sir," he growled, pausing in the doorway and thrusting out his jaw. "Nothing'll ever happen aboard a ship that I can't handle. You can rest assured."

He glared around and pulled on his cap, jerking it down to an emphatic angle. With that he turned and climbed the companion-way to the deck, to relieve the mate.

The days passed, and life aboard became more hazardous as the ship neared the Horn. She was homeward bound, and the men were beginning to go about their work strenuously. The seas were breaking aboard steadily now, and they had to make every-thing secure for the heavy weather ahead. So they drove themselves desperately, with no inkling of the future, not knowing what was in store for the ship, totally unaware of any freak show that could pos-sibly appear and make their present trials look like so much child's play.

It was in the mate's watch when it happened. The ship was then in the Sixties, far south of Diego Ramirez Island, and further south than she should have been. She was too close to the South Shet-lands for comfort, wallowing in the middle of the danger zone for ice in the month of February. The wind had changed from the southwest to the south, and it was the height of suspense for a man to stand watch in a thick black night, as though alone in the howl-ing darkness, unable to see his hand before him, waiting for a shat-tering blow, a devastating shock in the night — the crashing into a berg, a towering mass, perhaps miles long and hundreds of feet high. With everything black before him, a pale line would first appear, the breakers. And then a wisp of cold mist would creep over the ship. Or again, there might be no warning, no sight nor sign of anything, just a blind rendering havoc in the dark and a quick freezing death for all hands.

Many of the foremast hands had seen these bergs. A sealer had once reported sighting an ice island that was fifty miles long with a range of mountainous ice reaching to an elevation of a thousand feet. Uncharted, the bergs — so the "Mariner's Directory" described them — "form obelisks, towers, and Gothic arches. Some exhibit lofty columns with a natural bridge resting on them of a lightness and beauty inconceivable. . ."

Therefore, because of this, and the fact that it was the month of February, the danger month, it would have been wise no doubt to lie-to during these short nights of the year. But it so happened that later during that passage the ship was fortunate. She had the moon with her. She had visibility, a clear view of the running seas when the clouds were torn apart.

And those were the conditions — a howling gale south of Rami-rez, and the moon — when this incredible but beautiful miracle came about, an event that was to break one man's spirit, drown another, and bring the life of a glamorous character to a pathetic and inglorious end.

To the man at the wheel it was just another short night, a storm and the moon. And in the moon-flooded storm the sea was all alight, a vast view of a cold, illuminated world. The scaffold of masts and yards swinging under the moon, held a single patch of sail like a pale banner, a reefed main topsail straining alone. And high above the swinging mass, high in the wild spaces of the night, the racing clouds streamed, torn and disheveled, across the lighted areas of the sky.

On the silky slope of a swell there was a green glow from the starboard light; and the swell was surging into an enormous bank, its sides rising smooth and appalling, and then it was moving toward the ship, as if a hill were moving. An acre of water folded over, glittering and tumbling and flooding the deck, and burying the dark gear in a torrent of lather. And in the heavy lulls of the storm the distant moaning of the winds could be heard, droning like a host of phantoms riding away in the night.

But then the clamour returned, rising nearer, approaching and bringing the clouds, the larger masses to hide the moon. They came, and suddenly the world was darkened; the great sea was black and cold. The winds struck — full, with an orchestration of shrieks and howls tearing through the rigging; and in the darkened moment there was a pang of dismay felt, an intolerable loneliness. But the clouded moment passed and was driven away, and again the whole sea was clear, bathed in a weird light — a white, wind-torn plain, spreading far out in a wild and raging spectacle. The bow of the ship was lifted and held steady over a trough. And when it was dropped, crashing in a billow of foam. The ship shuddered, and a ghostly plume curled up, curving over the bow and covering the deck, as a reef is covered.

Across the scene a dark figure moved, wading through the wash and leaning into the wind. Faint snatches could be heard, the man's voice hailing the afterdeck. Then abruptly the voice was cut off, lost in a sudden gust.

The black figure seemed to float on the glistening side of a cataract. He was raised smoothly and carried overboard, and swept sliding into the sea. He vanished for an instant and then bobbled into sight, riding high on a passing hill. Under the moon, he was a small black thing on a hill of froth, a floating oilskin jacket and a lifted arm, drifting by on a luminous slope. Then he was gone, out of sight, passing away into the wake of the ship, and into the wild distances of the night.

In the shelter of the weather-cloth the man at the wheel said, "That was the lookout, sir." He waited but received no answer. The ship kept on, and the man spoke again, loud and anguished, That was the lookout, sir." But the shadowy outline of the mate remained still. He stood at the forepart of the poopdeck, against the rail, peering over the canvas dodger, and gave no sign that he had seen or heard anything. The man at the wheel was astonished. He knew it was of no use to bring the ship about. No boat or man would last in that sea. Nevertheless he wondered, gazing uneasily at the flickering lighted compass card.

It should have been a moment of disgust, he felt, at the lack of activity shown, of interest even. The man on lookout had climbed down from the top of a forward deckhouse. He had struggled aft, calling out in the gale, hailing the mate, trying to tell him something. Then the ship had plunged, carrying him away, and the mate had stood silent, insensitive, aloof as ever, and evidently far removed from these casualties of the sea.

With one watch below, and with half of the mate's watch down with frostbite and sickness, and the few on deck hiding and sleeping it off somewhere, perhaps huddled on the sheltered side of a lifeboat, too exhausted and sick at heart to stay awake — with all this slumbering and resting allowed there was now only the mate and the helmsman alive enough to be aware of anything.

The man at the wheel, receiving no response, stared about him dazedly. Something was wrong. He could feel it. There the mate stood, a bulky heap against the rail. Why hadn't the man answered him? There was something strange here, he knew. He glared around. What was going on, anyway? He wanted to know. He let his gaze drop to the compass and jerked at the wheel savagely. Then leaning on a spoke he glanced aloft at the yards, at the lone reefed topsail, and up at the sky. And then his breathing stopped, and his heart sank like a stone.

[175]

He let go of the wheel and stood straight, cold as death, as though the blood were draining out of him. He stared, stunned, gaping up like a frozen corpse, his eyes wide in the moonlight with wonder and horror.

For there, floating high above him, gleaming against the raveled sky, was a green moonlit vision, a massive sight of spires, minarets, domes, skyscrapers — a whole city of ice. It was high up and dead ahead. The lower part was shrouded in mist, while the turrets and pinnacles stood towering clearly, glittering, soaring into the sky like a spectral metropolis, sparkling with the starry glints of green and white crystal. And the ship was heading toward this, sailing toward a scarf of pearly, shimmering fog at the base of it. There were no breakers; the ship was to the lee of it all, as if she might be entering a bay. With the larger part of the berg, perhaps miles of it, having drifted northerly across the bow, another part could be already closing in on the starboard quarter. There was no sound above the squall, nothing but the steady, undeviating drifting of the mass to meet the ship, presaging a swift and terrible end.

The sight grew higher, rising nearer, and the moon was suddenly blotted out. The edifices became a monstrous silhouette looming in the sky, making the ship appear like a toy tossed on a miniature sea. The black form of the mate was now deep in shadow. He hadn't moved. He had given no order, no call to all hands to brace up and wear ship. Nothing whatever. Another second and it would be too late. There would be no wind to ricochet off the berg and send the single sail aback. They would merely drift, cut off from the wind, and glide into a murderous cliff with its white veil of icy mist. And that would be the grinding, splintering finish, bringing the whole top hamper down upon them, and crushing the ship as a man would crush a cigar.

She sailed on, still keeping her course. A minute passed, and the wind fell off. The pitching and rolling slowed down to gentler movement, a steadier keel. She began to act strangely then. As if sensing the danger, she seemed to move cautiously, slowly, making only a slight wash, a thin rippling wave at the water line. She covered another few fathoms, the fog-hidden berg running toward her. And then, with the topsail hanging flat against the mast, she entered the mist.

The man at the wheel gasped. To him, it was like passing into a chamber of icy vapor, and being suddenly made sightless, wrapped in a cold prickly substance. At first there was a frosty crackling and tinkling in the air, a faint musical sound about him, somewhere about his head, and then he found himself in a region of peace, surrounded by utter stillness, sudden and complete silence.

Nothing stirred. All was shut off — the storm, the moon, the sea. He was still there, sightless, alive, a shocked, conscious being braced against the binnacle, rigid and aching from tension. He could see nothing at that moment. He could hear nothing. It was as if he existed in a dead, breathless world, a void. Then after an interval the curtain parted, dissolving away, and he was left as though alone in a clear space, an open luminous area steeped in a faint greenish twilight.

He lifted his head and saw, on each side of the ship, high cliffs of ice sliding silently by, like the walls of a gorge. Then above him a distant ceiling arched over the ship, a high roof having the glaze of an iridescent grotto. The starboard and port lights cast their green and red glow on each wall, and on the ledges and galleries of ice on each side, on the tiers and balconies, causing them to sparkle as if they were incrusted with gems. And into the cathedral silence of the vaulted passage the ship either moved or the walls moved past her. All the man's numbed mind was aware of was a galaxy of colored flashes, of fairylike stars twinkling in a huge cavern around him. The twisted, sinewy, braided icicles hung in portieres from above, and through the strands of ice the ruby and emerald gleams were seen reflected prismatically from the crystal points and crags far ahead. In this unearthly stillness, through a tunnel of goblin lights and shadows, the ship seemed to pass on, without a sound, without a tremor.

The dreamlike journey continued, perhaps through an hour, a night, an aeon. Time for the man didn't exist anymore. Distracted he stared up at the awful glistening canopy creeping by high above the masts, making the ship look diminutive, no more than a tiny model in a vast shadowy case. He was about to close his eyes when faintly he noticed the black shape of the mate stretched out on the deck. What was he doing? he fretted. Sprawled there like that? He spoke softly to the silent figure. "Mister Mate," he whispered, and a booming voice came echoing back to him, rebounding out of the depth like a hollow clanging of a gong.

He sank down, crouching on the grating and covered his face with his hands. He could take no more. "Mister," he whimpered. "For the love of God!" And when the echo reverberated hollowly from wall to wall, from the clefts and ridges and the far reaches of the tunnel, he shook and moved with terror. He crawled toward the prostrate mate and peered closely. He knew before he touched him that the man was dead. He drew his hand away and gave a shuddering sigh. "Mother of God!" This was too much. Where were they? He breathed anxiously, afraid of making a sound, afraid of that hollow booming voice again.

Still the eerie beauty of the bejeweled cavern glided steadily by, unfolding ahead like a panorama, then widening as it approached and continued past the ship. The ceiling, tinged with an opalescent flush, narrowed to a distant aperture, to a phantom archway far within, which began to loom with a pale rising glow, swelling into a silvery halo. The growing light came slowly, spreading along the walls of the passageway and enveloping the forepart of the ship in a ghostly pallor. Then toward the increasing glimmer, with brightening outlines, as a craft drifting to the mouth of a cave, the ship crept on and out — into the morning light. Into the gray daybreak she passed, and into the sudden whistling tumult of the wind and the open sea once more.

It was a pale, clear scene now, a deluge boiling and hissing in the sudden daylight. The frenzy had returned, shrieking through the shrouds and bringing a mountainous wave with it. And once again the bowsprit was lifted, straight and steady, clear-cut in the dawn, and again it was lowered, dipping as gentle as a curtsy, until, with a shattering roar, the sea broke and cascaded over the forward deck.

It had been a freak adventure in which the ship had passed cleanly through, untouched, unshaken. And the berg had gone on its way, veiled in its wreath of mist. In the channel of a long corridor beneath the berg, the ship had been enclosed for miles by cliffs of traveling ice, while remaining still, motionless, as the berg passed over her.

But now she was out in the howling sea again, swinging wildly, unmanned, with her masts sweeping in a wide arc across the sky. And flat on the poopdeck, the lifeless form of the mate lay in a flurry of spray, stretched out in the rising dawn like a dark bundle left athwart the deck. He had collapsed, falling straight as a pole, his arms stiff by his sides, his eyes wide and staring.

A few odd things were scattered around him — a set of white perfect teeth, a black curly wig fluttering along in the scuppers, and a bearskin cap sliding about, leaving him bareheaded, his scalp yellow and scaly and as bald as an egg. And this, together with the rivulets of rouge and the streaks of dye staining his cheeks and dirty gray beard, made him clownish to look at, a sad and frightful thing having the toothless grin of a painted old man.

The maindeck was deserted in the morning light. The wheel bucked violently, abandoned, as the seas struck the ship on the beam, listing her over. Then from another direction a rushing sea righted her again. The weather came from all points, shifting from abeam to astern, while the ship yawed in the chaos, floundering about uncontrolled. And alone, crouched on a grating, the tears streaming down his face, the helmsman nodded and laughed idiotically.

And, in the midst of all this, Mr. Hawkins stepped on deck to relieve the mate.

CHAPTER XXIII

The Night The Navy Buried John

E.F. OLIVER

T HE colored signal flags soared up the halyard and bellied out abaft the towering tripod of the flagship USS *Arkansas*. From the halyards on a score of battleships flashed an acknowledgement to the strangest signal ever to originate on a United States Navy man-o-war:

> PREPARE TO BURY KING JOHN BARLEYCORN X BURIAL
> PARTY OF PALLBEARERS AND MOURNERS WILL CALL.

Thus was heralded a cocktail party never to be equaled — a party beyond Elsa Maxwell's wildest dreams — an around-the-fleet saturnalia not recorded in official naval records but which would be inscribed indelibly in the unwritten annals of the sea.

The year 1914 got under way on an ominous note for the United States Navy. The shadow of war darkened Europe while at home a new, blue-nose, Secretary of the Navy, Josephus Daniels, commenced his tour of office by firing a broadside at the officer corps which sent them staggering to their respective wardrooms for a nerve bracer — Daniels issued his famous "bone-dry" order to take effect July 1.

> GENERAL ORDER NO. 99 ... "THE USE OR INTRODUCTION
> FOR DRINKING PURPOSES OF ALCOHOLIC LIQUORS ON BOARD
> ANY NAVAL VESSEL, OR WITHIN ANY NAVY YARD OR
> STATION, IS STRICTLY PROHIBITED, AND COMMANDING
> OFFICERS WILL BE HELD DIRECTLY RESPONSIBLE FOR THE
> ENFORCEMENT OF THIS ORDER."
>
> Signed *Josephus Daniels*
> SECRETARY OF THE NAVY

The order was aimed at the officers' wine mess, a sacrosanct institution passed down from the British Navy. Daniels reasoned, since the abolishment of grog for enlisted men back in 1862 had been so beneficial, that the officers should be allowed to share in the benefits. But the officers in the coal-burning battleships, long accustomed to a leisurely tot after a hard day's steaming, reacted as though torpedoed in the backsides. The order was not only a blow to a standard of living, but it was considered an affront to the honor of each officer.

The bone-dry order caught the powerful Atlantic fleet with its anchors down in the tropical port of Vera Cruz, Mexico. The *mañana* land was in the throes of revolution and with Europe in a state of smoldering unrest, the major powers kept heavy naval units on the scene. In addition to the flagship *Arkansas*, the Stars and Stripes flew from the battleships *Connecticut, Florida, Wyoming, Louisiana, Vermont, Virginia, Georgia, New Jersey, New York, North Dakota*, and a score of auxiliaries. Other men-o-war, soon to be protagonists in the impending World War I were: His Majesty's Ships *Bristol, Berwick, and Suffolk;* the *Descartes* flew the French Tri-color; the German battleship *Dresden;* the Dutch *Kortenaer;* and the Spanish *Emperador Carlos V.*

Before bidding adieu to the States, the officers had prepared well for a long and thirsty campaign. Now, as the hot June wore on toward the hour of midnight, June 30, the careful preparations haunted them — it was unthinkable to jettison the precious cargo. Wine mess meant more than the term implied. Theoretically only wine and beer were stocked. However, a naval officer, like a Boy Scout, is always prepared. The inventories, in addition to listing the prosaic wines such as burgundy and port, also showed strange names — *Able* wine (bourbon), *Baker* wine (gin), *Charlie* wine (scotch), and so on through the phonetic alphabet. The officers of pre-World War I vintage, in addition to being accomplished seamen, were connoisseurs, with few peers, of alcoholic libations.

There seemed to be but one solution — transport the "wine" ashore and consume it at leisure. With Pancho Villa keeping his pistols hot, the fleet would be anchored for many weeks. A reconnaissance party, ably led by First Lieutenant Richard A. Malley, established a beachhead on a palm-shaded stretch of white beach called Los Cocos. There, unhindered by State Department protocol, he negotiated the first lend-lease contract in U.S. foreign relations — a thatch-roofed cantina for an officer's club.

Spirits were high and flowing that night as the word spread through the fleet that the marines had landed and the situation

[181]

was well in hand. The prospect of watching the sun set while guitars strummed "La Paloma" to the beat of popping champagne corks brought broad smiles of anticipation. But the anticipation was short lived. Word of the pending invasion spread and the natives grew restless. As the first personnel boat, loaded to the gunwales with "wine" nosed up on the wet sand, it was met by unsmiling customs officials who demanded a duty of one peso for each bottle. In a day when the lowly ensign only made fifty dollars a month, how could the officers raise some fifty thousand pesos?

While regrouping from the Los Cocos counter-attack, the officers received a fusillade from their exposed rear — the U.S. Army. A letter of condolence arrived in a black-bordered envelope: "The officers at West Point, feeling the deepest sympathy for their brother officers in the naval service at this time . . . have furnished and set apart a drinking room at the officers' club for the sole use of any commissioned officer of the Navy visiting us. . . Naturally, only grape juice and lemonade will be served to naval officers in the bar."

Hoarse cries of outrage, mingled with toasts vowing eternal vengeance upon the Knights of the Hudson, reverberated throughout the fleet as glasses were filled and refilled. Drastic measures were necessary if the mess was to be liquidated by the deadline. It was agreed that consumption must be increased — doubled, indeed trebled. A spartan determination was brewed in the wardroom country in each man-o-war as every officer vowed to carry his load and a little more. Men who before had drunk only beer selflessly shifted to bourbon. One bottle men became two bottle men. The officers faced each new dawn gallantly with eyes red and heads throbbing, shaken but resolute in their cause — liquidate the "wine."

The glorious effort, above and beyond the call of duty, was not enough. On the morning of the last day of June, it became apparent there was only one course of action remaining — drink the "wine" in one supreme, bacchanalian effort. Bury King Barleycorn with full military honors — a wassail that King Neptune himself would long remember. It was a challenge to test the fiber of a fighting man, but as the United States Navy has met every challenge in its history, gallantly and with no thought of self, the officer corps prepared for the maximum effort. For as the noble Publilius said, "No one knows what he can do until he tries."

And what could be more proper than to invite the officers

from the foreign men-o-war to attend the funeral services? Naval officers, representing the brotherhood of the sea, a fraternity not renowned for temperate habits, would make fitting pallbearers for the burial of such a distinguished personage.

As the torrid sun inched away from its zenith, the officers readied themselves for the joust with the Demon Rum as knights of yore, anticipating what promised to be a memorable night in many illustrious naval careers. At H-hour-minus-one the harbor of Vera Cruz was a placid mirror. The men-o-war swung lazily at anchor on water silvered by a crescent moon. On board the German battleship *Dresden*, the officers held their steins at the ready position while the *kapitan* exhorted them to console the bereaved Yankees and "*Vergiss nicht, dass wir mit schnapps erzogen waren, and jetzt machen wir den Kaiser stolz.*" (Do not forget we were raised on schnapps so make the Kaiser proud.)*

Two cable lengths away lay His Majesty's Ship *Bristol*. Captain Nathaniel F. Main, RN, stood before his officers with a warm gin and bitters raised high and thundered, "Let's jolly well show the bloody blighters 'ow it's done. . . God save the King."

As the clang of six bells shattered the quiet and echoed across the harbor, execute signals soared aloft to be two-blocked on taut tri-stays — the burial ceremony was officially under way. The first shot in the epic struggle to wipe out the "wine" was downed in every ship.

"Wardroom, junior officers and warrant mess provided an abundance of food and drink for all comers," the late Vice Admiral Wilson Brown recalled. There was something for the most discriminating imbiber — bourbon, scotch, rye, gin, cognac, armagnac, schnapps, madeira, rum, tequila, cointreau, curacao, kirschwasser, drambuie, absinthe, maraschino, pernod — not to mention the wine.

Each man-o-war strove to outdo the others in decoration. The USS *Connecticut* won first prize. The warrant officers' mess was transformed into a replica of a Wild West saloon with bar, brass rail, mirror, spittoons, gambling equipment, and an alluring nude behind the bar.

On board the dreadnought *Washington*, a menu was prepared

The Dresden *was sunk by the British Navy off Chile on March 14, 1915.* — EDITOR.

[183]

to delight the heart of the most sophisticated *bon vivant*. Lieutenant Commander Edward S. Moses, the chief engineer recalled:

"The menu was a gastronomic conception of genius. The first course was a fruit cocktail mostly of green and red maraschino cherries floating to the brim with maraschino. Our soup was a turtle soup rich in mulligatawny. The fish course was Lobster a la Newburg with a double shot of sherry for the sauce. The Roman Punch was a modern day frozen Bacardi. The roast was a tremendous Virginia razorback ham most generously basted with Moet & Chandon Cordon Bleu '92.

"The dessert was a fruit cake with pungent hard sauce which had been saturated with Martel 1887 from the time the order was bruited until the farewell night. The fruit cake was served with generous bowls of brandied peaches. Then Café Brulot with the strict injunction that each cup had to be filled over half full of coffee."

Extra boat crews were pressed into service and assigned the job of ferrying the funeral parties from ship to ship. As the night wore on the ranks swelled as every gig and launch which could float joined the funeral cortege. The smooth mirror of the harbor was crisscrossed with serpentine wakes and dotted with bobbing "dead soldiers." The balmy tropical night was punctuated by popping corks, laughter, and ribald sea chanties in five languages.

One young officer, Lieutenant William F. Halsey, drowned out others with his bull-like voice as he lustily gave forth with an impromptu rendition of the Whiffenpoof song:

"We're gentlemen sailors from over the lee,
Bound tonight on a Navy spree.
Lord, have pity on Daniels and me.
Bah! Bah! Bah!"

The pallbearers had a most hazardous mission — climb the dreadnoughts' ladders which became longer as the party grew louder. Many a dauntless mourner tripped over his sword and fell headlong — to be fished from the drink none the worse for wear after a salt water chaser. The mourners were met on the quarterdecks with formality. On the USS *North Dakota*, the skipper greeted the mourners while an honor guard of officers stood wavering at attention with brooms.

Among the mourners were Lieutenant Commander Ernest J.

[184]

King, and Ensigns Marc Mitscher, Thomas Kinkaid, and John McCain who acquitted themselves in a manner in keeping with the heroism to be accredited to them some thirty years later.

On board the *Connecticut* at the height of the revelry, one of the junior officers almost joined John Barleycorn. Overcome with the spirits of the affair, a desire to become an aviator overwhelmed him. Reeling over the deck skylight he shouted, "Look out below." His launching was a success but he lost altitude rapidly and made a three-point landing two decks below. The doctor related the pilot made no sound as his legs were set but smiled broadly when assured he would receive the purple heart for the sortie.

As the stroke of the witching hour drew near, the sour strains of "Auld Lang Syne" gave way to the sombre notes of Chopin's "Funeral March," followed by the haunting echo of taps. Tears fell freely and dropped unnoticed into many a half-filled glass.

Aboard the *New Jersey* a bottle of beer was encased in a coffin and a Marine honorguard stood at stiff attention as King Barleycorn slipped over the side forever. On every ship as eight bells tolled out the deadline, officers stood at weaving attention with glasses raised high in a thundering toast to the end of an era. As the glasses were emptied they were smashed against the steel hulls in one last magnificent, though futile, gesture of defiance.

Today, half a century later, the United States Navy, the Queen of the Seven Seas, is, thanks to Josephus Daniels, officially the "dryest" fleet of all. The spirit room key was laid away forever. . . but it would be a martinet indeed who would insist on inspecting all the dunnage in officers' country.

CHAPTER XXIV

Until The Owners Return

WILLIAM C. CAMPBELL

W E eased through the fog off Newport one evening last summer and anchored to the north of The Dumplings not too far from a big, straight-stemmed schooner that looked like an old Gloucesterman. After chow, we rowed over and looked at her stern. *"Coronet,* Portland," it read in rounded, old-fashioned lettering. Her topmasts were housed, no sails were furled on her spars, and she flew a United States Power Squadron flag.

Coronet! Fifty years of mystery and death, fifty years of appearance and disappearance, of "no comment," and of curious visitors being repelled at the gangplank were implicit in the name of the vessel — if she turned out to be the same *Coronet* that had kept the tongues of three continents' waterfronts wagging, off and on, for nearly three generations.

"Is this the schooner that used to anchor off South Freeport, Maine — the one owned by the Sandfordites?" we asked a lean, middle-aged chap who appeared on deck.

He nodded assent.

"May we come aboard?"

"Sorry — the owners are ashore. Can't let you."

Wanting to make sure that our suspicions were correct, we asked, "Isn't this the same yacht that came back to Portland about fifty years ago, all battered and with everybody aboard down with scurvy?"

"Not all," he replied laconically. "My dad was mate on her — and he was all right."

We asked again if we might come aboard, but the man only smiled and shook his head. "Come back in a couple of days," he said. "The owners'll be aboard then. . ."

The fog really set in that night. When it began to lift next morning, we looked across the water. The *Coronet* had hauled her

[186]

anchor and quietly slipped out to sea, disappearing — as she had time and again during her long career — into the protective fog.

She's an old lady, the *Coronet,* wherever she may be today. She's over the three-quarter century mark by now. But decades before she became a mystery ship, she reigned as a New York Yacht Club queen; engaged in transatlantic races; rounded the Horn twice; and finally smashed into another schooner, with only minor damage to herself, when returning from a cruise to Newfoundland.

The Newfoundland cruise in the summer of 1898 just about ended her career as a pleasure yacht; thereafter, she was out of the news for a dozen years or so. When next brought to public attention she had assumed a major role in one of the century's most unusual sea tales — and in the spectacular life of the state of Maine's only nationally influential religious leader.

Designed by Smith and Terry, the *Coronet* was built by C. & R. Poillon, Brooklyn, in 1885 at a cost of about seventy thousand dollars. Captain Christopher S. Crosby, who was her sailing master for many years, supervised the schooner's construction at the direction of the owner Rufus T. Bush, a Brooklyn merchant and pioneer oil man.

The *Coronet* was a good-sized 174-tonner, 123 feet on the waterline and 133 feet over-all, with a 27-foot beam, and 12-foot 6-inch draft. At one period in her career she was the largest sailing yacht flying the New York Yacht Club burgee.

The Bush family made one transatlantic run in her during the summer of 1886, the year she was launched. Bush soon realized that he had a fast vessel and on his return to the States put up a ten-thousand-dollar wager as challenger for a race from New York to Cork, Ireland. Caldwell L. Colt, owner of the *Dauntless,* picked up the challenge and engaged Captain Bully Samuels, one-time skipper of the clipper *Dreadnaught,* to take command of his schooner for the race.

The two vessels set all sail off Owl Head, Bay Ridge, on March 12, 1887, and headed for Ireland. They were almost evenly matched, although the *Dauntless* logged the best single day's run — 326 miles against the *Coronet's* 291 — during the entire race. However, the *Coronet* crossed the finish line off Rock's Point, Cork Harbor, fourteen days nineteen hours and three minutes after leaving Bay Ridge. She beat the *Dauntless* by thirty hours, but subsequent comparison of the two logs showed that the latter had sailed one hundred and twelve miles farther than the *Coronet* during the crossing.

Owner Bush kept his schooner busy during the next few years. She made a New York to San Francisco passage around the Horn in one hundred and five days — which was fast for even the square-riggers of her period. Later, she circumnavigated the globe in thirteen months, made four cruises to Europe, and two to the West Indies. In 1893, Bush sold the schooner to Arthur Curtis James, the railroad tycoon, an active yachtsman who gave the *Coronet* as little dock time as her previous owner. Commodore James took her around the Horn again, heading for San Francisco for fitting out in anticipation of a voyage to Japan in the spring of 1898.

It was during this passage that the first indication occurred that after years of trouble-free cruising the *Coronet's* luck might be changing. Heading south, she rounded Cape Stiff in a fine breeze early in February, fifty-five days out of New York. As she cleared the Cape, one of the crew shot an albatross. Thereafter, the good weather vanished and the schooner fought gales and driving rains for the next fortnight. She finally docked at San Francisco on April 1, one hundred and seventeen days out of New York.

With the owner's party of nine and a crew of ten, plus a cook, two helpers, and two stewards aboard, the *Coronet* sailed from San Francisco to Yokahama in just under two months, making the run (with a stop at Honolulu), between April 25, and June 22. She returned to the States in September, making a 4600-mile transpacific passage in thirty days. Her return from the West Coast was even rougher than the westbound Horn passage. Rounding the Horn she had to fight for every mile under reefed sails, her deck awash for days on end.

Her last trip under James's ownership ended in a collision. On his return from a cruise to Newfoundland in the summer of 1898, the *Coronet* plowed into the British schooner *Stella Maud* in thick fog off Point Judith, Rhode Island. The *Coronet* lost her martingale, a little paint, and started a few planks forward, but otherwise she was undamaged.

For the next few years the *Coronet* experienced neither cruises nor misadventures worthy of note. But when she did reappear in the news, she was international headline material.

The history of the "new" *Coronet,* from 1910 until the present, was interwoven with that of a powerful, successful religious leader who flourished in Maine at the turn of the century and for a decade thereafter, almost to the beginning of World War I. The career of the Reverend Frank W. Sandford became inextricably involved with that of the schooner; and Sandford's tragedy, years after the event, could still have had the end effect of causing the *Coronet* to slip her mooring and steal away in the Newport fog in 1962.

On January 1, 1893, Sandford, a regularly ordained Free Baptist minister in his thirties, broke away from his New Hampshire parish to found his own evangelical society. He settled on a few barren acres at Durham, Maine, a small farming community near Lisbon Falls. Sandford's material and evangelical successes were phenomenal. Almost from the outset he attracted men, women, and money to the communal religious community he founded at The Kingdom, as he named his colony.

Within a few years he and his followers had acquired about four thousand acres of land; farms and homes; and with the volunteer labor of members of the sect, had built a huge main building — Shiloh — where the offices and common living and dining rooms were located; a meeting-house large enough to seat six hundred people; Bethesda, the hospital; a children's building; and a number of homes for leaders and officers.

The Kingdom, Incorporated, became a flourishing business, financed to a great degree by the results of Sandford's edict that all new members must turn over their worldly goods — even to gold wedding rings — to The Kingdom upon admission to the Shiloh fold. At one time his followers were estimated to number well over six hundred.

At the height of his career Sandford was described as "a handsome and attractive and gentlemanly man of nearly sixty. He is a most interesting preacher and probably the longest sermonizer in the world. . . His last sermon at Shiloh lasted ten hours... He leaps from the platform, a distance of several feet from the ground, and walks about his audience shaking his Bible and vociferating and then leaps back on the platform again." He was . . . "a physically impressive and symmetrical man (whose) dark eyes seem to indicate both geniality and stern determination, and he has a voice which could simulate that of a general on the field of battle."

Revivalist and evangelical sects, from those having elements of free love to the disastrous Palestinian Emigration Society of the 1860's, sprang up, matured, and died in Maine throughout the nineteenth century. But Sandford and his Shilohites, members of The Kingdom (also known as The Holy Ghost and Us Society), were distinguished by the fact that of all the Maine-generated sectarians, their influence was national in scope. Sandford drew financial support and converts from all over the country. Indeed, if a contemporary account is to be believed, Sandford once had "upwards of a thousand followers, including a Japanese lady, an African king, and a man from Texas."

There was nothing mysterious about the Shiloh organization. But from the beginning Sandford and his adherents were subjected to ridicule and persecution, primarily because they differed in behavior, conduct, dress, and manner of worship from those around them. Once having surrendered all of their wealth and goods to the Shiloh administrators, new members became part of a close, communal society.

The Shilohites had been largely Methodists and Baptists and, as one of the leaders expressed it, followed "the teachings of the Holy Bible to the letter. Our movement founded entirely on a religious basis of the highest sort, applied the Bible and its teachings to every situation" — a tenet whose practice was ultimately to lead Frank Sandford to disaster. To this fundamental belief was added that of "the appeal of the Bible as the literally inspired word of God . . . the final argument for the truth of their belief in Sandford as a prophet and leader." "Miracles" in obtaining material things were attributed to the power of prayer — a man and a woman, one stationed in each of the two towers of the main Shiloh building, prayed constantly day and night — and misfortunes were attributed to lack of faith.

One more important factor distinguished Sandford from other religious leaders of his century. In order to spread his faith overseas, he disdained the common practice of financing the transportation of a few missionaries here and there. Instead, he conceived the idea of a whole fleet of his own ships filled with evangelical Shilohites who would carry the gospel of The Kingdom throughout the world. Sandford bought several small yachts, including a Maine pinky, the *Ripple*, and the steam yacht *Barracouta*, formerly the *Alsatia*. He formed The Kingdom Yacht Club so that none of his vessels would have to clear in each port and, in the spring of 1910, acquired the *Coronet* for ten thousand dollars.

The *Coronet* became Sandford's flagship, key to his grandiose plan "to send forth a hundred vessels and convert the heathen from Panama to the polar regions." The exact sequence of events during the fateful eighteen months of the *Coronet's* cruise under Sandford's command is not too clear. But it is known that she cleared Portland in June 1910, with Sandford and about forty-five followers and crew aboard. The schooner sailed back and forth between Hatteras and Newfoundland for several months before making an Atlantic crossing to the Mediterranean and Palestine. She then sailed back past Gibralter and headed south along the west coast of Africa. There she was joined by the *Kingdom,* the former 586-ton barkentine *Rebecca Crowell,* which Sandford had bought in 1907.

The *Kingdom* was wrecked on the African coast. Sandford burned her, then picked up her thirty-five survivors who had taken refuge at Bathhurst, Gambia. The badly overcrowded *Coronet* recrossed the Atlantic to South America, but Sandford refused to land at any port in order to replenish his stores. In July 1911, the schooner left Panama astern and, at Sandford's direction, headed north for the Arctic. Just how far or how long he and the *Coronet* would have gone on, nobody knows. But a series of gales during the northward passage gave the vessel such a severe beating that she had to make port — or sink.

When she limped into Portland in October of 1911, her topmasts were gone, her canvas hung in shreds, and her hull was leaking so badly that only round-the-clock pumping kept her afloat. But more importantly, most of the Shilohites and crew members were near starvation, many had scurvy — and six persons had died at sea.

Sandford was brought to trial in U.S. District Court, Portland, in December 1911, charged with being directly responsible for the six deaths resulting from malnutrition and disease. And it was at this trial, begun just a week before Christmas, that the whole story of the *Coronet* began to be lost from public knowledge; when newsmen began to get the Shilohite comment that other newsmen were to hear, in one form or another, for ensuing decades: "We are peace-loving Christians who just want to be left alone."

There are no public records of the cruise of the *Coronet*. Even — to still further obscure the trail — the official transcript of the trial is missing from its container in the Court Records Center. News reports are sparse and contradictory. For example, one states that Sandford accepted no counsel, and offered no testimony in his own defense. Another report has it that, on the contrary, he held the jury spellbound for an hour-and-a-half with his impassioned eloquence.

But a few bits of testimony were reported, such damning evidence from the survivors of the cruise as that "they had been forced to fast for twenty-eight days, eating one meal a day of cornmeal mush and bread"; and that they "had lived on two biscuits a day — literally starving to death." Sandford's tremendous power over followers and crew alike had forestalled mutiny. But his adamant refusal to replenish supplies, trusting to the power of prayer to provide for their material needs, created the frame for disaster.

Sandford was convicted on a charge of manslaughter on the high seas. Judge Clarence Hale sentenced him to ten years in the federal penitentiary, Atlanta. Released for good behavior after having served only a few years of his term, Sandford disappeared from public view after a brief visit to Shiloh. His death at the age of eighty-six was announced by the Society in 1948.

The self-styled "Elijah" Sandford's dream of a world-encompassing fleet of missionary ships, carrying his word to the heathen ended in a federal penitentiary. But the *Coronet* continued on, a tangible sea-going mystery that is still very much alive fifty years after she barely made Portland, death and disease in her wake. Until 1948, she was berthed there almost constantly, most of the time at the Randall and McAllister wharf. Captain E. S. Knight was long caretaker of the vessel, allowing nobody aboard and giving out no information. The schooner was periodically hauled out and kept in repair until, in 1946, the Marine Railway and Repair Company, South Portland, began a complete fitting-out job on her.

By early 1947, the *Coronet* had two big diesels installed, new masts stepped, and planking, companionways, and a completely new stern added. Nobody knew for certain who was paying the bill, where she was going, nor who would be in command. Like the man aboard her in Newport last summer, the repair yard head would say only that he was acting on order of the owners. At any rate, the cost of the new engines and general overhaul was estimated at one hundred thousand dollars — paid for, no doubt, by The Kingdom, Incorporated, since The Kingdom still owns her.

For the next few years the *Coronet* appeared and disappeared at intervals until in 1954 she changed her home port to Gloucester. Two years later she showed up in Portland again, anchoring off the Grand Trunk pier in a heavy fog after a trip in weather that had held up all other Portland-bound shipping. She continued to come and go without warning; within the last couple of years, she has again been moored at a Gloucester wharf.

Where is she today, on what cruises, in what waters? There is no question that she is an active, handsome schooner yacht with a set of powerful diesels in her hold. Headquarters of The Kingdom have been moved from Maine to Dublin, New Hampshire, but a few hundred Maine believers hold regular Sunday services in the old Shiloh meetinghouse; and still practice in strict adherence to Biblical teachings that characterized Sandford's precepts.

But strangers are not welcomed, either at Shiloh or aboard the *Coronet*. The Sandford followers and their descendents, after almost three-quarters of a century of exposure to suspicion, ridicule, and notoriety in one form or another, have had enough. At sea, or in some fog-enshrouded harbor, mariners and yachtsmen may see the *Coronet* as we did. Yet none are likely to be invited aboard this twentieth century Flying Dutchman — not until the owner returns. Which is a fine, polite way of saying: "Never."

CHAPTER XXV

Home To The Meadow

FARLEY MOWAT

MY father was not the only man in Saskatoon to know the frustrations and hungers of a landlocked sailor. These were a good many other expatriates from broad waters in the city, and he came to know most of them through his work, for on the library shelves was one of the finest collections of boating books extant. Some of my father's staff — who did not know a boat from a bloat — were inclined to take a jaundiced view of the nautical flavor of the annual book-purchase list, but, after all, he *was* the chief librarian.

Aaron Poole was one of those who appreciated my father's salted taste in books. Aaron was a withered and eagle-featured little man who had emigrated from the Maritime Provinces some thirty years earlier and who, for twenty-nine years, had been hungering for the sound and feel of salt water under a vessel's keel. The fact that he had originally come from the interior of New Brunswick and had never actually been to sea in anything larger than a rowboat during his maritime years was not relevant to the way Aaron felt. As a Maritimer, exiled on the prairies, he believed himself to be of one blood with the famous seamen of the North Atlantic ports; and in twenty-nine years a man can remember a good many things that ought to have happened. Aaron's memory was so excellent that he could talk for hours of the times when he had sailed out of Lunenburg for the Grand Banks, first as cabin boy, then as an able-bodied seaman, then as a mate, and finally as skipper of the smartest fishing schooner on the coast.

Aaron's desire to return to the sea grew as the years passed, and finally in 1926, when he was in his sixty-fifth year, he resolved his yearnings into action and began to build himself a vessel. He married off his daughters, sold his business, sent his wife to California, and got down to work at something that really mattered. He planned to sail his ship from Saskatoon to New Brunswick — and he intended to sail every inch of the way. He was of that dogged breed who will admit no obstacles — not even geographical ones like the two thousand miles of solid land which intervened between him and his goal.

He designed his ship himself, and then turned the basement of his house on Fifth Avenue into a boat works. Almost as soon as her keel was laid, some well-meaning friend pointed out to Aaron that he would never be able to get the completed ship out of that basement — but Aaron refused to be perturbed by problems which lay so far in the future.

By the time we arrived in Saskatoon, Aaron and his boat had been a standing jest for years. Her name alone was still enough to provoke chuckles in the beer parlors, even among those who had already laughed at the same joke a hundred times. It was indicative of Aaron's singular disdain for the multitudes that he had decided to name his ship *The Coot*.

"What's the matter with *that?*" he would cry in his high-pitched and querulous voice. "Hell of a smart bird, the coot. Knows when to dive. Knows when to swim. Can't fly worth a hoot. Who the hell wants to fly a boat?"

Aaron's tongue was almost as rough as his carpentering, and that was pretty rough. He labored over his ship with infinite effort, but with almost no knowledge and with even less skill. Nor was he a patient man—and patience is an essential virtue in a shipbuilder. It was to be expected that his vessel would be renamed by those who were privileged to see her being built. They called her *Putty Princess*.

It was appropriate enough. Few, if any, of her planks met their neighbors, except by merest chance. It was said that Blanding's Hardware—where Aaron bought his supplies—made much of its profit, during the years *The Coot* was a-building, from the sale of putty.

When my father and Aaron met, *The Coot* was as near completion as she was ever likely to get. She was twenty-four feet long, flat-bottomed, and with lines as hard and awkward as those of a harbor scow. She was hogged before she left her natal bed. She was fastened with iron screws that had begun to rust before she was even launched. The gaps and seams in her hull could swallow a gallon of putty a day, and never show a bit of it by the next morning.

Yet despite her manifold faults, she was a vessel—a ship—and and the biggest ship Saskatoon had ever seen. Aaron could see no fault in her, and even my father, who was not blinded by a creator's love and who was aware of her dubious seaworthiness, refused to admit her shortcomings, because she had become a part of his dreams, too.

Mother and I were expecting it when one March day Father announced that he was taking a leave of absence from the library that coming summer, in order to help Aaron sail *The Coot* to Halifax.

Saskatoon took a keen interest in the project. Controversy as to *The Coot's* chances for a successful journey waxed furiously among the most diversified strata of society. The Chamber of Commerce hailed the venture with the optimism common to such organizations, predicting that this was the "Trail-Blazer step that would lead to Great Fleets of Cargo Barges using Mother Saskatchewan to carry Her Children's Grain to the Markets of the World." On the other hand, the officials of the two railroads made mock of *The Coot,* refusing to accept her as a competitive threat in the lucrative grain-carrying business.

But, on the whole, the city was proud that Saskatoon was to become the home port for a seagoing ship. Maps showing the vessel's route were published, together with commentaries on the scenic beauties that would meet the eyes of the crew along the way. It was clear from the maps that this would be one of the most unusual voyages ever attempted, not excluding Captain Cook's circumnavigation of the globe. For, in order to reach her destination, *The Coot* would have to travel northward down the South Saskatchewan to its juncture with the north branch, then eastward into Lake Winnipeg. From there the route would turn south to leave Manitoba's inland sea for the waters of the Red River of the North, and the territories of the United States. Continuing southward down the Minnesota River to St. Paul, *The Coot* would find herself in the headwaters of the Mississippi, and on that great stream would journey to the Gulf of Mexico. The rest of the trip would be quite straightforward—a simple sail around Florida and up the Atlantic Coast to the Gulf of St. Lawrence.

Sailing time (announced by banner headlines in the local paper —MOWAT AND POOLE TO SAIL WITH MORNING TIDE) was fixed for 8 A.M. on a Saturday in mid-June and the chosen point of departure was to be the mud flat which lies near the city's major sewer outlet on the river. The actual launching had to be postponed a day, however, when the ancient and gloomy prediction that Aaron would have trouble disentombing *The Coot* from his basement was found to be a true prophecy. In the end, a bulldozer had to be hired and Aaron, with the careless disdain of the true adventurer, ordered the operator to rip out the entire east wall of his house so that *The Coot* might go free. The crowd which had gathered to see the launching, and which at first had been disappointed by the delay, went home that evening quite satisfied with this preliminary entertainment and ready for more.

Father and Aaron had reason to be thankful for the absence of an audience when they finally eased the vessel off the trailer and into the Saskatchewan. She made no pretense at all of being a surface ship. She sank at once into the bottom slime, where she lay gurgling as contentedly as an old buffalo in its favorite wallow.

They dragged her reluctantly back on shore and then they worked the whole night through under the fitful glare of gasoline lanterns. By dawn they had recaulked *The Coot* by introducing nine pounds of putty and a great number of cedar wedges into her capacious seams. They launched her again before breakfast—and this time she stayed afloat.

That Sunday morning the churches were all but deserted, and it was a gala crowd that lined the river shores to windward of the sewer. The mudbank was the scene of frantic activity. Father and Aaron dashed about shouting obscure orders in nautical parlance, and became increasingly exasperated with one another when these were misunderstood. *The Coot* waited peacefully, but there were those among us in the crowd of onlookers who felt that she hardly looked ready for her great adventure. Her deck was only partly completed. Her mast had not yet been stepped. Her rudder fittings had not arrived and the rudder hung uncertainly over the stern on pintles made of bailing wire. But she was colorful, at least. In his hurry to have her ready for the launching, Aaron had not waited for the delivery of a shipment of special marine enamel, but had slapped on whatever remnants of paint he could find in the bottom of the cans that littered his workshop. The result was spectacular, but gaudy.

Both Aaron and Father had been the recipients of much well-meaning hospitality during the night, and by morning neither was really competent to deal with the technical problem of stowage. The mountain of supplies and gear which had accumulated on the mudbank would have required a whole flock of *Coots* to carry it. Captain and mate bickered steadily, and this kept the crowd in a good humor as the hours advanced and the moment of departure seemed no nearer.

The patience of the onlookers was occasionally rewarded, as when Aaron lost control of a fifty-pound cheese—a gift from a local dairy—and it went spinning off into the flow from the sewer. The audience was entranced. Aaron danced up and down on the mud-flat, shrilly ordering his mate to dive in and rescue the cheese, but the mate became openly mutinous, and the situation was only saved by the prompt action of two small boys armed with fishing poles who caught the truant cheese and steered it gently back to shore. They would not touch it with their hands, nor would anyone else, and long after *The Coot* had sailed, that cheese sat on the flat, lonely and unloved.

Mutt was prominent during these proceedings. He had been signed on as ship's dog and the excitement attendant on the launching pleased him greatly. When willing hands finally pushed *The Coot* out into the stream, Mutt was poised on the foredeck, striking an attitude, and he was the first part of the deck cargo to go swimming when the overloaded vessel heeled sharply to starboard and shook herself free of her encumbrances.

The Coot came back to the mudbank once again. Mutt withdrew under the growing mountain of discarded supplies for which there was no room aboard the ship. It was not so much the sewer that had discomfited him, as it was the heartless laughter of the crowd.

Just before noon they sailed at last, and *The Coot* looked quite impressive as she swung broadside-to under the arches of the New Bridge, accompanied by a flotilla of thirty-six sodden loaves of bread that had fallen through the bottom of a cardboard container which

Aaron had retrieved from the wet bilges of the boat, and had in-cautiously set to dry upon the canted afterdeck.

Riding my bicycle along the shore path, I accompanied them for a mile before waving farewell and then returning to the city, where, with the rest of Saskatoon, I settled down to await reports of *The Coot's* progress.

Our newspaper had outdone itself to cover the story properly, for it had enrolled all the ferrymen along the river as special cor-respondents. The ferries were located every dozen miles or so. They were square scows, fitted with submerged wooden vanes that could be turned at an angle to the current so that the water pressure on them would force the ferries back and forth across the river, guided and held on their courses by steel cables that were stretched from shore to shore just below the surface. The ferrymen were mostly farmers, with little knowledge of wider waters than their own river, so the newspaper representative who visited them (himself a fugi-tive from a seaport town) had given each of them a careful briefing on the proper manner of reporting commercial shipping.

When, for five full days after *The Coot* left us, there was not a single report from a ferryman, we began to worry a little. Then on Friday night the operator of the first ferry below the city—some fifteen miles away—telephoned the paper in a state of great agitation to report an object—unidentifiable due to darkness—that had swept down upon him just before midnight and, after fouling the ferry cable, had vanished again.

The mysterious object was presumed to be *The Coot,* but the reporter who was dispatched to that section of the river at dawn could find no trace of the vessel. He drove on down stream and at last encountered a Ukrainian family living high above the riverbank. The farmer could speak no English and his wife had only a little, but she did the best she could with what she had.

She admitted that she had certainly seen *something* that morn-ing—and here she stopped and crossed herself. It had looked to her, she said, like an immense and garish coffin that could never have been intended for a mere human corpse. When she saw it first it was being hauled across a broad mud flat by—and she crossed her-self again—a horse and a dog. It was accompanied, she continued, by two nude and prancing figures that might conceivably have been human, but were more likely devils. Water devils, she added after a moment's thought. No, she had not seen what had happened to the coffin. One glance had been enough, and she had hurried back into her house to say a prayer or two before the family icon — just in case.

The reporter descended to the river and there he found the marks left by the cortege in the soft mud. There were two sets of barefoot human tracks, a deep groove left by a vessel's keel, and one set each of dog and horse prints. The tracks meandered across the bar for two miles and then vanished—including those of the horse. The reporter returned to Saskatoon with his story, but he had a queer look in his eye when he told us what he had seen.

As to what had actually happened during those five days when *The Coot* was lost to view, my father's log tells very little. It contains only such succinct and sometimes inscrutable entries as these: *Sun. 1240 hrs. Sink. Again. Damn. . . . Sun. 2200 hrs. Putty all gone. Try mud. No good. . . . Wed. 1600 hrs. A. shot duck for din., missed, hit cow. . . . Thurs. 2330 hrs. Rud. gone west. Oh Hell! . . . Fri. 1200 hrs. Thank God for Horse.*

But the story is there nevertheless.

It was in an amiable and buoyant mood that Father and Aaron saw the last of Saskatoon. That mood remained on them for three miles during which they made reasonably good progress, being forced to make for shore—before they sank—only four times. At each of these halts it was necessary to unload *The Coot* and turn her over to drain the water out. Aaron kept insisting that this would not be necessary in the future. "She'll soon take up," he told my father. "Wait till she's been afloat awhile."

As the day drew on, the initial mood of amity wore thin. "She'll take up all right," my father remarked bitterly as they unloaded *The Coot* for the twelfth time. "She'll take up the whole damned river before she's done — that's what she'll do."

By the time they established their night camp they had covered a total distance of six miles, and *The Coot* had lost what little putty still remained in her. Her crew slept fitfully that night.

On Monday there was little difficulty keeping the water out, since there was no water — only a continuous sand bar. It was a terrestrial day, and they hauled *The Coot* the entire two miles that they made good before sunset. The three days which followed were of a similar nature. Mutt began to get footsore from sand between his toes. Because they spent so much of their time slithering and falling in the river muck as they attempted to haul *The Coot* a little farther on her way, both Father and Aaron abandoned clothing altogether and went back to nature.

They kept making new discoveries about their vessel and her equipment, and these were almost all discouraging. They found that in the monstrous pile of stores left behind in Saskatoon had been the fuel for the stove; the ammunition for the shotgun, though not (alas for an innocent cow) for the .22 rifle; the ax; blackest of all omissions, three bottles of Jamaica rum. They found that their sodden blankets were in an equally unsanitary state. They found that all the labels of the canned goods had washed away, and they discovered that the two cases of gleaming, but nameless, cans which they had supposed held pork and beans actually held dog food intended for Mutt.

I do not wonder that the log had so little to say about those days. I only wonder that *The Coot* continued on her voyage at all. But continue she did, and on Thursday evening her crew was rewarded by at last reaching relatively navigable waters. It was nearly dusk by then, but neither mate nor skipper (both of whom had become grim and uncommunicative) would be the first to suggest a halt, and Mutt had no say in the matter.

They pushed *The Coot* off the final sand bar and slipped away downstream into the darkness. At midnight they fouled the ferry cable, and lost their rudder.

That loss was not so serious as it seemed to them at the time, for before dawn they were aground again — and again trudging over the mudbanks with the towropes gnawing into their bare shoulders.

They had paused for a while in order to cook a dismal breakfast when my father, happening to glance up at the high bank, saw the horse. Inspiration came to him and he leaped to his feet, shouting with elation. He was no longer shouting when, after having hiked for five miles over the burning prairie in order to find the horse's owner, and to arrange temporary rental, he came wearily back down the banks of the river to rejoin *The Coot*. Aaron greeted him with unwonted joviality and a momentous announcement. "I've found it, Angus!" he cried, and held aloft one of the precious bottles long given up for lost.

[201]

It was the turning point of the journey.

By noon the amiable horse had dragged *The Coot* across the two-mile flats to open water once again. Aaron allowed the horse to wade a little way out from the shore in order to float *The Coot*. He was about to halt the beast in order to untie the towrope when my father's genius renewed itself. "Why stop him now?" Father asked.

Aaron looked at his mate with growing affection, and passed the bottle. "By God, Angus," he said, "for a librarian you've got quite a brain."

So *The Coot* proceeded on her way under one horsepower and, since the river seldom was more than three feet deep, the horse experienced but little difficulty in his strange role. When, as occasionally happened, he struck a deep hole, he simply swam until he could touch bottom once again. And when the water shoaled into a new sand bar, *The Coot's* passengers jumped ashore and helped haul.

The use of a river horse was a brilliant piece of improvisation and it might well have sufficed to carry the voyagers to Lake Winnipeg — where they would assuredly have drowned — had it not been for the flood.

When the rain began on Saturday afternoon, Father and Aaron took *The Coot* to shore, hauled her a little way up on the flats, covered her with a big tarpaulin, and crawled under the canvas to wait out the downpour. The horse was turned loose to scale the high banks and forage for himself, while the two men and the dog relaxed cozily in their shelter over tins of dog food and dollops of rum.

The rain grew heavier, for it was the beginning of one of those frightening prairie phenomena — a real cloudburst. In less than three hours, three inches of water fell on the sun-hardened plains about Saskatoon and that was more than the total rainfall during the previous three months. The ground could not absorb it and the steep-sided gulches leading into the valley of the Saskatchewan began to roar angrily in spate. The river rose rapidly, growing yellow and furious as the flow increased.

The first crest of the flood reached *The Coot* at about five o'clock in the afternoon and before her crew could emerge from their shelter, they were in mid-stream, and racing down the river at an appalling clip. Rudderless, and with only one remaining oar — for Aaron had used the other to support a tea pail over an open fire a few days earlier, and then had gone off to sit and think and had forgotten about oar, tea, and fire — there was nothing useful that *The Coot's* crew could do to help themselves. The rain still beat down upon them, and after a brief, stunned look at the fury of the river, they sensibly withdrew under their canvas hood, and passed the bottle.

By seven o'clock the rain had moderated to a steady drizzle, but the flood waters were still rising. In Saskatoon we who waited impatiently for news of *The Coot* were at last rewarded. The arrangements made by the newspaper began to bear fruit. Reports began arriving from ferrymen all down the river, and these succeeded one another so swiftly that at times they were almost continuous. The telephone exchange at the newspaper office was swamped with messages like this one:

SPECIAL TO THE STAR:

SAILING VESSEL, COOT, OUTBOUND IN BALLAST FROM SASKATOON, SIGHTED AT INDIAN CROSSING AT 7:43 P.M. ON COURSE FOR HALIFAX, THAT IS IF SHE DON'T GO BUSTING INTO THE BIG ISLAND BAR AFORE SHE GITS PAST COYOTE CREEK.

The Coot got by Big Island and Coyote Creek all right, for at 7:50 P.M. the watcher at Barners Ford reported that she had just passed him, accompanied by two drowned cows, also presumed to be enroute for Halifax. At 8:02 she went by Indian Crossing . . . at 8:16 she sideswiped the Sinkhole Ferry . . . at 8:22 she was reported from St. Louis (Saskatchewan, not Missouri) . . . and so it went.

In the city room at the newspaper, reporters marked each new position on a large-scale map of the river, and someone with a slide rule calculated that if *The Coot* could maintain her rate of speed, she would complete her passage to Halifax in six more days.

By nine o'clock that evening the darkness of an overcast and moonless night had so obscured the river that no further reports were to be expected from the watching ferrymen. However, we presumed that on Sunday morning the observers would again pick up the trail. A number of people even drove out at dawn from Prince Albert to see *The Coot* go past the junction of the two branches of the river. They made that trip in vain. The flood passed and the river shrank back to its normal, indolent self, but no *Coot* appeared. She had vanished utterly during the black hours of the night.

[203]

All through that tense and weary Sunday we waited for news, and there was none. At last Aaron's son-in-law called on the Royal Canadian Mounted Police for help, and the famous force ordered one of its patrol aircraft up to make a search. The plane found nothing before darkness intervened on Sunday evening, but it was off again with the following dawn.

At 11 A.M. on Monday the following message was received in Saskatoon:

> COOT LOCATED FIVE MILES NORTHWEST FENTON AND TWO MILES FROM RIVERBANK. AGROUND IN CENTER LARGE PASTURE AND ENTIRELY SURROUNDED BY HOLSTEIN COWS. CREW APPEARS ALL WELL. ONE MAN PLAYING BANJO, ONE SUNBATHING, AND DOG CHASING CATTLE.

It was an admirable report, and indicative of the high standards of accuracy, combined with brevity, for which the force is justly famed. However, as my father later pointed out, it did not tell the entire story.

Mutt, Aaron, and Father had spent the whole of Saturday night under cover of their tarpaulin. Even after the rain stopped they did not emerge. Father said that this was because he wished to die bravely, and he could do so only by ignoring the terror and turmoil of that swollen river. Aaron said it was because they had found the second bottle of rum. Mutt, as usual, kept his peace.

When the light grew strong on Sunday morning, Father began to hope that they might yet survive and, pulling aside the canvas, thrust his head out for a look. He was stupefied by what he saw. *The Coot* had evidently managed to cover the entire distance to Lake Winnipeg in less than ten hours. His bemused mind could find no other explanation for the apparently limitless expanse of brown water that stretched away on every side.

It was not until late afternoon, when the flood waters began to subside and the tops of poplar trees began appearing alongside *The Coot,* that the illusion was partially dispelled. It had vanished totally by Monday morning when the voyagers awoke to find their vessel resting on a broad green meadow, surrounded by a herd of curious cattle.

The crew of *The Coot* now proceeded to enjoy the happiest hours of their journey. There was no water in the boat, or under her. There was no sand or mud. The sun was warm. Aaron had found the third of the missing bottles, and Father had procured a side of home-cured bacon and five loaves of homemade bread form a nearby Dukhobor settler. Mutt was having a time with cows. It was a fair and lovely place for storm-tossed mariners to drop their hook.

The idyll was disturbed by the appearance of the search aircraft; and shattered a few hours later by the arrival of Aaron's son-in-law as a passenger in a big red truck. A conference was called and the cruise was declared to be at an end, despite Aaron's blasphemous dissent. *The Coot* went ignominiously back to Saskatoon aboard the truck.

When he was safely within his own house, Father frankly admitted to us that he was delighted to be there, and that he had never really had much hope of seeing home again.

But there is a curious postscript to the story of *The Coot*. One day in the autumn of the following year my father received a letter from Halifax. It contained nothing save a snapshot which showed a funny little craft (unmistakably *The Coot*) tied up alongside that famous Lunenburger, the *Bluenose*. On the back of the snapshot was a cryptic message, scrawled large in purple ink. "Quitter!" it said.

Father would have felt badly about that, had not his friend Don Chisholm (who was assistant superintendent of one of the railroads at Saskatoon) shown him a waybill sometime earlier. It was an interesting document. It dealt with the dispatch of one flatcar, "with cargo, out of Saskatoon, bound for Halifax." And the name bestowed on that flatcar for the journey by some railway humorist was writ large on the bottom of the bill.

It was *The Cootie Carrier*.

CHAPTER XXVI

A Jar Of Fish Oil

W. R. JOHNSON JR.

The morning was clear and cooled by a freshening easterly wind as Robert Barr's sloop *Lonely Bird* slipped her moorings and sailed out of Nassau Harbor. The ragged and much patched mainsail billowed and drove the heavy little fishing smack through the first of the sea chop outside the bar.

When clear of the chain of keys west of the harbor entrance, Barr went forward to set the equally ragged jib and to lash the rusty anchor to the samson post. He used strands of a former anchor line as lashings, for he was a poor man; a fisherman and occasional pilot for American sportsmen. He had lived his forty years in the Bahama Islands, most of it on the sea. Yet, as so many like him, he could not swim. In his years on the sea he had acquired a wealth of local knowledge. He took his knowledge for granted, as he did his way of life.

Barr could navigate by the bottom when out of sight of land. He could tell of approaching storms from the pattern of weather and the cloudiness or clarity of a jar of fish oil he kept below in the cabin. He was familiar with almost every harbor and hurricane creek in the Bahamas.

He had once navigated across the coral-studded Yellow Bank at night in a raging norther and gained the safety of an anchorage. His experience was vast and varied, and he had all the local knowledge a man could desire. But he maintained the childlike awe and respect that superstition gives the honest man. He believed in *scuttles* and *dupees,* those multi-legged creatures that rise from the great sea deeps at night and snatch men from the decks of ships. He believed in mermaids, the blonde women who sit on barren rocks and comb their hair. He never claimed to have seen these things, but he knew people who had.

[206]

Like most seamen, he had an abiding fear of lightning and fire at sea, and of waterspouts. For these things he had remedies. For lightning and fire he carried a mysterious polished stone known as a "thunderstone" which protected him. For waterspouts, which he called "devils' tails," he would take out an old rusting machete and swing it a few times to make the spout pull up into the clouds. This he believed, and these things he practiced in all sincerity. The traditions and lore of his way of life were as honest as was Robert Barr. But as are humans, they were fallible.

The gray-green hills of New Providence had dropped astern by noon and the easterly wind was increasing so Barr handed the jib. They ran on under main alone with the tricing lines taken up to keep the deep foot of the sail out of the lumping seas. Barr lit his clay pipe and looked westward where he knew the island of Andros lay with thunderheads looming over its steaming land mass. He was bound for Nicolls Town and then around into Lowe Sound to fill his well with fish and return to the market in Nassau. The price of grouper was up that winter, and he knew where there was a ledge full of hungry ones. He would hook up some conchs, bait his lines, fish for a week or so and return to Nassau.

The little sloop ran well downwind, and Barr sat calmly at the tiller smoking his pipe. Around noon he noticed a darkness in the northwest; a hump of solid cloud crowding the clear sky as it grew. Barr knew right away that a northwest gale was coming. The wind veered to the southeast and increased until the *Lonely Bird* was running down the crests of each sea and struggling up the slope of the next.

With great difficulty he brought the boat up into the wind and reefed the sail by tying a line around it several feet in from the clew. With the sail reefed and set he lay off and headed south.

"No'th Bight now!" he said aloud to his boat and settled at the helm intent on the new landfall, and the growing menace of the cloud bank in the north. At one time he shook his head and clicked his tongue. "Da fish oil didn' cloud befo' dis one. Maybe it need replacement."

By midafternoon the whole dome of the northern sky was gray-blue. Barr had picked up the tops of the pine trees at Cargill Hill and was intent on making North Bight anchorage before the storm

[207]

hit. *Lonely Bird* drove hard through the lumpy cross seas pitching her clipper bow into an occasional swell. She was an old boat but strong and well built. The fish well made her sluggish, as it did all native boats, but it also added to her stability.

North Bight finally opened as the trees on Big Wood Cay rose into view. At the same time the wind flattened out and a terrific cross sea took over and began tossing the little smack about. The boom came crashing across and broke before Barr could take in the sheets. "Oh, Gawd, now I done it!"

With a roaring high in the sky and a hissing on the water the first cold gust of wind hit the *Lonely Bird*.

Just before sunset Barr had run up the jib in a desperate effort to beat inshore, but the lack of wind and the confused sea had prevented any headway. He had tried sculling but he knew he couldn't reach North Bight in time, so he sat and waited. When the norther hit it drove the little boat offshore and deeper into the Tongue of the Ocean. Barr sat at the helm trying to keep the boat directly before the wind. He was cold and the night was dark. The cloud cover had obscured the stars, but he knew that he was headed south and east into the great cul-de-sac of the Tongue of the Ocean, an area that was relatively unexplored and unfrequented by boats.

He had heard how the ocean "ran out" there into myriad channels that themselves ran out onto barren sand flats. It was said that on those flats there was no life. Not even the black-head gull or the high-flying frigate bird came there to feed. And he remembered also the stories of the deep blue holes, and how *scuttles* passed through them into the ocean holes of the interior of Andros Island. He had seen those holes of sea water in the interior of his home island and had caught sea fish in them and watched the tide rise and fall just as in the sea.

But the thoughts that filled Barr's mind that wild night were of the moment . . . each moment. The urgency of what to do now and next to keep the boat from broaching manifested itself in the reflexes of experience that took no conscious thought. Barr and his *Lonely Bird* worked together as one living unit for survival.

Barr had been in other storms and in other tight spots, but never as bad as that . . . never blown offshore with no safe harbor to run down on. Nassau was out of the question, even if he could carry sail. It was all he could do to keep her dead before the wind so she would not broach.

No thought of sleep came until the jib blew out with something like a shotgun blast. Then Barr's heart sank, and he lost hope. He sat at the helm shivering as cold seas swept around him. The strands of canvas blew away before him in the night.

Dawn came cold and steely-gray, filtering through the driving spume and sea mist. Barr left the helm and crawled below where the small and once neat cabin was in shambles. The useless fish oil was a scum over everything. Bilge water sloshed from side to side and splashed against the bulkhead of the empty fish well. He managed to open a can of corned beef and took it on deck to eat. When he finished he realized thirst, and only then noticed that the water keg had been swept away during the night.

Sunlight filtered through the overcast and warmed him somewhat. He, like everything on the boat, was wet. A chill passed through him and he realized that the wind had veered more to the northeast.

"It die out soon," he said to the boat. "Den we see what we can do." The warmth and food cheered Barr and made him optimistic. "I got a sculling sweep yet. We get along with dat somehow..." He stood and stretched in the light of day as the sun grew stronger and warmed him more... "even if I got to scull back to Andros."

Barr talked to his boat all morning, and the wind began to pipe up from the northeast. At noon running under bare poles he saw green reflections on the bottom of the scudding overcast in the south.

"Dat's Hurricane Flats. Dat's shallow bar and deep dead en' channel comin' up." He began pumping the boat to lighten her.

Lonely Bird hit the first bar with a shattering smash. The next wave swept her decks but carried her across into enough water to float her, and another sea lifted her up and over the next bar. She ran headlong into a gently sloping bank, and the waves drove her hard up on it canting her over on one bilge and finishing the job by filling her with water. During this Barr had hung stubbornly to the tiller. He was lifted and smashed to the deck, but he hung on giving up hope of life but not physically giving in to death. When

[209]

they came to rest, there was only the sound of waves beating against the hull.

That night the wind shifted to the southeast and the sea went down to light chop. At low tide only a foot of water lay around the boat. Barr lay in shock and sleep on deck by the tiller.

He awakened at dawn to a dryness in his throat and a hollowness in his stomach. He looked below and found a small piece of rotten conch meat and a tin of corned beef. He found his fishing gear and baited a line with the conch and cast it far astern. He could not see the blue water of the Tongue of the Ocean, but he knew it lay to the north. A channel was visible a half-mile to the east. Aside from that there were only the sky and sand banks.

The sand! White and yellow with not a rock or sea fan or sponge to break the glare. No schools of fish. Nothing but the whiteness of the sand bottom and the green water channel to the east.

Barr rigged an awning as best he could with a few shreds of canvas and the sculling oar. The sun rose and the heat increased. At first he basked in it remembering the chill of the night, but soon thirst and fear of thirst drove him to the little patch of shade.

Nothing took his pitiful bait. Innumerable times he pulled it in and found only waterlogged stinking conch. He took to examining the bait and found no change, not a scratch on it. No fish had tasted it; not even a crab, or a sea hermit, or a goat fish had come to it. At sunset he ate more of the corned beef, but it only increased his thirst.

The night was bad for Barr. Dreams of food and water haunted him. He awoke many times gulping the precious sweat running down his face thinking it to be cool spring water. He dreamed of rain squalls and deep blue oceans of freshness. He lay on deck in the predawn calms and prayed for dew that he could lick from the decks as he had seen cats do. But no rain or dew came to Robert Barr.

The motor schooner *Heantie* had run in as close as possible onto the sand banks. A half-mile to the south there was a hull careened on its side, its mast angled, with streamers of line from it blowing in the breeze.

Two men waded back from the wreck and swam the few yards to the schooner. They climbed up the bobstay and were met by the captain.

"It's Barr, Cap'n. He dead," said one man.

"Just recent dead," put in the other.

"An' what so strange," said the first, "is dat de water aroun' his boat is wellin' up fresh."

CHAPTER XXVII

Safe In The Belly of the Sail

ANTHONY ANABLE

Outwarly, Dad was a product of his times — 1856 to 1904 — a true Victorian in speech, demeanor and attire. Added to this was the life-long burden of carrying and living up to the formidable name of Eliphalet Nott Anable, bestowed on him by his parents in honor of his great uncle, Eliphalet Nott, a sturdy, circuit-riding Presbyterian clergyman of the early nineteenth century who, in the course of an active life as a minister, inventor, and educator, set an all-time record of sixty-two years as president of Union College at Schenectady, New York.

Dad's life-long love of boats began at the tender age of seven at Bellport, Long Island, on the Great South Bay. His attire for a sail in his later years, as my father, on the shoal, inland waters of the New Jersey coast was quite correct for that period — a spotless panama hat, silk shirt with demountable starched collar and cuffs, a flowing madras necktie and a pair of immaculate white duck trousers, pressed to a knife-edge crease. Picture that ensemble of late Victorian finery on a wiry, athletically built man of medium height and build who had pale, watery blue eyes peering out at you through gold rimmed pince-nez spectacles above a sandy-red mustache and goatee, and you have a good likeness of my old man about ready to go for a sail.

Happily, below that formidable appearance, which gave an utterly wrong impression of the inner man, there lay a captivating sense of humor. A love of life and people and a spirit of adventure, led him into and out of all types of scrapes to the never-ending consternation of my dear mother with her rather somber Holland-Dutch antecedents. He was great fun with his contemporaries who affectionately nicknamed him "Liph" and with me, his only child, and my childhood friends, who lived during those pleasant far past days, in anticipation of what strange thing Dad would do next.

[212]

Our summer home at then-unspoiled Bradley Beach, New Jersey, around the turn of the century, witnessed many a prank of his which utterly upset my mother, but completely delighted me and the boys and girls of that period. One Fourth of July, when he had spent Mother's monthly household allowance to buy vast quantities of Paine's fireworks, he set himself, in all his sartorial splendor, on fire and raced like a flaming torch into the ocean to quench his personal pyrotechnical display.

On another evening, he was the ring-leader of a group of men who burned up a God-awful looking row of benches which Mr. Bradley, founder of Bradley Beach, had erected on top of the sand dunes between our house and the ocean.

Then there was that Sunday evening when Dad and a friend simulated complete and disorderly intoxication on the boardwalk as they passed the minister and his wife, who exclaimed "for shame, look dear, those are the two men who passed the plate at this morning's service."

One family custom was never broken: the devoting of all Dad's birthday, September 1, to him and to whatever he wanted to do — which brings me to his last birthday, his forty-seventh, when I was seven and, in Dad's judgement, old enough to learn to sail.

That first lesson in sailing was a bit of a hair-raising experience, but it did succeed, as he hoped it would, in starting me off on some sixty-odd years in the sport he loved so well, and which, in turn, became for me a lifelong avocation.

September the first, 1904, dawned clear and bright, as dad, clad meticulously in his silk shirt and white ducks, descended the stairs to his favorite breakfast of codfish cakes and bacon cooked in deep steaming fat. "Annie," he said, or words more or less to the same effect, addressing my mother, "it is high time our boy learned to sail and today is as good a day as any to begin." Unknown to us, he had arranged, a day or two before, to rent a small catboat on Shark River, a shallow body of water between nearby Avon and Belmar, New Jersey.

Mother looked at Fraulein and Fraulein looked back. Neither could swim, and Mother was deathly afraid of boats. But it was Dad's day! A basket lunch was dutifully prepared, and about ten in the morning we four set out in a hired, horse-drawn surrey for the dock where the catboat *Frolic*, awaited us. Dad was happy as a clam, mother morose but determined to grin and bear it as a good wife should. Fraulein muttered to herself in German that nothing good could come of this venture. And I? I, in my boyish way, was delighted with my father's plan of the day, and sure that a real adventure with some humorous overtones lay just ahead. And so it turned out.

The breeze was a moderate southerly as *Frolic* cleared the dock and headed upstream. Dad, happy in his native element, salt water, kept up a lively running commentary on the proper handling of a small, centerboard boat. All of this, obviously, was for my edification and I ate it up. Mother and Fraulein were haughtily indifferent, their only concern apparently being how long the sail would last and how soon they could get back again on terra firma. After a while I was permitted to take the tiller under close supervision.

As luncheon time approached, the southerly built up a bit, as it customarily did in these parts, I was entranced by the spray scudding across the weather bow, the singing of the wind in the rigging and the gentle hiss of the water as it swept along the submerged lee rail. Dad, in his seventh heaven, explained the dangers of an unpremeditated gybe as we came about smartly and ran downwind towards Scott's, a popular shore dinner emporium in Avon in those days. Mother and Fraulein continued a dignified, haughty silence, quite unimpressed.

As *Frolic* approached the dock at Scott's, dad sighted a rowboat tied up on the beach, and a comparatively smooth body of water in the lee of the dock. Suddenly he had one of his famous double-barreled ideas. Turning to mother he shouted above the sound of the increasing wind: "Annie, here's what I am going to do. I plan to run *Frolic* in to leeward of that dock, gybe her all standing, and upset her about a hundred yards offshore. That will teach our boy not to fear upsetting, because all of us will land safely in the belly of the sail and be able to scamper back aboard on the half-submerged weather side via the mast which will then be lying on the water."

"Liph," replied mother in no uncertain terms, "you know I can't swim a stroke. If you do this, I'll never speak to you again."

Fraulein turned white. "Mr. Anable," she said, "if you do this, I will immediately give notice. This time, sir, you have gone entirely too far."

Dad, nothing daunted, retorted: "Quiet, you two women; this

is the one day in the year when I am permitted to have my way without female interference. My plan goes through. Steady all, hold on, here we go."

And go we did as Dad put *Frolic* into a neat gybe with her sheet belayed. Over she went to a chorus of female squeals, and into the mainsail we were pitched, quite unharmed but decidely damp, especially our women folk with their picture hats and veils, long skirts and open parasols. I followed them along the semi-submerged mast to the high side of the boat, floating clear a foot or so above the water, suppressing my laughter with all the power within me. It truly was a humorous sight. Never will I forget the mortified expressions of those two women, and their soggy finery.

Dad, while swimming ashore to commandeer the rowboat and rescue his family, turned on his back and shouted to us, "Well, that wasn't so bad, Annie, was it? Think what a lesson this has taught our boy. If he ever carelessly gybes a boat he has only himself to blame, and he will never forget today." There was no reply from the ladies — only dark looks from mother with a "wait till I get you alone" meaning. Poor Fraulein was too angry to reply.

Dad got the rowboat, put *Frolic's* anchor out, set us ashore, and got a local tradesman to drive us home in his delivery cart — all in complete silence.

All's well that ends well, they say, and so it went. Mother, like the good sport she always was, forgave Dad, Fraulein stayed on with us, and Dad enjoyed the experience to the utmost. He boasted shamelessly at the shore and at his New York office about how he had taught his son not to be afraid of the water and possible capsizing, and had started his sailing career off in the right direction with a baptism by total submersion.

Dad's end came only six weeks later; and without him as a teacher I had to go about the mastering of the art of sailing the hard way, on Barnegat Bay at Bay Head, New Jersey, in cat-rigged sneakboxes. But Dad was right, and my vivid recollection of that capsizing has ever since enlivened and enriched my enjoyment of the sport I learned to love, just as he had loved it before me, and which my son equally enjoys and will carry on long after I embark on my last voyage.

[215]

Chapter XXVIII

"Puly Dificalt" Was Right

ARTHUR HOPPE

ORDERING a yacht by mail, and I speak as an authority, involves you in the whole question of international understanding. As everybody knows, this is a frighteningly important question these days. Most experts in the field — senators, syndicated columnists, and the like — keep telling us that inadequate cultural exchange programs, high tariffs, and other such barriers are the major blocks to proper international understanding. Maybe so. But on this one occasion when I got personally involved in the subject, the only real barrier to international understanding was that half the time neither Mr. Okamoto nor I knew what the other was talking about. Even Mr. Okamoto, now that we are good friends, politely admits this tended to make things "puly dificalt."

Mr. Okamoto, to get the cast straight, is Yutaka Okamoto, the son in Okamoto & Son Boat Yard of Yokohama. He is not to be confused with his father, Mr. M. Okamoto, who enters this chapter only near the end when he forgets the anchor and mooring rope. The younger Mr. Okamoto handles all the American correspondence for the firm because, it was explained to me, his English is better than Mr. M. Okamoto's. The latter, I assume, is monolingual.

Ham had supplied Mr. Okamoto's address. (Perhaps I should have been forewarned. It was etched on his memory.) And I kept it tucked away in my wallet during the two weeks of the great debate. Once Meriwether succumbed, I forbore and waited a full twenty-four hours before dashing a letter off to Japan so as not to show undue haste. Thus it was the following night that I excused myself from the table and hustled off upstairs to the typewriter while she banged the pots around in the kitchen. I don't know what had gotten into Meriwether so suddenly. Before dinner, we'd had what should have been one of the best Children's Hours ever. I mean we really had something to talk about.

[216]

"Isn't she beautiful?" I had said.

"Who?" she said.

"The boat. The *Fleur Bleue*. Isn't that a lovely name? Melodious yet not — well — grandiose."

"Hmmm."

"Anybody would fall in love with her." I had gotten up and was pacing back and forth, waving my martini. "When I first saw her from the stern — hasn't she got a graceful stern? — I knew right away. . . just like that!"

"Oh?"

"I think I know what it is that makes her beautiful. Every line, every splinter of wood, every single little piece is purely functional. There's a reason for everything. It's a functional beauty, a clean sweeping beauty. Nothing hidden. No defects artificially enhanced. Isn't she wonderful?"

"Oh yes."

"A toast," I said. "A toast to the beautiful, wonderful, lovely *Fleur Bleue*."

"I've been meaning to tell you," said Meriwether. "You're drinking too much."

As I say, I don't know what got into her. I don't drink too much. But I wasn't going to argue. I was going to get that letter off. It wasn't that I didn't trust Meriwether to stick by the bargain; it was just that I didn't see the need for further discussion, especially with the mood Meriwether was in.

The letter — I have the thick file of my correspondence with Mr. Okamoto here before me now — reflected my enthusiasm. I opened with a proper oriental bow: "I have been fortunate enough to see Mr. Hammett Gaines's *Fleur Bleue* class sloop. Please accept my congratulations for a beautifully designed, exceptionally well made boat."

And then I got right down to business.

"I am very much interested in purchasing a *Fleur Bleue* class sailboat for myself and my family. I understand from Mr. Gaines that the price is $2500 F.O.B. Yokohama, including sails, mattresses, bow pulpit, jib winches, sink, water tank, outboard motor bracket, mooring line, and boat hook, but without a head or inboard engine.

"If this information is correct, please let me know as soon as possible, and I will airmail you my contract for immediate construction. I should like delivery of the boat by March 1."

My letter was dated October 30. Ham had said the boat would be built in three months. But he had added vaguely that "It might take a little longer," and with what I now realize to be admirable delicacy, that Mr. Okamoto "didn't much like to be hurried." So, eager as I was to lay hands on my beauty, I set the delivery date at March 1 to allow Mr. Okamoto a full five months of uninterrupted craftsmanship.

In one respect, Mr. Okamoto seemed as enthusiastic as I. I had an answer to my letter in just nine days. While speedy, the reply wasn't exactly gratifying.

"I am very sorry," he wrote, "in Japan was metal material and shipping charge rise up from early this year then price was higher than Mr. Gaines boat. I thank you and hope for your good order."

This did little for my good order. It wasn't the obscurity of the letter that got me, it was the clarity of the estimate enclosed: not $2500, but $2772.

"Do you know," said Meriwether, "they wanted ninety-eight cents a pound for lamb chops at the Purity Market today? I tried three other stores and I finally got some for ninety-four. I do hope they're all right."

But also enclosed in Mr. Okamoto's letter were the *Fleur Bleue's* blueprints, a symphony of meticulous white lines on thick paper the color of deep, open ocean. And lettered in a draftsman's neat hand across the top was the legend:

FLEUR BLEUE RACER CRUISER
WINNER OF OSHIMA RACE
IN FREQUENTLY TYPHOON

That did it. I was hooked. For I coud see myself, barechested, gripping the tiller and laughing disdainfully into the teeth of a frequently typhoon. Unfortunately, Meriwether refused to see the value of the boat that could conquer a frequently typhoon.

"Don't you see?" I explained. "She can go through anything."

"Not with me aboard it."

"Not *it, she,*" I said, for this inexplicable predilection of Meriwether's to call boats *it* had been bothering me. "Boats are feminine. They are as feminine as you, dear. And when she gets here, I know you'll learn to love her."

[218]

Mindful of ninety-eight cent lamb chops and all that, I tempered my native American enthusiasm with my native American business prudence and got off a letter to Mr. Okamoto that night saying $2772 was far too much for such a flimsy little craft. I said I noticed from his itemized estimate that those romantic sounding but unessential doodads, such as the bow pulpit and jib-sheet winches, totted up to $183. In line with the old horse-trading theory of splitting the difference, I graciously advised Mr. Okamoto that I would be willing to do without these attractions in order to keep the price down to $2500. In other words, I was asking him only to drop his offer from $2772 to $2683; I would then sacrifice the $183 worth of luxuries and — presto! — we would be back at the original figure.

This letter almost broke up our budding international friendship. I don't know whether it was my new business-like tone or the complexity of the bargain. Whatever it was, Mr. Okamoto retired into the depths of his Japanese shell. A month went by. On December 12, I sent a cablegram: "PLEASE REPLY SOONEST." I think he may have enjoyed the "soonest." Another week passed. Then, on December 23, the long-awaited envelope, with the familiar inscrutable Buddhas on the stamps, turned up in the mailbox. I ripped open the envelope with trembling hands and read:

"Okamoto & Son Boat Yard and wishes you a Merry Christmas and a Happy New Year."

During the weeks that followed, as I wrote one plaintive letter after another and received no reply, I began to develop a fatalistic oriental understanding of the unimportance of time. I moped about the house, imagining and discarding a hundred reasons why the mail brought no word of my *Fleur Bleue*.

"I know just how you feel, Daddy," said Dazey, hugging me as I sat slumped in my easy chair. "You know that Roger Cipriolani? Now he won't even speak to me." And she began to cry, squeezing out the bitter tears of unrequited love.

It was good to have sympathy. Meriwether was no help. Her initial pique, which I found bearable, had given way to an irrepressible cheeriness, which I found unbearable. She would whisk about the house, flicking away with a duster and singing, "No letter to-day-yay" — a very soulful tune.

On January 19, after more than two months of silence, my penance was well rewarded. The letter from Mr. Okamoto began by

[219]

apologizing for the "dary in repling" to my "letters and teleglam," explaining that he had been "puly busy" with year-end inventory and all. Besides, "In Japan puly dificalt make estimate in Dicemver because every thing gone up every year." He said he was terribly sorry, but "we are puly hard cut off $2500 that yours says . . . but this time we going to cut off price to $2600 F.O.B. Yokohama. After yours please tell $2772 before we said."

"Hah!" said Meriwether triumphantly. "See? He's jacking up the price on you. Just like Purity. Do you know lamb chops are . . ."

"Hah!" I said triumphantly. "He's jacking *down* the price. Look, he isn't leaving off the bow pulpit, the winches, and all those other extras."

"Oh?" said Meriwether. "You know I don't understand those things."

And I cheerfully explained that Mr. Okamoto's letter meant he was willing to deliver the boat for $2600 *with* the $183 worth of extras, instead of accepting my magnanimous offer of $2500 *without* them. To put it another way, he was saying he couldn't possibly build the staunch little vessel for the ridiculously low figure of $2683; the very best he could do was $2600. International understanding, I was beginning to see, really does work both ways. I had my order in triplicate on its way by airmail before the day was out.

There was more to Mr. Okamoto's letter, such as: "We delively for your boat end of may," and "We wont go to San Francisco and race your bay this summer please help me." The first was disappointing as I had dreamed of delively in March so that I might be sailing by springtime. The second left me nonplussed. I even thought it a little uncalled for, since I hadn't even invited Mr. Okamoto to race on our bay. But such negative bumptiousness didn't sound like Mr. Okamoto, and I puzzled over the phrase until I cracked it: "Wont" means "want" in Mr. Okamoto's English. At last, the Rosetta stone.

That letter started me on the way to becoming one of the world's few living authorities on Okamoto's English. As the months followed one another and he faithfully answered my questions about equipment and construction details, my proficiency became astounding. Here, for the benefit of cryptographers and philologists, are some sample exercises in this rare script:

Q. Could Mr. Okamoto prepare the boat for the installation of an engine?

A. "Shaft and propeller cost plus $40 includ engine bed, please send me catrogu, and shaft through side because must to keep clear of rudder shaft."

(This is child's play: Mr. Okamoto would be glad to install the propeller, shaft and engine mountings for an additional $40, but I should send him a picture of the engine from a catalogue, so that he would know where to place these objects. The propeller shaft must be offset to keep it out of the way of the rudder.)

Q. Could he supply fenders and life rings?

A. "Japanese fender is very pure, life rings, too, you fix in stats better."

(For the intermediate student: Japanese fenders and life rings are of poor quality, so one would be wiser to purchase them in the United States.)

Q. How about an anchor for the boat?

A. "We have 2d hand Dunhorse ancor from U.S. Navy that 30 Lbs., one but biger for her but price only $17."

(A cunning problem because it demands technical knowledge — namely the technical knowledge, acquired through numerous telephone calls to nearby naval bases, that the United States Navy had never heard of a Dunhorse anchor. A Danforth anchor seemed the closest likelihood. The rest, of course, is a snap: a thirty-pound anchor is too big for the boat, but the price is right.)

I wrote that I'd love the 2d hand anchor, but was wisely rejecting Japanese fenders. As for the engine, I had decided against it. The engine was Meriwether's idea. I had inadvertently left one of my magazines open to an article entitled, *"Why* Diesel Engines Are Safe."* Meriwether, attracted by the last word, read enough to discover diesel fuel couldn't explode. She did.

"Why didn't you tell me about this?" she said. "We can put one of these diesel things in the thing."

So I priced diesel engines. The price, with fuel tanks and whatnots, was a solid one thousand dollars, which was an awful lot of lamb chops.

"I'm going to buy you a nice outboard motor for your birthday," I told her.

"I'd rather have a surprise," she said.

[221]

So I surprised her. I bought her a head. For us iron men in wooden ships, I figured, a wooden bucket is fine. But for a lady, like Meriwether, I could see that a real, flushing head would be a delightful gift and might make all the difference. Mr. Okamoto, in his incredibly honest fashion, advised me that Japanese heads were very pure. Luckily, I came across an ad in one of my magazines placed by a fine old reputable Rhode Island firm — "A Head That Will Lift Your Heart!" It was a beauty. "All castings made from virgin metal in our own factory . . . gleaming white vitreous china bowl, sparkling solid brass pumping handle . . ." I got an order off right away, asking them to gift wrap it and to make sure it arrived before March 7, Meriwether's birthday.

It arrived March 5. Meriwether called me at work, all excited by the big, mysterious packing crate. And she prevailed on me to let her open it that evening, even though her birthday was still forty-eight hours away. She loves surprises so.

"What," said Meriwether as she tore at the wrappings, *"is that?"*

I won't describe the scene that followed. Sometimes women are terribly juvenile. But I do think the whole affair might have gone better if they hadn't forgotten to gift wrap it.

I suppose I should have spent more time trying to understand Meriwether during those difficult days. But I was having enough trouble trying to understand Mr. Okamoto. What did he mean "bottom paint must lunching before dry"? Or, "tyde up jib crew these cost $15"? What I didn't understand, I ignored. And I regret ignoring tyde up jib crew. I assume had I dispatched Mr. Okamoto $15, he would have shipped me several small Japanese sailors secured in a neat bundle. And, as it turned out, they would have come in handy.

These intellectual challenges were not enough, however, and I spent most of my days and much of my nights dwelling on dreams of the unbelievably rosy era that would dawn when the boat arrived. The days seemed as endless as they do to a small boy waiting for Christmas. Mr. Okamoto had promised to let me know three weeks ahead of time the name of the freighter which would carry my little vessel across the broad Pacific. This meant, I figured happily, that I should be getting a letter by May 10, at the latest, if he were to make delivery by the end of that month. I could hardly wait. May 10 finally came. So did May 11, May 12, May 13. . . . At 10:30 A.M.

on the day of May 28, the postman casually dropped an airmail letter from Japan in our mailbox.

"Puly soon now," the letter read, "I can sent to you pictur of your boat with planking on."

"That's too bad," said Meriwether.

But even Mr. Okamoto realized he couldn't stop there. And he went on to say he was enthusiastic about a suggestion of mine, made several months previously, for converting the cockpit into a double bed so we could sleep above decks on warm nights.

"I understand for your idea of cockpit," he wrote, "and I like your idea too because summer time very nice place for sleep puly kool."

Puly kool was right. I'm afraid I forgot all those hard-learned lessons about the value of patience and understanding. I fired off my reply at 11:07 A.M. asking him bluntly when the hell he was going to make delivery. There went Mr. Okamoto, right back into his inscrutable oriental shell. And he didn't let out a peep all through the month of June.

That, let me say, was a mighty trying month. It wasn't only Mr. Okamoto; it was Meriwether. And it wasn't that she was grouchy; it was that she was cheery. She would bounce around the house singing that infernal, "No letters today-yay. . . ." And I would stomp upstairs to get off another bulletin to Japan, demanding, commanding, or more often, just plaintive. The trouble was that Meriwether couldn't seem to comprehend the seriousness of our situation. My vacation was scheduled for July, and one of the foremost *we coulds* in the great debate had been the incentive that *we could* spend two glorious, sun-filled, fun-filled weeks cruising in what is known as the Delta — a network of hundreds of miles of narrow, meandering slough where the San Joaquin and Sacramento rivers join some fifty miles inland from San Francisco. The idea had a measure of appeal even for Meriwether. We had driven through the area by car and what appealed to her was the narrowness of these quiet sloughs — never would she be more than twenty-five feet from dry land.

But as June waned, it became increasingly clear that the boat was not going to arrive in time for my July vacation. Meriwether suggested — I'm sure she was being facetious — that we could spend the two weeks at some silly resort. But, obviously, there was only one

[223]

course of action. I would have to change my vacation dates. As any-one who has worked in a large office can testify, such a project equates with squaring the circle. In our office, the vacation list some-what resembled a General Motors parts list. To it were appended seniority lists and such warnings as: "72 Hrs. to Choose" and "No More Than 3 Off At One Time!"

It was the creation of an assistant managing editor named Jano-witz, a thin-lipped definitely unfriendly gentleman. He had entered each name in its proper little square. In ink. And he regarded the work as immutable as the stone tablets of Moses. Yet my plight was so desperate that I was actually screwing up my courage to approach him with a direct plea of hardship, a foolhardy dream at best. But then, as though an unseen hand intervened, a fellow reporter thoughtfully misspelled the middle name of the publisher in a pic-ture caption, thereby producing two scratched-out squares on the chart, beginning with the one labeled "Aug. 6." While Janowitz was by no means pleased at the thought of inking over my name in the July boxes and penning it into the August squares — "That'll make a hell of a mess," he said — he finally acceded.

But even with this act of grace, by the end of June, I was get-ting downright panicky. I simmered and I stewed and, on July 2, I boiled over. I picked up the phone and said, "Get me Japan!" It would have been a more impressive scene if Meriwether hadn't been standing at my side with our three-minute hour glass egg timer in hand, ready to make signals like a radio director. The receiver emitted vague clickings and whirrings accompanied by far-off disembodied voices which seemed filled with cosmic foreboding.

"Sun spots," said the operator. "I am sorry, sir, we have tempo-rarily lost communication with Japan."

They had lost communication with Japan. I viewed the sun spots as divine interference. "Star-crossed," was the way I put it. Meriwether, who had calculated the call would cost twelve chops for the first three minutes, agreed the sun spots were an omen. She took it awfully well. The sun spots delayed the call three days, but when I did eventually get through to Mr. Okamoto, the connection was as clear as a bell.

"Harro?" said Mr. Okamoto.

"Hello — Mr. — Okamoto — How — are — you?" I said carefully, my fingers tapping the telephone stand nervously as the sand began flowing through the egg timer.

"Fine," said Mr. Okamoto distinctly. "Thank you."

"When is my boat going to be finished and what ship is she coming on?" I asked, all in one breath.

I could hear Mr. Okamoto's reply, which sounded startled, but I couldn't understand any part of it. I suddenly realized that my months of study of Mr. Okamoto's language had totally failed to prepare me for this oral exam.

"*When?*" I repeated.

This time his answer was more voluble and I did make out one word, which was "boat." The rest was undecipherable.

"What?" I said.

We kept this up until the last grains of sand were sifting down and Meriwether was making scissor-like motions with her fingers.

"Well," I said, giving up, "thank you, Mr. Okamoto. It was nice talking to you."

"Thank you very much," he replied, quite clearly. "I liked talkink to you."

"What did he say?" Meriwether asked politely as I hung up.

"Not much," I said.

"Well," she said, "nothing ventured, nothing lost."

But the expensive transpacific call did do some good. For, five days later, at long last, a letter arrived from Mr. Okamoto.

"Thank you very much for your telephone of today," it began. "I am very soory delay to delively. Boat finish 16th of this month and I wont Ship 19th of July."

"He won't?" said Meriwether hopefully.

"He will," I said confidently. And he did.

The big white freighter carrying the precious cargo steamed through the Golden Gate shortly after dawn on August 1. I was waiting at the bridge in our car, a sleepy Meriwether beside me, the children dead to the world in the back. I shepherded the ship down the bay and into her pier, fearful that any moment she might strike a rock or explode or inexplicably sink from sight. Somehow the captain kept her afloat, but he took forever nudging her into her berth. It took even longer for the longshoremen to begin peeling back the covers of the forward hatch as though unwrapping some mammoth present. And then, there she was! Gleaming mahogany hull, dark green decks. .

"But you ordered white decks," Meriwether said.

"Well," I answered philosophically, "we can all accept minor imperfections in those things we love."

"I know what you mean," she said.

"But isn't she beautiful?" I said. "Look at the way her transom gleams in the sunlight."

"Very nice," said Meriwether and went off to sit in the car.

For me, it was a long, swirling heavenly, dreamlike day. I just couldn't believe she was here at last. I didn't eat lunch and I couldn't eat dinner, and that evening I hurried up to my typewriter to compose a final, glowing letter to Mr. Okamoto. The boat, as I remarked, only a little pointedly, was well worth waiting for. I didn't even mention the dark green decks. Unfortunately, however, she also seemed to have arrived without her Dunhorse anchor and her mooring lines, as per contract. Since I had her in my grasp, I felt I could afford to be bold, and I did mention these omissions, in passing, at the bottom of my letter.

Mr. Okamoto was quick to apologize. He himself had been out on a "130 mils ocean race" at the time the boat was shipped and was "very sory my father forgot ancor and mooring rope." He said he was flying to San Francisco on business. "I have introducing letters to Mayor of San Francisco from Mayor of Yokohama," he explained. "Can you help me, I won't see him."

And as for the money he owed me for the anchor and rope, "I already changed you doller to yen then puly difficalt change yen to doller now. I pay you at San Francisco in this month."

I thought this was a truly fine gesture and I should say right here that Mr. Okamoto was as good as his word, going to no end of trouble to hunt me down and fork over the dollars. It certainly is one world and it is even more certainly true that in international friendship, mutual understanding is of the gravest importance. For proof we need look no farther than the closing lines of that final letter from Mr. Okamoto pledging to look me up and give me my money:

"I leave Japan 13th this month. I sure wont see you. I thank you."

Chapter XXIX

Life and Death of A Yachtsman

BRIG. E. F. PARKER

IT was getting light on the cold grey morning of November 24, 1922, when a party of Irish Free State soldiers marched their prisoner through the archway into the inner courtyard of Beggar's Bush Barracks in Dublin.

The prisoner was invited to take his stand at the place of execution. He asked that he be not blindfolded, then walked over and shook hands with each of the firing party, telling them to be of good cheer and do their duty as soldiers. They were young men and deeply moved.

He resumed his place, then asked his executioners to come nearer in case they were affected by the bad light. As the rifles were raised; he looked proudly and steadfastly over them. A command: an irregular burst of fire, and Erskine Childers fell. Yachtsman, scholar, writer, soldier, and irreconcilable republican, he died for Ireland's independence.

The independent Ireland for which he struggled, first against the British and later against his fellow Irishmen, is now an accomplished fact, and the compromise of an Irish Free State under British domination, which he would not accept, is buried in the limbo of the past. In Ireland he is a legendary hero — one of the founders of the nation; but outside Ireland, in the rest of the English-speaking world, it is as a yachtsman he is best remembered, and as the author of that splendid yachting thriller "The Riddle of the Sands."

Born of an English father and an Irish mother, both of whom died when he was young, he was brought up by his mother's family in their lovely Irish county mansion Glendalough House, Annamoe, County Wicklow. This was home to him and he loved it dearly. It was there he was captured before his execution and it was in that same house his wife died in 1964 at the age of eighty-seven.

At Glendalough he was not far from the sea and as a boy was

[227]

well acquainted with the fishing boat harbor of Arcklow and the sturdy craft which came and went there, with the little harbor of Wicklow, and with the yachts, coastwise traffic, and shipping of Dublin Bay and the port of Kingstown. In these waters he developed a love for the sea and an understanding of shallow waters with sandy bottoms which was never to leave him.

After completing a conventional British upper-class education at Haileybury College and Cambridge University, he was appointed as a Clerk to the House of Commons in the British Parliament at Westminster in 1895. As soon as he had established himself in London, he acquired a yacht, the *Vixen* — a shallow draft, gaff-rigged sloop of about thirty feet in length and nine-foot beam. She was very robustly built with double diagonal teak planking, and had a large centerboard. Uncomfortable and cramped below, heavy and slow to windward, she was not everyone's cup of tea, but for Erskine Childers she was eminently suitable for those shallow-water explorations among the sands, estuaries, and creeks of the Northern European littoral.

In the long Parliamentary recesses of those unhurried times, he could get away for weeks on end. Sometimes alone, sometimes with a companion, he sailed eastwards down the English Channel across the North Sea to the coasts of Holland and Germany. Among the Frisian Islands, through the creeks at the mouth of the Maas, the Scheldt, the Ems, the Weser, and the Elbe, up through the Kiel canal, and along the Baltic coasts of Germany and Denmark, he made his way. In the open sea in heavy weather he was calm, competent, and unruffled, but he was happiest exploring in shallow water. Drawing practically nothing with his centerboard up, he would go anywhere a duck could swim and with his robust hull and heavy ground tackle, running aground had no terrors for him. Exploring, recording, experimenting, he built up a fund of knowledge of shallow water navigation in those parts which has never been surpassed.

After four years of peaceful sailing and quiet parliamentary business, this calm was broken by the outbreak of the Boer War in South Africa in 1899. Erskine Childers, determined to be in at the beginning, took off as a volunteer in the Honorable Artillery Company — an organization of gentlemen volunteers — and spent the whole war as a horse driver in an artillery battery. After the war was over in 1901, he went back to his job in Parliament, but with a changed outlook. He had become a liberal with a strong anti-colonial prejudice and a confirmed belief in freedom for oppressed nations directed now toward Ireland, his adopted homeland. He also had a strong desire to resume his sailing which he did in his new yacht the *Sunbeam,* a fifteen tonner about forty feet long in which he started afresh his cruises in North Sea waters.

After his first season in *Sunbeam,* he wrote the "Riddle of the Sands." The plot (as most yachtsmen know) is based on two yachtsmen in a little sloop rather like *Vixen* discovering, among the creeks and inlets behind the Frisian Islands, a German scheme for the sudden invasion of the British Isles by troops, towed in barges, disgorging from tiny harbors behind the island curtain where they could easily be hidden away. With his extensive knowledge of the waters, the tale was plausible, convincing, and exciting. Its effect on British Naval thinking, and on the general public, was so profound that dispositions were altered to meet such a threat; and two naval officers who went (or were sent?) to investigate the possibilities of the scheme were seized and imprisoned by the Germans as spies.

Shortly after the publication of "The Riddle" — in 1903 — Erskine went to Boston, Massachusetts, as a representative of the Honorable Artillery Company of London to be entertained by the Ancient and Honorable Company of Artillery of Massachusetts. Shy, quiet, and retiring, he was happier at sea, or with his books than in the cocktail party circuit, and found the lavish Boston hospitality overwhelming. He was getting frantic when one day at lunch he met Mary Osgood. She too was quiet and determined, also attractive.

She had read "The Riddle" and others of his books, was mad keen on sailing, and shared with him a feeling of common cause against oppression and tyranny. The Osgood family had immigrated to New England in 1648 and were active in the American revolution from the time of the Boston Tea Party — that may have been a contributory cause.

In no time they were married and, as a wedding present, her father gave them the yacht *Asgard* which was specially built for them. *Asgard* was a 50-foot gaff ketch designed by Colin Archer and built by him to a very robust specification in Larvik, Norway. She was a small edition of Nansen's *Fram* of Arctic fame.

[229]

Molly Childers loved *Asgard* and went everywhere in her with her husband. Though slightly crippled (she had a spinal injury when young), she could navigate, steer, and work the ship; often they made long passages with only the two of them and a paid hand. Despite having a large sea-going vessel, Erskine never quite got over his passion for creeping about inshore. To quote from the log of one trip on which they visited Denmark, Sweden, Finland, and Russia:

"You cannot imagine the charm of cruising far north in midsummer. In Finland there was no night, really; sunset and dawn melted into one another and the color of the sea, islands, and sky were exquisite.

"Now, of course, we are down south again and things are more normal. It is a curious country, the Northern Baltic. The shore from Petersburg by Finland and Aland to Sweden is all fringed by tiny islands and rocks and shoals, but there are passages between them marked by buoys and lights, and if you like, and have a fair wind, you can sail in there like threading a needle or sewing a very intricate hem. It is delightful but very tiring work, and we have not done much of it, but most in the open sea."

During these halycon years, 1905 to 1910, Erskine got more and more concerned about the state of his unhappy country, Ireland, and he eventually resigned from the House of Commons to devote himself wholeheartedly to the cause of Home Rule. In this he had the full support of his wife who believed fervently in the cause, and who used her considerable charm and powers of persuasion to further its ends.

The ramifications of English-Irish politics of the period immediately before the first World War were so complex that it is impossible to make them comprehensible in a paragraph. It is enough to say that when the Ulster Volunteers started to arm themselves in 1914, Erskine Childers was convinced that the rest of Ireland would be unarmed and defenseless against the Ulstermen, and Home Rule would be in jeopardy unless the South armed, too. He decided to get arms for the Southern Irish Volunteers.

The revolutiontary fervor of both the Childers and their sailing experiences, were to be combined in this operation for *Asgard* was the chosen vehicle for the gun-running expedition.

He collected his crew in Conway, North Wales, on July 1, 1914. As well as the two Childers, there was a young attractive girl called Mary Spring-Rice, a British Army pilot, Gordon Shephard (on leave at the time), and two fishermen from Donegal. They set sail in fair weather down the Welsh coast, rounded Land's End, and made their way down the English Channel to Cowes, England, where they brought up in the anchorage. There they were met according to plan by another famous Irish yachtsman, Conor O'Brien, who brought his 60-foot yacht *Kelpie* to anchor alongside.

When plans had been coordinated, *Asgard* and *Kelpie* set sail from Cowes for their rendezvous in the North Sea with the German tug *Gladiator* which was bringing the arms. On Sunday, July 12, the *Kelpie* arrived first off the Ruyingen Light Vessel near the Belgian coast and took her share of arms on board. The *Asgard* arrived soon after, lay alongside the tug, and started to transfer the cargo from the holds of the tug into the saloon, cabins, gangways, and every bit of space aboard. The wrappings had to be taken off the rifles to get them in, and whole chunks were ripped out of the cabin to make space. The crew, both men and women, worked through the night stowing and lashing. By dawn 900 rifles and 29,000 rounds of ammunition were aboard. The yacht was low in the water and little space was left for living. The tug took them in tow for a short way, and then they set sail. They were on their own.

Beating, she heeled over so far, and got so low in the water, that Childers ditched four thousand rounds of ammunition; but he held on grimly to the rest and battled on. Off Plymouth, the British fleet were out exercising and *Asgard* was suddenly surrounded by warships. A shot was fired and hearts sank into boots. Preparations were made to heave-to and submit to search, but before they could act, the threatening warship sheered off and fired a shot in another direction. It was target practice. Hearts rose again and they continued.

It was uncomfortable going. Off watch, the two women could only crawl in under the doghouse and lie on top of the rifles with only a couple of feet clear below the deckbeams. The wind was fresh and mostly from ahead and cooking was almost impossible. Round Land's End, they were off the wind and with their sheets eased, made good progress to the north. They closed with the land near Milford Haven in South Wales, anchored close inshore in the dark, and put Gordon Shephard ashore in the dinghy. His leave was up.

From Milford Haven, it was only a short haul down the Irish Sea to Howth where they arrived on Sunday, July 26 — thirteen days after they had collected the arms from the *Gladiator*. A motorboat was supposed to come out and give them a signal if all was clear to land, but no motorboat showed. Childers drove straight in under sail and laid the yacht alongside the quay. All was well; the volunteers were there and so too was Gordon Shephard who took their lines. He had slipped away from his unit and taken the packet boat over.

Four coastguards had seen the landing and rowed across toward the *Asgard* but, swiftly appreciating the situation, they withdrew quickly. Later they fired off rockets to give an alarm. It was no use. "A thousand men with guns on their shoulders were marching on Dublin town."

Conor O'Brien's consignment an the *Kelpie* was landed successfully a week later on the Wicklow coast.

It is difficult at such a distance in time to understand the loyalties of those, such as the *Asgard's* gun-running crew, who were concerned with the struggle for Irish independence. They were not against England, they were loyal to her after their fashion; but above all they were for Ireland and freedom. Attractive, perky little Mary Spring-Rice, who was the originator of the gun-running idea, belonged to the family of Lord Monteagle which had a distinguished record of service to the Crown.

When World War I broke out, Erskine Childers, too, showed his loyalty to the King and reported at once for duty as an officer of the Royal Naval Volunteer Reserve. Strangely enough, those in authority used sense instead of a pin when choosing his assignment; he was sent to Naval intelligence and given the job of reconnaissance over those enemy-held North Sea coasts which he knew so well. To do this, he had to fly aeroplanes, and so he became one of the pioneers of British Naval flying. Flying suited his yachting skills and on one occasion he combined both when he crashed his plane in a minefield. Rigging a sail out of some wing fabric, he sailed the remains and himself out again and returned to base.

In the North Sea, in English bases, and in the Mediterranean, he served the Navy well. His astute brain, his gallantry (for which he was awarded the Distinguished Service Cross), and the practical common sense of his yachting background made him an excellent

[232]

pilot and a reliable reconnaissance officer. Yet all the time he had his eye on Ireland and followed closely the development of the Home Rule struggle. He was horrified by the 1916 rebellion (made possible by the arms he had smuggled in though that was not what he had brought them for); but later he gradually became convinced that a modified system of home rule was not enough and that a revolution following the lines of the 1916 rebellion was inevitable and necessary.

When the war was over, he returned to Ireland, threw up his British citizenship, and devoted himself (with his wife's full support) to the republican movement. He came to England in 1921 as the Secretary of the Irish Delegation to the Treaty discussions which were to seek a final ending of the age-old conflict.

The solution arrived at disgusted him. He was by temperament incapable of compromise, and would not accept an outcome which was less than the independence he thought essential. With his columns of faithful republicans, he took to the hills and harried the newly founded establishment. Encouraged by the British, the Free State regime sought and eventually caught him in his boyhood home. From there he was taken to the prison from which he never came out.

His last words written in his cell when the feet of those who were to summon him to his death were already sounding in the corridor were:

"My beloved country, God send you courage, victory, and rest, and to all our people harmony and love."

CHAPTER XXX

Go On To Sea

AUBREY ANABLE

THE Monday morning newspaper carried the item: "Max Sorensen, caretaker of several retired barges belonging to the Seaboard Lighterage Company moored at the foot of East Broad and River streets, was found dead in a leaking dinghy offshore of Tybee Island yesterday, two miles from the mouth of the Savannah River. John Bailey, 34, deckhand aboard the U.S. Geodetic vessel *Sea Sprite*, spotted the drifting small boat shortly before sunset. Also rescued was a thirteen year old boy who, etc. . ."

It was a brief and prosaic obituary of a man with a dream. It deserved fuller treatment.

Had the newspaper writer been apprized of those other facts which were known to me, I am sure he would have extended himself. People may not understand dreamers, but they are generally sympathetic toward them much as savages respect the insane.

On the other hand, perhaps the reporter knew what he was doing. Undoubtedly, from his materialistic perspective, he must have reasoned that the passing of an obscure, lonely old man hardly warranted more space than he gave him.

Yet. . . .

I knew him only as Old Swede. He must have been about seventy years of age. Gnarled, he bent a bit to starboard because of some spinal affliction. His arms were thin but sinewy, his wasted neck corded, his eyes were a washed-out blue, but ever fastened on some horizon unseen by most others. He always wore a faded but clean pair of coveralls over a blue flannel shirt. On his grey and grizzled head was perched a peaked white cap without markings.

I met him first when I was a Western Union messenger boy working after school hours. Picking up and delivering telegrams was not our exclusive function. We ran errands for anybody who required our services in that direction, and was willing to pay the basic fifty-cent fee.

A call came into the company's office on Drayton and Byran Streets — only one block from the waterfront — requesting that a messenger be sent down to the foot of East Broad and River.

I was dispatched.

After a bone-jarring ride on my bicycle down the cobblestoned hill from the base of the Bay Street bluff to the wharf below, I found myself regarding several decaying barges which rested on the few feet of redolent, muddy beach available at low tide.

It was close to midnight. There was not another soul around. The river flowed smoothly seaward in ebony majesty with only an occasional muttering around the dock pilings. A gentle breeze whispered confidingly in my ear of places visited and yet to be explored. Now and then, I heard the timid twitterings of some wharf rats. Otherwise, quiet brooded like an unseen mantle over an area of the city usually completely deserted shortly after sunset.

I thought I had been sent on a wild goose chase, although a nearby telephone booth suggested validity for my trip. On the point of departing, I was stopped by a man's figure emerging from the housing atop the rear deck of one of the ancient lighters. He carried a glowing hurricane lantern.

"You bane Western Union boy?" a cracked voice hailed me in an obvious Scandinavian accent.

"Yes. You call for one?"

"Yah. Do errand for me, hey?"

"Sure. What is it?"

"Go get for old feller big bottle of beer from grocery store on East Broad Street."

"Okay. Cost you fifty cents service charge."

"Come aboard. Ay give you money."

I laid my bicycle on its side, and made my way up the two rickety boards tied together with frayed rope which served as a gangplank. Old Swede — as I ever after knew him — held out the money to me when I faced him.

"You come right back?" he probed anxiously, with an appealing, friendly little smile on his seamed, wrinkled face which revealed the few surviving teeth of his original store. "You don't take money from old man and not come back, hey, you nice li'l feller?"

I knew what actuated his apprehension. Some of my less conscientious young colleagues occasionally failed to fulfill their obligations after accepting payment; particularly when the client suggested the ingenuous character of my present negotiator.

"I'll be back," I promised. "Won't be long."

Nice li'l feller or not, I had my scruples. I went back uphill, and within the half hour returned, puffing with my load, a gallon bottle of beer. I deposited it on the deck before the old man who sat staring dreamily out across the river in the precise spot I had left him. I held out the change due him from my purchase in his behalf.

"You keep money," he told me kindly, "You nice li'l feller."

Taken by my surroundings at this witching hour . . . placidly flowing river sliding on its irresistible course to the open sea . . . the distant lights reflected in its mysterious bosom from the Gulf Oil docks on the opposite Carolina shore . . . the soft waterfront breeze cooling my sweat bedewed brow . . . I was reluctant to leave this soothing oasis.

The old man looked at me hopefully. "You maybe like stay awhile, li'l feller? Maybe you like talk a bit with Old Swede?" He hung anxiously onto my words. It was obvious I could alleviate some of his galling loneliness. Unable to think of anything better to do at this moment than return to the Western Union office, I agreed.

"Sure. Glad to."

"Wait!" said my companion. "I get glass for drink." He disappeared into the little house. A few seconds later, he was back with two large tumblers. These he filled to the foaming brim with beer. He gave one to me. "*Skoal!*" he toasted, and took a satisfying draught.

I hesitated, glass in hand. This would be my first introduction to a liquid boasting an alcoholic content in excess of that of sarsparilla. But not to be out-done by my fellow drinker's sophistication, I sacrificed my virginity.

I must confess I took small pleasure in this primary experiment with the tart blandishments of the brewer's art. Rolling the beer around in my mouth, I assumed, like spinach, it must be an acquired taste. With some effort, I swallowed it. At least it was wet, and it was cold.

[236]

Old Swede, having consumed his first glass, poured himself another. It slid down his throat with relished ease.

"It's nice down here," I remarked, as I took a seat on the second of the two broken chairs available.

The pervasive effluvia of dank river bottom mud titillated my nostrils. Some distance down the dock, the lights of a small freighter lit a limited area mysteriously her own. A few hundred feet up river, where the United States Coast Guard Cutter *Yamacraw* was moored, a radio sprayed a thin patina of dance music over the scene.

"Nice!" The old man echoed my word so explosively I was momentarily startled. "Is nice maybe for mud crab!" he declared with surprising bitterness. "Is nice maybe for lazy old alligator! Is not nice for feller who sail sea to sit on broken old barge stuck in stinking mud watching ships go past!"

I assumed some philosophical comment on my part was called for in return. Limited familiarity with the art caused me to flounder. To cover my confusion, I took a deep gulp of my beer and gagged with corresponding vitality.

With his fourth glass, Old Swede grew a little mellow. "Hey, Sven, you feller, what you say?"

For a second, I thought he was talking to someone else. He was not. Apparently, I had assumed a new identity in his mind: someone called "Sven" he had either known in his past or presently conjured up in a wandering mind. Child? Grandson? Young friend? I never knew, and was not to learn. "Sven" I was to my elderly companion, and "Sven" I was to remain for the time that was left to our relationship. It was not very long. Culminating as it did in tragedy flecked with nostalgia, it was only years later I was mature enough to relate it to its proper perspective.

"You t'ank Ay like this kind of life?" the old man asked me. "Bane sad t'ing for old deep water sailor to sit on busted barge. Seagulls better off. Got wings. Fly out any time. Old sailor ballasted with barnacles. Can't scrape off. He go in deep water now, they sink him!"

Warmed to the conversation by the effects of the beer I had drunk, and feeling, as a consequence, foolishly effervescent, "You mean," I interposed, "you want to go back to sea?"

He replied broodingly, "Not fit t'ing for sailor to die on mudbank so far from open water."

[237]

Speciously, I consoled him, "We're not far away. Only eighteen miles down river."

"Where Ay get ship?" he demanded loudly. "Who sign on old hand with yaw to starb'd? Ay been beached for good!" He sighed gloomily. "Marooned! Old sailor, he finish!"

I would have liked to offer some palliative words to relieve my companion's unhappiness. The adroitness to fashion them as comfortably as I wished, however, did not fall within my thirteen-year-old dexterity.

"You're not so old," was all I could lamely substitute for my conscious inadequacy to do better.

By this time, Old Swede was on his sixth glass of beer. I was ruing the completion of my first. I felt a little dizzy and mildly nauseous.

From its cupola atop the City Hall, several blocks to the west, on the bluff overlooking the river at the foot of Bull Street, the deep throated clock chimed the three-quarters of an hour. I was due off the job in fifteen minutes at one o'clock.

"Got to be going," I said. "Thanks for the—er—beer."

There was a lightness in my head, and an odd dispute going on between my legs as to the direction each wished to take. Likely I would have stumbled off the edge of the barge into the glutinous mud had not the old man reached out a hand to steady me.

"Ay t'ank you take too much ballast aboard," he chuckled. "Sven, you li'l feller."

"Well, good night," I said.

My companion rose to guide me down the short, improvised gangplank. "You come again maybe talk with old sailor," he prompted eagerly when he had seen me ashore. "Old Swede here all the time. Never go no place," he added wistfully. "Sit like old bird with busted wing on mudbank. You come again," he urged hopefully. "We talk and drink more beer. Yah?"

"Sure. I'll come again," I promised. "As for the beer—." I left my thoughts unspoken. "Good night."

"Good night, Sven, li'l feller."

I retrieved my bicycle. Because of the steepness of the cobblestoned grade, I had to push it before me.

Following this introduction to Old Swede, I visited him several times, but always in the light of day. If the river seemed more prosaic during that time, my talks with my elderly friend never lost any of their original charm for me.

Loneliness made him garrulous. In me, he found an attentive and sympathetic listener to his long-winded stories of vanished years at sea. He had done all I wanted to do; he had seen all I was hoping yet to see.

I was still "Sven" to him. After a few attempts to correct this misnomer, I gave it up, and was content to play the harmless, passive role of the unknown, shadowy personality he imposed on me.

Sunday was a day I particularly enjoyed in Old Swede's company. I had the whole day to myself, unfettered by the restrictions of school or afternoon employment. Corporeally, we went nowhere, adhesively limited as we were to our old mud scow stuck on the dank mudbank within spitting distance of shore.

But the magical voyages we took in conversation and fancy!

Several Sundays later, I was down at the waterfront, shortly after breakfast. The river was quiet, the morning sabbatically hushed. The little municipal ferry boat *Island Queen,* chugging across river to the Seaboard Airline Railway docks, was the only moving object visible. A lounging negro or two, fishing for fat eels off the stringpiece of the wharf, were the only humans in sight.

I came up to the cluster of decaying barges. Old Swede was not in view. I went aboard.

"Mister Swede!" There was no answer. I pushed open the door of the little shack. "You-all in here?" I called in British accent and Southern vernacular. (My parents had brought me to Savannah from London, England, only a few years ago.)

"That you, li'l feller?" The voice was tired and listless. In the sparsely furnished, scrubbed little interior of the shack, I made out the figure of my old friend lying on his bunk. In spite of the early morning heat, he was covered with several blankets.

I stepped down into the room. "Sleeping late?"

"Ay bane tired," the old man answered. His face looked peaked, and his complexion was pallid and marked by a faint, bluish tinge.

Looking at him wonderingly, "You all right?" I questioned. "How come you're covered with all those blankets?"

"Cold," he said. "Ay bane cold."

I disputed the assertion. "It's hot! Going to get hotter by noon!"

[239]

Old Swede smiled ruefully. "Ay t'ank Ay get lazy in old age."
He pushed the blankets aside. "Ay get up. Sit in sun." It took an
obvious effort for him to get to his feet.

"Had breakfast?"

"No appetite. But Ay like to have cup of coffee."

"Want me to put the pot on the stove?"

"You do that, li'l feller. Ay wash up."

Coffee pot in hand, I left the shack. On the wharf nearby was
a fresh water spigot. I filled my receptacle and returned to the scow.

The old man had slipped into his flannel shirt and coveralls.
Laboriously he was pulling on the pair of sneakers he customarily
wore. With one shoe on, and the other in his hand, he paused in
his task to steady himself by holding onto the edge of his bunk. "Ay
feel bit dizzy," he apologized for his action.

"The coffee will make you feel better." I struck a match I
found in a box to one side, and lit the small kerosene stove.

When he had drunk a cup of the hot liquid, the old man
seemed to be more like his former self. "We go topside," he stated.
"Today we have fine fun!"

"What are we going to do?"

"We spend day on river. We take rowboat, and we go have
fun!"

"Gee!" I exclaimed with enthusiasm. "That'll be great! But
where are we going to get a boat?"

"Plenty tied up alongside."

This was true. They belonged to various negro owners who
used them during the week to ferry passengers across the river at
ten cents a head. These latter were too impatient to await the
scheduled crossings of the city ferry.

Since he accommodated the proprietors of the rowboats by
permitting them to tie up to his barge, as well as letting them stow
their oars and oarlocks aboard, Old Swede was able to avail himself
of any of them whenever he so desired.

Bubbling with pleasure in anticipation of our Sunday on the
river, I filled an empty gallon beer jug with fresh water, packed a
pullman-sized loaf of bread and a substantial square of cheese from
my companion's food locker, and we were ready to go.

The Savannah River has a strong current. Surface whirlpools
and areas of curling water visible at close view attest to as much. So,

when Old Swede and I shoved off from the side of the scow in our rowboat, all I had to do was to make for midstream, and there let the river have its will with us.

It was not long before we were carried beyond the city's eastern limits. We found ourselves moving smoothly between far stretching expanses of gently waving marsh grass. To me it was an adventure we had embarked upon worthy of any spirited navigator. Lounging on the thwart, leaning indolently on shipped oars, I drank in the colorful panorama of green swamps, yellow river, and blue summer sky.

The sun grew hotter as we drifted. Close to the water as we sat, we received the full effects of the heat intensified by the reflected rays. Old Swede rested quietly on the stern thwart. Periodically, he wiped the sweat from his brow with a red checked handkerchief.

Soon my perpetual appetite asserted itself. I took several slices of bread, parted them with indelicate chunks of cheese, and then devoted myself to absorbed mastication. My companion declined my offer to make him a duplicate of my sandwich. He contented himself with a mouthful of water.

I was enjoying myself thoroughly. Several time I tried to draw Old Swede into innocuous conversation, but he showed no disposition to share in my exuberance. Presently I posed a pertinent inquiry to which an answer could not be avoided.

"How far we going down river?"

"To sea!" returned my companion in husky tones.

That was all right with me. The sea, however, was still a matter of some ten miles off.

"All the way?" I queried.

"The sea!" repeated Old Swede tensely. "We got to make sea!"

"Be almost another three hours before we get to the mouth of the river," I said. "And its getting awful hot!"

The old man looked at me in some surprise. "Ay feel chill in air."

I heard him with astonishment. Tanned as I was by months of indifferent exposure to our southern sun, I was now, nevertheless, feeling its bite. The exposed areas of my body were showing a dull red tinge. Old Swede leatherly face, basically fair skinned, was beginning to assume a truly disconcerting color. It was not a wholesome outdoor look, but a disturbing mixture of unprepossessing blue and red mottled tints verging on the purplish.

Squinting at the sun, I said, "It's after twelve. Maybe we had better row ashore and take shelter awhile under that clump of scrub palms."

"No! No, Sven, li'l feller!" The old man's voice was so urgent in discouragment of my proposal that I became automatically infected by the tension I recognized behind it, and without understanding why. "Is no time!" he declared with palpable anxiety. "We got to get down to sea."

Why the destination to be achieved was so vital, I could not fathom. But my friend's poorly concealed excitement imparted to his words a sense of such extreme importance, I could not ignore them. Temporarily stampeded by the mysterious and frightening significance they seemed to have, I began to row rapidly. This manifestation of personal insanity I soon gave up as the sweat drenched my shirt and trousers.

We continued to drift with the current.

Soon we were abreast of old Fort Pulaski of Georgia Civil War fame — now a national monument — with its time-worn walls and ball-scarred ramparts. It disappeared when we rounded a bend in the river.

In another hour, we were off the little wooden frame waterside home of the celebrated "Waving Girl" as she was known in ports the world over.

And there she was: a slender figure on the small front porch waving a handkerchief as we floated by. . . waving. . . waving. . . until we disappeared from her view around another curve of the waterways. She had lived many lonely years in her little house, surrounded by empty, far-flung muddy fields of marsh grass — ever since the man she was to have married went off to sea and never returned. From that time on, she had never failed to greet every passing ship in the manner she had done to us, every boat, big and small. At night, a light shone uninterruptedly in her window as a beacon of hope. There was not a ship that passed up or down the river which did not blow its whistle in greeting or farewell to the faithful creature mantaning her pathetic vigil. She had become a legend in her lifetime throughout the seven seas.

In the distance ahead, I could see the rearing white Tybee Island lighthouse on the far edge of the Fort Screven reservation, at that time a small army installation, now, since its military deactivation, a real estate development. The marker meant we were within sight of the sea.

The river widened considerably as we approached its mouth. There was a noticeable freshening of the breeze. Yet the sun had lost none of its virulence. It was only practical that we should consider landing in the vicinity of the lighthouse.

I mentioned this desirability to Old Swede. He rejected the suggestion fiercely.

"We go on to the sea!" he rasped. His breath came in small gasps. "Sven, li'l feller," he implored, "we go on to sea! You do like old feller say!"

My friend's alarming appearance now had succeeded in making a disturbing impression even on my previously youthful imperceptiveness. I thought he looked ghastly as he lay in a state of apparent exhaustion on the bottom of the boat, the back of his head resting on the thwart.

"You like some water?" I asked uncertainly resorting to the one panacea I could think of likely to mitigate his obvious discomfort.

He did not reply. The boat began to rock gently as the smooth surges of the tidal current began to manifest themselves. Soon we were dipping in rolling swells. Miniature scrolls of spray tumbled from our bow. The wind grew brisker.

We had passed the river mouth.

Old Swede suddenly sat bolt upright. He stared at the horizon with the look of one who had had some impossible promise fulfilled. It was as if a great burden had been lifted from his heart. Falteringly, he removed his cap to let the wind finger his sparse grey hair. He took a deep breath of the salt air to fill his lungs to the utmost. After many a weary year, old friends had met once again — or so it seemed to me as I watched his strange performance.

Holding onto the sides of the boat to brace myself against the roll, I now spoke firmly to my companion.

"We better head back a ways until we pass those breakers, and make shore at Fort Screven. We get too far out, we might have trouble putting back."

Old Swede did not answer me. He had slumped back against the thwart, chin on his chest.

I glanced about me with some dismay. For some time now, I had been aware of several inches of water sloshing over the bottom of the boat. Parts of the calking had opened. Although I was not unduly alarmed by this development, it added nothing to my peace of mind, for we had swept farther to sea than I liked.

Apparently oblivious to the water washing against his legs and thighs, the old man appeared to have dozed off. I decided to take matters into my own hands now.

I turned the boat about. The tide was running against us. With every foot gained by struggling with the oars, three were lost between strokes. Frankly viewed, the situation was upsetting.

Panting from my exertions, I gave up. Old Swede still slept, wedged in the corner of the boat. When I scanned the receding shore line, I was surprised to see how small the bathers looked on the beach. For the first time, I began to worry about the effect my prolonged absence from home would have on my parents.

Then she hove into sight: a white painted, yacht-like vessel. She looked as if she might pass by some distance off, but suddenly, she changed her course and bore down on us. Presently we were alongside each other. . .

Back in the city, the coroner said Old Swede had died of congestive heart failure. How he had survived those gruelling, heat-packed hours on the river was a matter for considerable speculation.

But that was because the coroner did not know Old Swede as I did — as neither did he understand the driving compulsion the old man felt to spend that Sunday on the river.

CHAPTER XXXI

A Little to the S'uth'ard

HAROLD COOLEY

IN this day of electronic wonders such as radio direction finders and depth recorders, much of the old thrill has been removed from navigating in thick weather. It might be fairer to say that much of the risk has been removed. I suspect that the thrill remains. I wouldn't know because I never have been shipmates with any of these modern gadgets.

There's one thing I do know about, however, and that's the non-electronic wonder of the natural instinct of sea-fairing men which guides them to a chosen destination like homing pigeons, thick weather or thin. This is the story of a personal experience with one such man.

The whole thing began in the winter of 1937 when I read an article in a Portland, Maine, newspaper about a lighthouse keeper at a lonely post on Gannet Rock out in the middle of the Bay of Fundy. So vividly did the article portray the solitude of that tall black and white striped lighthouse which warned all vessels away from a terrible expanse of ledges and shoal water that I visualised a visit to the spot on my next cruise Down East.

I sent the newspaper clipping to the Coast Guard station on Grand Manan Island and asked for advice about my proposed visit to Gannet. The advice came promptly and it boiled down to not attempting to run in thick weather because of the strong Fundy currents and the absence of any shelter at Gannet. It also told me that the lighthouse keeper was in the habit of talking, by short wave, with a ham operator in Portland.

It was easy to locate the ham in question and a few days later I talked with the Gannet keeper. I told him that I was having a 30-foot motor sailer built and that I was planning a shakedown cruise to Gannet the coming July. In my enthusiasm, I even named the day that we should get there. He, in turn, was equally enthusiastic about the prospects of a visit and repeated the Coast Guard warning about attempting the trip in the fog.

"Even the local fishermen keep away from here in thick weather," he said.

Well, that was that. At long last my staunch little ship was finished — a sea-going thirty feet of good white oak and mahogany from the board of "Wink" Warner, powered by a Chrysler Ace motor and with an ample spread of sail.

We sailed out of Portland right on schedule — my brother Blake, the indestructible secretary of the Boston Yacht Club, and two mutual friends making up the crew. A fair wind and clear weather encouraged us to make a night run to Northeast Harbor. That was the end of the fair weather.

The next day, when we were abeam of Petit Manan we entered the great fog barrier of the Bay of Fundy. We had no electronic listening or sounding devices but we did have one of Wilfred White's fine compasses and had had plenty of opportunity on the run from Portland to check it out and find it comfortably free from deviation.

With a good fix on Petit Manan, we laid a course for the whistle off the Little River, throttled the motor to give a steady six knots, furled the sails, checked the time and let her go. As I remember it, it's thirty-five miles from Petit Manan bell to the whistle a couple of miles off Little River Head and that's a pretty long leg in the fog. We got a fix on the horn on Mistake Island after about sixteen miles and about ten miles farther along we caught the booming diaphone horn on Libby Island a couple of miles inshore. Everything was checking out nicely and we ploughed along for the Little River whistle about an hour and a half ahead.

It was getting along toward dark when our time ran out and we shut off the motor to listen for the groaner. No sound. You couldn't see much beyond the bowsprit and the moderate breeze was from the south or southeast and we estimated we had a little farther to go. We started the motor and ran another five minutes, which meant half a mile, shut off again to listen. Still no sound.

Blake was navigating and I was on the wheel. We held a quick consultation and decided to go another half-mile. At the end of that five minutes we still heard no sound coming through that thick blanket of fog. We were satisfied that we had sailed a good course and that we should be on target, so we headed off to port on the course from the whistle to the bell at the mouth of Little River, slowed down to about three knots and set four pairs of eyes straining ahead through the fog for a landfall or anything that would lead to one.

After about ten minutes we decided that we simply had to be close to shore and changed course to starboard to coast for a few minutes. Suddenly there was evidence of a strong current crossing our bow from the direction of shore. We were certain it was the current of Little River emptying into the bay.

And just then we heard the whistle we had previously been seeking — upwind on the starboard bow. We decided to head for it. With darkness falling we had to be sure of our river entrance. Stopping the motor to listen at short intervals, we finally ran the whistle down and I was never happier to see an aid to navigation. Our course to the bell at Little River proved to be accurate and in a few minutes we were safely anchored off Cutler, and mighty glad to be there. It had been a long day.

The next day dawned rainy and miserable and the fog was still pea soup. We decided to lay over a day not only to get acquainted with Cutler but also to have plenty of time to lay our courses with tidal allowances to Grand Manan which was about eleven miles east-southeast of our Little River whistle. Our target was to be the whistle off Southwest Head right under the two-hundred-foot Gull Cliff. We figured that such a bold headland would scale up any self-respecting fog and that we would see the cliff before we hit its base.

After clearing away breakfast the following morning we poked out into the Bay, picked up our whistle and proceeded on our two-hour run. The visibility was, as usual, negligible and when we had about run out our time we had all hands staring ahead for a landfall which seemed more possible than a sight of the whistle we eventually wanted to pick up. My own gaze was riveted across the port bow looking for that two-hundred-foot cliff. Suddenly the fog ahead seemed to darken. I called to Blake, "Look how black that fog is out there." I hadn't finished the sentence before it wasn't fog at all. It was Gull Cliff and we were actually in the rollers at the base. I spun the wheel to starboard and we retreated down the back of the sea that had intended to toss us ashore. It was that close.

A later inspection of the Canadian large scale chart of the area showed that we had made our landfall at the only place that would have permitted such close quarters to the beach. The adjacent shore was littered with boulders running well out to sea.

As we sheered off, the lighthouse keeper above us on the cliff sounded his fog bell vigorously for our benefit. With that extra assurance of our exact position, we had no trouble finding the whistle and rounding into Seal Cove where we tied up to a huge mooring buoy hoping that no local fisherman would come in and kick us off later.

That afternoon a dory came alongside through the fog rowed by a man I'll never forget. He was an ex-Coast Guardsman — a husky gent in his late sixties who had heard of our intended visit to his friend on Gannet. He asked if we'd mind if he came along and we told him we'd be mighty glad to have him, for more reasons than one. It seemed the answer to our navigating problem the next day, and it was.

Our Guardsman captain was aboard right after we had finished breakfast. The fog seemed thicker than ever. We had not yet seen the shore line of Seal Cove in which we were moored. The captain gave our ship a complete inspection. He gave special attention to the mast and its rigging.

"How tall is that mast?" he asked. We told him it was forty feet.

"And how long is the boat?" We told him she was thirty feet on deck.

"Thirty-foot boat and a forty-foot mast," said he. "Around here, we'd have a thirty-foot mast in a forty-foot boat."

Nevertheless, he approved of all he saw and we prepared to get under way. At that point I turned to the Guardsman.

"Captain," I said, "I suspect you've been out to Gannet a good many times, fog or no fog. How would you like to pilot us out?"

He grinned and said he would be glad to do it. It's quite possible that he was more than glad to do his own navigating rather than trust ours but he was kind enough not to say so. As we headed out of the cove he stood in the middle of the cockpit with his back to the compass and to me on the wheel and advised, "You want to come out of here about sou'west." That checked close enough to our chart work of the day before and we held to that course for about ten minutes.

Then the captain turned around and commented, "Seems as though we are a bit too close to the shore on this course. Better come a bit to the s'uth'ard."

I moved over a point or so and he said, "That's good. Hold her there for about an hour."

Now there was some really casual piloting. "A bit to the s'uth'ard and for about an hour." Our chart was in the cabin keeping dry and there was nothing to do but follow the captain's instructions. He had lived a lifetime with that Bay of Fundy current and was personally acquainted with every wave in the Bay. His instinct, I decided, could be as good or better than our chart work. I suggested that the watch below might buy the captain a drink and that seemed quite in order with him. There was no sun and we had no yardarm so what the hell — we all had one.

When we had run about an hour I called "time" to the captain. He was still standing in the middle of the cockpit balancing to the gentle heave of the ship. We were under power at our usual rpm's for fog running and had made about six miles in the captain's "about an hour."

"Shut off the motor," he ordered, "and we listen. We ought to be there."

As the quiet settled down I heard a noise close aboard that sounded like a gas engine.

"What's that noise, Captain?" I asked.

"Oh, that's Don's compressor. He's keeping up pressure on his whistle."

And, at that moment, out of the fog came a tall black and white lighthouse, literally right on top of us. It was only a glimpse we got. We were sliding past at about four knots on the current.

"You'll have to get an anchor overboard," observed the captain. "There's no harbor here and we're making four knots to leeward."

Our thirty-five-pound anchor was all ready and we dropped it from the bowsprit chock and paid out on the rode until we had a good angle and it took hold. By that time, of course, we were alone in the fog again, the lighthouse having long since been swallowed up in the white blanket.

"Now," said the captain, "I'll row a couple of you ashore in the tender for a visit with Don and then the second couple can go."

"Well, said Blake," here's part of a couple that will stay right here."

One of the others also decided to stay and the third joined me in the tender the captain had already brought alongside. He sat on the middle thwart and rigged out his oars. Heading into the current he started to pull with powerful strokes.

"You want to take it a bit easy," I warned him. "Those aren't dory oars you've got there. They're just light drugstore spruce and it wouldn't be good to bust 'em right here."

The captain eased up a trifle but still had to keep the pressure on to make headway against the fast-running current. As for me, I couldn't help thinking what a damn fool proposition the whole thing was. Here we were out in the middle of the Bay of Fundy in a ten-foot dinghy with a total stranger rowing us through thick fog in search of a rock island with a lighthouse—no grub or water on board and a reasonable chance of missing the light entirely and having one hell of a long row to the nearest lee shore.

While I was engaged in such thoughts, all of a sudden, there was the lighthouse, dead ahead and close aboard. We pulled the tender up on the rocky lee shore, secured the painter to a boulder and climbed up the slope to the little house alongside the light. We found Don lunching with his wife and little daughter. They were indeed excited by our visit.

When Don shook hands with me he said, "We were looking for you yesterday." Think of it. Six months before I had told him, over the short wave radio, that we expected to see him on the twenty-second of July and this was the twenty-third because we had lost a day in Cutler. That gives you an idea of what a small world that lighthouse keeper lived in and how much our visit had meant to him.

Well, we chatted a while and then I began to get anxious about the boat. I asked the captain if he thought he could find her. He smiled and answered, "Found the lighthouse, didn't I?" So we said good-by to the keeper and embarked in the dinghy. The captain took up the oars and proceeded down current. Suddenly, right ahead, was our little ship. I swear the captain smelled his way to her. We climbed aboard and weighed anchor.

"Now," said the captain with a smile, "I brought you out here. Suppose you take me home."

I'm not sure that wasn't a damn brave suggestion. At least,

he didn't know all the computing Blake had done to determine the course back to Seal Cove on that particular set of tide. He just turned the job over to us and accepted a twelve-ounce hooker of Scotch and soda.

Little need be said about the next hour and ten minutes but it saw the best navigating job ever turned out by a Cooley. We stuck to our calculations and the first thing we saw was that big mooring buoy in Seal Cove that we had left a few hours before. We saw no trace of the shore line . . . just that buoy.

The captain was delighted and insisted that we take advantage of the high tide and run up the cove to the dock at the head so the people could see the boat. That we did and I guess the whole population of Seal Cove turned out. The captain had a field day. He told them how we had brought him home from Gannet and then proceeded to buy a drink for every male adult . . . with our Scotch.

We needed gas and water. All formalities having been completed we returned to our mooring buoy.

The next morning we left for the westward, still not having seen anything of Seal Cove but that dock area. But if one is enriched by experience, then I'm a millionaire. I'll never forget the way the captain hit that target eight miles out in the Bay of Fundy with its tidal currents without looking at a chart or the compass.

"A little to the s'uth'ard," he said, "for about an hour."

CHAPTER XXXII

The Mysterious Hand

HILAIRE BELLOC

W E awoke early one morning to the noise of the loud clapping of water upon the bows, and I put my head out of the skylight to see little dusty clouds going too quickly across the heaven, and a freshening breeze blowing up from a little south of west, so that all the harbour water was dancing and alive. But the glass was high, and there was no reason why we should not take the sea again, only we must wait for the ebb (which would come in about three hours' time, nearer nine than eight o'clock). For, in that blanketed part of the river down below, we should never get the *Nona* out against the flood.

Nevertheless, I asked my companion whether it might not be wise to take another man, for we were going down the coast, where the rare harbours were shoal, and not easy to enter, and also small, and lay so that, with such a wind, one would have to beat up to them. An extra hand would be an advantage.

Such a hand, therefore, after minute inquiry and searching questions, did we ship; then, all things having been done in their order, and sail set with the second jib and two reefs in the mainsail and one reef forward, we got up the anchor and let her down for the sea.

The hand we had shipped (promising him his journey home by rail within three days at the most) was very well got up in sailor fashion, with his jersey and his peaked cap, the latter worn a trifle to one side, after the fashion of those who are daring, and challenge Aeolus. His trousers, it was true, did not spread out at bottom, like elephant's feet or the mouths of bells, as do the trousers of sailors upon the stage. On the other hand, he would give them a theatrical hitch from time to time—a gesture symbolic of the Main in Drury Lane. He had nothing to do as we dropped down-river, for all was trim. He sat and smoked, and watched the water before him with wistful eyes. I think he was by nature a man sad or saddened; and he was very silent.

On the bar there was no end of a lump, and, as we were blanketed by that high cliff, the *Nona* took it uneasily, chucking up and down with flapping sails and rolling damnably, but in a few moments the strength of the ebb had swept us far enough out to catch the wind again, and we set a course full-and-by; right out for the open, for the large. For we designed to beat in again after a few miles, and so make our way down-channel towards the Cornishmen.

There was certainly quite enough wind: "All the wind there is," as an old Irish sailor said to me once during an Atlantic gale so abominable that he and I could not walk against its icy, sleeting December fury, but had to crawl forward tugging along the rail by main force, all up the windward side. . . . That was a passage worthy of remembrance, for we took three weeks between Europe and the Delaware, the engines and the old frame quite unfit for their task; and in that cheap passage, also, I learned from a stoker two songs: one called *The Corn Beef Can,* and the other called *The Tom Cat.* They are of the great songs of this world.

A man should learn all the songs he can. Songs are a possession, and all men who write good songs are benefactors. No people have so many songs as the English, yet no people sing less in these last sad days of ours. One cannot sing in a book. Could a man sing in a book, willingly would I sing to you here and now in a loud voice *The Corn Beef Can* and *The Tom Cat,* those admirable songs which I learned in early manhood upon the Atlantic seas.

There was more wind, indeed, than I liked. We took in the third reef, and went about on the starboard tack after we had run out so far that we thought we could fetch, upon this tack, the next harbour. As we came near to that town, and saw its roofs far away appearing and disappearing again behind the crests of unpleasant seas, the *Nona* heeled suddenly to a much too angry gust. I heard a crash coming from below, and with it the voice of my companion crying, "Come down quick and help!"

The crew (if I may call him so) was sitting forward, hunched up, clutching the weather shrouds, and not happy. I called him to come and hold the tiller, while I should go below to help, and I warned him that she was pulling hard, although she was under three reefs, for we had nothing forward now but the third jib. He looked over his shoulder in a very ghastly way, and shook his head from side to side, as though despairing to be heard in such a wind. I was within a few feet of him, and I bawled: "COME AND TAKE THE TILLER! QUICK." but again he miserably shook his head, and clung to the shroud. Then did I, commending myself to St. Elmo (which is a false name, for his real name was Peter, and even Gonzales, and he was the man who was so shocked to find all the Galicians lapsed into a Pagan darkness and living in open fun), struggle to make some shift of keeping the tiller up with my right arm stretched back while I craned my head through the cabin door to see what was going on below.

The stove had gone adrift in the lurch. There was oil all over the place, and a mess of crockery, and everything on the weather side had leapt to leeward, and some little of it trailed in the oil of the floorboards. It was not more serious than that; for, luckily, the stove was not alight. I shouted to my companion that I could not leave the tiller. I bobbed up my head again, and found that even in that short moment she had almost swung into irons. I put her around just in time, and we raced and flew, breasting the seas for that farther little misty harbour town.

The *Nona* is like those women who are peevish and intolerable under all conditions of reasonable happiness, but come out magnificently in distress. I lie; for the *Nona* is never peevish and intolerable. What I mean is that in easy weather she is a little sluggish on the helm, and has one or two other small faults, excusable after the fortieth, the fiftieth, year: for she was launched before Plevna, though it is true, a year or two after Sedan. She has her mortalities; but in a sea-way she is magnificent. With her few inches of freeboard, her old-fashioned straight stem, her solid grip upon the water, she takes the sea as though she belonged to it, and so she went that day, riding in high-bred fashion, worthy of all praise, and praise she received from me as she leaned over and took the combers one after the other. I gave her perpetual encouragement: for no boat will do her best unless she is sufficiently flattered.

Thanks to that increasing wind, the passage was short enough, and what we had said would at most take three days was accomplished between a morning and an evening, for it was still broad daylight when we passed outside the group of rocks of which the chart warned us, and stood within a mile or two of the now distinct houses of that little harbour town, all full of Cornishmen.

But the wind still rose, and for the wind to rise when day is falling is a very bad sign. I had no desire to ride it out in the open, and I proposed to get in under the lee of the land (for there was a sort of point there), and not to drop anchor till I could be sure of plenty of water in the harbour later on, when I should make for it on the flood.

My companion came up on deck, from settling things below, and we cast about anxiously for a place where the anchor might be let go.

It was not an easy calculation. She was driving pretty fast. One had to get well under the shelter of the low point, and yet to leave plenty of water beneath one in which to swing. I asked him to go forward and get all ready, and the crew would help him. But the crew did not do so.

The sea being now calmer (though the wind was still rising) because we had come under the lee of the point, the crew did, indeed, stagger forward; but he still held on manfully by the fore-stay, and looked curiously on my companion's activity with the anchor as at a novel and a pleasant sight. Beyond that he did noth-ing; but I think he was proud of keeping his legs so long as he could grasp that forestay. It is no use to argue nor much use to command in the face of imbecility.

I shouted to my companion to let go the chain when I thought the right moment had come, and at the same instant brought her up sharp.

The anchor took the ground. We were in, perhaps, five fathom of flood water; for it was full evening, though still light. When we had so lain for a quarter of an hour or so, taking stock of every-thing around, I asked my companion whether we could not, with the last of the light and the last of the flood, make harbour. The wind was still rising, but we should be running before it towards the not distant pier. Rounding that stonework, we should shoot right into the wind's eye, when it probably would be broken by the hillside of houses beyond, and, even though we did not know how far the harbour might still be when dried out, we should be in safety, with plenty of water beneath our keel for an hour or two more, while we inquired where we should berth. So we decided to risk it, though perhaps wiser men would have ridden out the night where we lay.

She certainly took a great deal of water aboard during that short mile or two, with more and more breakers as we got farther and farther from the protection of the point. Once, when she buried badly, I was afraid the sprit might snap, for I had not housed it. But she carried through all right, though the sprit bent like a willow wand, and we rounded in the gloaming, shot past the pier end, and dropped anchor immediately inside.

A man hailed us from the shore; we threw him a line, and he showed us where to berth in water that would just or nearly float us, even at the lowest of the tide.

The crew was no longer indolent, now that he had left behind him the pitiless waste of the seas and felt once more beneath his feet the solid strength of England. He did what he was told in fastening warps and putting out fenders. Then came the moment for payment: wage and the railway fare home. Before he went over the side I asked him gently whether he had ever been to sea before. He said: "Oh, yes, in a manner of speaking." I asked him whether he had ever handled a tiller. "Not by rights," he said. "Not in such a boat as this." I asked him whether he had any fault to find with the boat. He said: "No she is a very good boat so far as I can see, but I do not pretend to understand these things." He went over the side into the darkness. He was and he remains a mystery.

Was he a Charon man who pulled a ferry from shore to shore? Or was he a man who lounged about on the quay, dressed as his companions were dressed, but timid of tumbling water? Or was he a vision? Or a detective? Or an actor? Or one of those writing men who pretend to go to sea in boats, but never .do? I cannot tell. I never saw him again.